ME, MY FAMILY, OUR LIVES

Me, My Family, Our Lives

A Memoir, and More

DAVID GERARD

Illbird Press

CONTRIBUTORS

Contributing content, stories, historical events and information, and ideas to this book are the following: Mary Shelor, William J. Jurkiewicz, Linda Jurkiewicz, Susan McGinnis, Gail Row, Audrey Jurkiewicz, and Phillip and John Pitts.

Publisher: Illbird Press, Tulsa, OK
illbirdpress@gmail.com
Web: www.illbirdpress.com

Design/Production: David Gerard

Copyright © 2021 by David Gerard

All rights reserved. No part of this book may be reproduced or transmitted in any form or by any means, electronic or mechanical, including photocopy, recording, or any information storage and retrieval system, without written permission from the publisher, except in the case of brief quotations embodied in the critical articles and reviews.

First Printing, 2021

ISBN: 9780996962124
EPUB: 9780996962155

Printed in the United States
10   9   8   7   6   5   4   3   2

A NOTE

I remember riding the bus home one day from high school, and Karen Sue Dragoo, who was one year older than I and whom I knew from my one year at Moore School, the first grade, was sitting next to me. I had not seen or talked with her for several years, and because we had been together in the early years of school, we didn't know a lot about each other. So as we talked, she asked about my family. I told her that I had four sisters and two brothers.

She said, "You must be Catholic."

People understood that was the case then with Catholics, just as people understand today that some religious people promote and engender big families.

Although my family was typical of Midwestern, Catholic families of a previous era, my family was also a special family, individual in its own right. My purpose in this account, with the help of my siblings, is to convey some of that uniqueness on the pages that follow. I wanted to write down some of our story, and mine, before no children of Anne and William Jurkiewicz were left to tell anything of themselves and their lives.

As in any story, the events are clouded by time, by new perspectives and feelings, and aging, hardening brain cells. I apologize for the darkening clouds, but even those eventually become part of the story.

DGJ

1990 REUNION

In June 1990, my family and I met with my brothers and sisters and their families for a reunion at a rental on Grand Lake just south of Grove, OK. John Miles took the photo of us, which included (back row) Jared Jurkiewicz, Cole and Mike Jurkiewicz, Mary Shelor, me, Annie McGinnis, Farrell McGinnis, Steven Lamb; (middle row) Mom, Mary Jurkiewicz, Audrey Jurkiewicz, Susan McGinnis, Rich Lamb, Bill Jurkiewicz, Richard and Kathy Lamb; (front row) Noah Jurkiewicz, Linda Jurkiewicz, Matthew Shelor, Caleb Jurkiewicz, Jessica Jurkiewicz, and John McGinnis.

CONTENTS

	A Note	v
1	The Circumstances of My Birth	1
2	St. Joseph, Missouri	5
3	14 East Hyde Park Avenue	23
4	God's Acres	29
5	6602 King Hill Avenue	37
6	Stefan and Ahafia Jurkiewicz	57
7	Phillip and Draga Zuptich	67
8	William Bill Jurkiewicz	79
9	Anne Marie Jurkiewicz	95
10	Accidents and Injuries	113
11	The Day Kennedy Was Shot	121
12	The Valley	125
13	Christian Brothers High School	135
14	Minnesota Trips	141

15	New York/Washington D.C. Trip	145
16	Other Trips	151
17	Colorado Trip with Bill	165
18	The University of Missouri-Columbia	169
19	Ten Fathoms Restaurant	175
20	West Texas Cowboy	179
21	Meeting Audrey McKinnon	189
22	William Joseph Jurkiewicz	195
23	Kathleen Anne (Jurkiewicz) Lamb	207
24	Mary Draga (Jurkiewicz) Shelor	209
25	Susan Joanna (Jurkiewicz) McGinnis	219
26	Michael John Jurkiewicz	222
27	Linda Elizabeth Jurkiewicz	225
28	Audrey Jo (McKinnon) Jurkiewicz, in her words	231
29	Birdwatching	237

| 1 |

The Circumstances of My Birth

My mother told me one time that she didn't feel well the day I was born, November 21, 1952, but she attributed her upset stomach to the beans she ate the night before. So she was reluctant to head to the hospital right away. My mother never said that her pregnancy that led to my birth was out of the ordinary or difficult, only the thing about the beans.

When she did get to the hospital, my mother said that a nun at the hospital, St. Joseph's Hospital, visited her during the day to check on her. Nuns did that in those days to check if patients had spiritual needs besides the physical needs they were there for.

My mother told the nun that she had had three girls in a row after her firstborn, a son. She said that she really wanted another boy, not another girl. My mother said the nun pulled out a holy card with St. Gerard on it and gave it to her. The nun told her to pray to St. Gerard, the patron saint of expectant mothers, for a boy and he would hear her prayer.

My mother said that is what she did, and voila, she got a boy.

I never told my mother this, but I told many people when I have related this story that my mother really should have been praying more than nine months earlier if she wanted a boy, not the day before I was born. I also joked a few times that St. Gerard may have really been a powerful saint because I may have been a girl in

My mother holding me with Mary seated and Bill and Kathy standing. The photo was taken outside our East Hyde Park Avenue home with the west side of our next-door neighbor's house behind us.

my mother's womb and he miraculously changed me into a boy the day of my birth just for my mother.

Me at Hyde Park in an old-style swing, one in which the wooden front bar raises up in order to put the child in the seat.

Regardless, in gratitude for St. Gerard giving her a boy, my mother gave me the middle name Gerard. She said that she was set on David for a first name, that she always liked that name, and one of her favorite characters from the Bible was David of the Old Testament. From what I heard her say, she named me after him.

However, a nun in grade school, when I was preparing for Confirmation, told me that I couldn't be named after King David. She said good Catholics in those days were supposed to be named after a saint, one canonized by the Church, which King David was definitely not.

The nun told me that if I wanted to claim David as a Catholic name, I would have to say I was the namesake of St. David, a Welsh bishop who lived in the 500s. I remember looking up the history of St. David of Wales, and I was not impressed by his life or legacy. Compared to King David, St. David was milquetoast. So I have always claimed King David as the inspiration for my first name.

There are not a lot of photos of me as a toddler, but in most, I am without a shirt. But I am wearing cool socks.

I was born at 11:55 PM on Nov. 21, just five minutes away from the next day. I am not superstitious, but the dates for a person born under the sign of Scorpio is Oct. 23 to Nov. 21, so I am right at the cutoff date for being a Scorpio. Another five minutes and I would have been born under Sagittarius as my brother Michael was.

I have often wondered what astrologists say about borderline-born people. But I have never been interested enough in astrology to look it up. In high school, because other students talked about that sort of thing and we

A St. Gerard holy card and medal that Jessica purchased for me years ago. On the back, it states, "Glorious St. Gerard, because ... you bore without murmur ... the calumnies of wicked men, you have been raised up by God as the patron and protector of expectant mothers."

went through "The Dawning of the Day of Aquarius," I frequently read the daily horoscope in the newspaper. I never put any faith or trust in them, even if they seemed to relate to my life.

My mother said that there was a complication during my birth, that I was a "blue baby." She said that the pediatrician, Doctor Wadlow, said the umbilical cord was wrapped around my neck, cutting off the blood supply which caused my face to turn blue.

I looked up blue baby once, and there is a blue baby syndrome that is actually a result of poor blood flow in a newborn that has nothing to do with the umbilical cord.

Susan has gotten into our mother's makeup and highlighted her lips, and the left sleeve of her dress, with lipstick. I believe I was holding my lips tight to keep her from putting some on me. We are in our bedroom at East Hyde Park.

A birth that results in the cord wrapping around a baby's neck is actually called a nuchal cord birth. With a nuchal cord, according to health websites, the baby can suffer from a slow heart rate or complete stoppage of the baby's heart which could end in a still birth. The sites make no mention of the baby turning blue, though they say babies might have red or purple splotches. The sites also say nuchal cords happen in about one-third of all births and they are usually not serious; the cords are not wrapped tightly, but loosely enough to be unwound by the doctor.

So I'm not sure where my mother got the idea that I was a blue baby. And while the idea that I was a blue baby is very dramatic, it doesn't sound as if I was in as much difficulty as my mother stated. Or maybe she had the reason for my "blueness" attributed wrongly, as she may have misunderstood the doctor or read some wives tale or folklore into it after the fact.

As my birth certificate states, I weighed nine pounds at birth. I was not the biggest newborn for my mom, however. Michael, who is two years younger than I, weighed ten ounces more than I did.

Our mother, Anne Jurkiewicz, loved to embroider, and this is one of the pieces that she did. She liked to sit and sew or embroider evenings while watching television.

| 2 |

St. Joseph, Missouri

I and my brothers and sisters were born in St. Joseph, Missouri. When we were living there, the population was about 72,000. The population has stayed about the same for 100 years.

Susan's husband did the electrical work on the Pony Express Stables when the museum was remodeled. This photo is from the early 1990s on a visit to St. Joe. Left to right: John McGinnis, Caleb Jurkiewicz, Jessica Jurkiewicz, Jimmy Fields, Noah Jurkiewicz, John Miles and Linda Jurkiewicz.

In the 2020 Census, the population was reported to be 74,875. In 1900, the population was recorded at about 100,00, and St. Joseph would have been the 34th largest city in the United States at that time. It is about the 500th largest city now.

The town received its start from Joseph Robidoux, a French trader, in the 1800s, and became most famous for being the eastern terminus of the Pony Express. A statue of a horse and rider stands on the west end of Civic Center Park, where Francis and Frederick avenues meet. The statue sits on a high rectangular base, almost impossible to climb, so the one time we took photos there, we only stood in front of it. But whenever we traveled downtown, the statue offered a constant reminder of the town's past history.

The original stables are located on Ninth and Penn streets, and the building is now a national museum. It was renovated in the 1980s, I believe, and Susan's husband, Farrell McGinnis, and his company did the electrical work, rewiring the whole building to carry a greater electrical load. He pulled the old breaker box out of the building and gave it to me. I've forgotten now where I reused it.

A drawing I did with Prismacolors of several buildings and statues in St. Joseph. Jesse James' home is the white-washed building at the bottom left.

One other event vied with the Pony Express for being the top highlight from St. Joe's past, and that was the assassination of Jesse James by Bob Ford. When we were growing up, we would drive by a house on the Belt Highway that was privately owned and touted as the house where James was killed. The owners had moved it from the center of the city to the outskirts and the highway for greater tourist exposure. A sign out front declared visitors could see the floorboards soaked with blood where James hit the floor in 1882 after Ford shot James in the back of the head. Eventually, the city bought the house and moved it to the grounds of the Patee House Museum, near where the house originally stood. We always wondered what that blood stain looked like, but Dad would never pay the entry fee for us. Some other kids at school, whose parents had more money and less sense and who paid for their children to go inside, said the stain wasn't red, but a disappointing brown. The city patched up the house after its move. It's a nice white-washed building with green trim now. I still have never seen the inside of the house, nor the wood soaked with Jesse's blood.

St. Joseph is also famous for being one of the starting points for the emigrant trails west. I can remember watching a few western movies where the migrant characters were leaving from St. Joseph. We were always proud, of course, to hear our hometown recognized by Hollywood. According to historical records, the emigrants were outfitted in the downtown area; then they loaded onto ferries to cross the Missouri River. When we grew up, we crossed into Kansas on highway US 36, which was a much easier crossing, a concrete arc over what looked like a small stream. I once built a raft out of driftwood and floated from St. Joseph to Atchison, Kansas, about 20 miles away. When I was floating on the river, the shores seemed much farther apart, much farther than when I crossed the river on a bridge.

The Carnegie Library in South St. Joe, where my siblings and I used to go almost weekly for books to read. The head librarian, Mrs. Plummer, was a kindly woman who patiently endured our boring verbal book reports during the summer reading programs.

When I floated downriver out in the very middle, I felt the shores were miles apart, and the gurgling, sucking noises of the muddy waters made me think I'd never make it to either shore. However, near Atchison, a towboat and barge coming up the river motivated me to abandon my un-steerable raft, and I swam with haste to the Missouri shore.

When we grew up in St. Joseph, the downtown was the center of town, only we didn't call it downtown. We always said we were going uptown. We lived in the South End of St. Joseph, and uptown was about three miles north on King Hill Avenue which turned into Sixth Street at the viaduct where the train depot and big switching yard were. The center of the city was actually the western edge of town that fronted the Missouri River.

The spring before I was born in November 1952, heavy snow melt and deluges to the north sent the Missouri out of its banks from South Dakota to northwest Missouri. At St. Joseph in July, the rushing waters cut a new channel, leaving Rosecrans Field, a military Air Force post, without a land connection to St. Joseph. Getting to Rosecrans Field now requires going through Kansas.

Downtown St. Joseph was still a thriving business district when I was a child. The center was a collection of red-brick warehouses and commercial and industrial buildings impressive to look at and very aesthetic. There were many beautiful buildings, including the Buchanan County Courthouse, the Robidoux Hotel, the St. Joseph Central Library, the U.S. Post Office, and the Missouri Theater. We went to the Missouri Theater often, as well as the Trail Theater, which was near the Missouri. The downtown library was, and still is, a light tan limestone and marble building with high windows and a big lobby at the entrance with a checkout and information station in the middle. The lobby looks

In 1995 on a visit to St. Joseph, Bill showed my children how we used to climb on the ledge around the Carnegie Library. We weren't supposed to do it in the 1960s and surely not in the 1990s.

up at an open second floor with a protective iron railing. The building seemed huge since we were used to the South End's little Carnegie Library. We didn't go to the central library often, but when we did, we were always excited.

Mom and the girls liked to shop at The Paris. They went there when they had something fancy to go to, but prices must not have been outside our feeble reach since it seems we went there often. Mostly, we shopped at the United Department Store, which had a basement and two or three upper floors. I remember the marble stairs in that building were wide and open. The floors had different items on them. It seems toys were in the basement and clothes on the first floor. We did a lot of shopping at Townsend's too, which was mostly for clothing. We went into Eshelman's Music store because the girls took piano lessons and Mary also had accordion lessons. She didn't go to Eshelman's for lessons, but we bought music there. I believe she did take accordion lessons somewhere downtown, and sometimes Mike and I had to go along and sit in the waiting room, listening to several accordions going at one time. We also ended up attending accordion recitals as a family and listening to *Lady of Spain* multiple times in our life. The highlight of the recitals, though, was a big, heavyset kid who rocked back and forth as he played, which somehow seemed very comical to Mike and me.

Jackson in 2017 walking atop King Hill, overlooking South St. Joseph. The red-brick building in the middle with the cupola is the former Livestock Exchange Building, now abandoned and deteriorating. The electrical power plant is to the right, and to the left is Triumph Foods, a pork processing plant.

But we didn't have to go downtown to shop. The South End then was its own little town. When other residents of St. Joe heard you were from the South End, they treated you as if you were from a foreign country, and the connotation was that you were a tough or a lower-class citizen. That was a carryover from the early 1900s, when the meat packing industry was big in the South End and mostly immigrants worked at the plants.

Swift and Armour had huge plants located along the Stockyards Expressway, just west of Lake Avenue. The Livestock Exchange Building, a big, four-story, beautiful red-brick building with a steeple on top, overlooked a huge complex of wooden stock pens that stretched for a mile or more. The stock pens were always full of cattle. The smell was overwhelming when we drove by them, and one of the ways uptown was through the stockyards. The cattle pens were to the north of Illinois Avenue after crossing the railroad tracks, and the hog pens were to the south with a loading dock facing the street. We kids always looked for dead hogs lying on the loading dock when our parents drove by, and usually a dead hog or two with their distended stomachs were there.

The stockyards contributed immensely to St. Joseph's development from the turn of the Twentieth Century. When the cattle prices were given by any radio station while we were growing up, the St. Joseph market prices were quoted right along with the Chicago and Kansas City market prices. The St. Joe stockyards attracted thousands of immigrants, including our grandparents, and the South End was especially noted for its enclave of Poles, Ukrainians, and other nationalities from Eastern Europe. Even those of us who were second-generation Americans were disparagingly called Polacks, Bohunks, or Hunkies.

The stockyards and packing houses weren't the only big farming-related businesses there either. Huge grain silos and storage complexes lined the Stockyards Expressway, along with a rendering plant, a walnut wood processing plant, and the railroad yards, and the city waste treatment and power plants were there. All of those industries added to a mixture of smells that were unpleasant but economically important to everyone who lived in the South End.

In 1984, I took Jessica and Caleb on a visit to the swine pens still remaining at the old stockyards next to the Exchange building. At one time, swine and cattle pens extended up and down Packers Avenue, but they are gone now.

The rail yard was always busy too. There were several tracks that went south out of town, and we hated driving west to Lake Contrary or trying to cross to the Stockyards Expressway because we just knew there would be trains to hold us up. The trains went out of town in a hurry, but when they rolled in, we were in for a long wait as the trains slowed to stop in the yards. I remember waking up in the night in the house on King Hill hearing trains sound their horns at crossings. You never had to wait long to hear one. The sound of their horns was a constant presence.

Because of the nearby industries, we had a couple of important commercial centers in the South End: The Valley, where my dad had his store along King Hill Avenue; and The Junction, which was along Lake Avenue. Both had clothing stores, hardwares, insurance agencies, groceries and pharmacies, banks and doctors, though I don't remember any dentists being in either. Our parents didn't take us to the dentist regularly, and I didn't go much until I was seventeen and had a couple of bad teeth. Then Mom took me Downtown to Dr. Barr, who was unlike any dentist at that time or now. He had a plain office, no fish tanks, magazines or pictures on the wall. I don't even remember a receptionist. We showed up for our appointments and went straight to a room, where Dr. Barr, who seemed to be 70-plus years old, fixed our teeth and out we went at half the price any other dentist charged. He was bare bones dentistry, but he was a good dentist.

But he wasn't in the South End with all us Bohunks. The Mareks lived two doors south of us. The Miljavacs and the Kovacs lived down Fulkerson Street. We went to school with the Mihelichs, Swartzes, Pawlowskis, Yurkoviches, Goucans, Koveleviches, Mihelskis, Caloviches, Kalamons, Ziberskas, Hasiaks, Kobzejs, Zawodneys, Shtohryns, Cupryks, Halamars, Jakymiaks, Kalahurkas, Wisneskis, Zapalas, Mazurs, Mareks, Szczepaniks, Jirkovskys, Borkowskis, Basztas, Brewkas, and Bolonyis. There were only a few Hispanic families, the Gallegoses, Riveras, Chavezes. The Hispanic neighborhood was on the north side of the South End, and we went one time to their church, a small church between King Hill Avenue and the Stockyards Expressway. It closed though even when we were young, and its members began attending St. Patrick's and went to school there. We would meet some of them in the Catholic high schools. Sometimes on our way home from Downtown when we were little, we would stop at a Hispanic man's house along Sixth Street and buy tamales. I don't remember if the Barbosas started out there or not, but the Barbosas had a notable restaurant at one time in one of St. Joseph's old Downtown buildings, a castle-like structure. On our first date, Audrey and I went to Barbosa's Restaurant.

Mom, Kathy and Billy outside the Ukrainian Tavern in South St. Joe. As the name implies, the hall was founded by Ukrainians, who also belonged to a Ukrainian Society based in the US, which aided new immigrants and offered $1,000 life insurance policies. Dad bought the $1,000 policies for all of us children, cashing them in when we turned 18. Then he told us that we needed to purchase our own life insurance policies.

We had some good restaurants in the South End in our day. The Hoof and Horn in the Junction near the Stockyards was probably the best, but we never ate there. It was too expensive. We went to the Bucket Shop, a clapboard building on Lake Avenue that was half bar and half restaurant. My Aunt Anna, Dad's sister, worked there in the kitchen. The Bucket Shop was noted for its beefburgers, ground beef seasoned and placed in a hot dog bun. We went there fairly often. There was also the El Rancho, which wasn't Hispanic, but a place for sandwiches and meals. Occasionally we went to Galvin's, a restaurant that was in a home and customers ate whatever they were cooking that day. Usually, it was a chicken dinner with mashed potatoes, gravy, and beans or peas, and apple pie for dessert. The Mareks and Gnats, who had small stores, made ethic Eastern European sausage, and we often shopped there, but they didn't have restaurants. The Valley had a restaurant, Betty's, but we never ate there. I don't know why. If we went to a little diner, we went to Spot's farther north. I was in Betty's a lot, though, because when I was at Dad's shop, he would often send me to Betty's to get him cups of coffee. Betty had a brother, Norman, who was almost blind. He would hold the pot and cup so close to his face as he poured the coffee that I thought he would pour it on himself.

Our favorite place for ice cream was the Dairy Queen at King Hill and Missouri avenues. It was an old-fashioned Dairy Queen with no inside seating, where customers went to a window to order and waited outside for their ice cream. That place was always busy, but it was about the only ice cream place around.

The South End had a few public grade schools and the one high school, Benton. But we went to St. James Parochial School. We walked eight blocks from our house on King Hill and Fulkerson to Michigan Street where our grade school was behind the church. We walked whatever the weather, and most other children did too. On the way to school, we ran and jumped to see if we could reach the paint sign with a picture of a world dripping paint outside the front of the Valley Lumberyard. When we walked by our dad's shoe store, we waved and yelled, "Hi, Dad," and other kids imitated, or mocked, us with a yell of their own.

In the summer, when we weren't in school, we still weren't home. We ran the neighborhood, playing with friends. Mike and I played baseball with Chuck and Danny Hensley on the Hosea school grounds. With two on a side, we only played the left side of the field. A hit ball to right was an out. In the evening, the Miljavacs would come up to our yard and we would play a type of mass tag. I think we called it Monster. One person was it, and if the it person tagged you, both of you were now it, until only one person was left. When that person was caught,

Jessica and Caleb stand atop the hill across from where I grew up at 6602 King Hill Avenue and where Mike, Susan and I roamed when we were small. Hosea Elementary School, where Dad went to school, is the rectangular building above Jessica's head.

the game was over, and he or she started as the it person the next game.

On summer nights, because we didn't have air conditioning until most of us were in high school, we sat on the front porch talking, singing songs, watching cars go by. I remember reading a lot of books sitting and lying on the porch swing.

Mike and I played baseball. Since Mike was two years younger than I and the divisions only included players a year apart, we never were on the same team. We played almost all our games on the fields at Hyde Park. There were only two hardball fields until I turned 13. Then Hyde Park expanded the fields and there were five.

This was a 1990s painting I did that contains some St. Joseph memories. Most evident is the early religious training at St. James Parochial School, and the steeple is of St. James Church along King Hill and Michigan avenues.

The girls, until the renovation, had four fields. Kathy and Mary played there on a big field just north of the swimming pool. Kathy was a big hitter. The four home plates were at the corners of the huge rectangular field, and all four ball fields had no fences. So when a player hit a ball past the outfielders on one field, it rolled onto an adjoining field. I remember Kathy hitting a ball one time that rolled past the opposite outfield and onto its infield almost to the backstop. Mary was a good pitcher with a wicked curve. She hit the ball well, too.

A terrible accident happened one night there. The youngest Kern girl, Jerri Lynn, 10, and another girl were climbing on a backstop, and Jerri Lynn slipped and fell to the ground. She broke her neck. Her oldest brother, Ronnie, a big, muscular guy, was there, and I remember him crying and telling people to stay back and leave room so the ambulance could get to her. It was nighttime, and we didn't hear until the next day that she was dead, but we suspected it that night.

A painting of the inside of St. James Catholic Church that I painted about 20 years ago. A young server boy is dreaming of cowboys, not saints.

When the park was overhauled, the four girls' fields were turned into one big boys' field, one for 15-year-olds and older players. It was a nice field with a six-foot high chain link fence around it. Ronnie and Rodney Wahlert were paternal twins a year younger than I who I often played with on the same team. Ronnie and his older brother Jackie were good ballplayers, Rodney only so-so, but he had heart. One time, someone smacked a ball all the way to the fence. Rodney chased after the ball with abandon, running not into the chain links, but right into one of the metal posts. Everybody gasped when he collapsed to the ground, thinking for sure he was out cold, but he bounced right up. Mr. Wahlert, Rodney's dad, was an assistant coach on my team, and he said, "It would take a lot more than a metal post to knock that boy out."

My grandfather helped found St. Joseph's Ukrainian Catholic Church on Virginia Street in the South End in the early 1900s. His funeral service was held there in 1971, and the congregation held a special service for my dad when he died in 1980, even though he had not attended regularly for years.

The outfield fence ended at East Hyde Park, and a row of houses lined the avenue looking across the street at the ball field. One time, Harry Thrasher, a big kid who could be mouthy and a bully at times, hit a ball and it carried all the way to the porch of one of the houses. That was the first time and the only time I saw a ball hit that far.

From the time I was nine until I turned sixteen, St. Joseph hosted the NAIA College World Series at Phil Welch Stadium on Southwest Parkway near 28th Street. The city or the NAIA, somebody, always allowed boys in Little League to watch a lot of the games for free. I remember going several years, and it seems Sam Houston, Grambling, and Grand Canyon made it every year. Major league scouts always came to the games to check out prospects, and they were willing to talk us kids if we sat down next to them and started asking questions. In 1967, Grambling came into the tournament with a record of 35-1. Ralph Garr, who would play for the Atlanta Braves for eight years, led Grambling and all NAIA hitters with a .585 batting average. In fact, every position hitter on the Grambling team, except for one, batted for more than .300. A guy whose last name was Patterson hit like .280, and I remember sitting next to him and asking him who he was. He said quite happily, "I'm the guy who hit under .300," and he was pretty popular among all of us young ballplayers. He was a real friendly young man. I also sat next to a scout from the Cincinnati Reds and talked to him about Ralph Garr. The scout wasn't big on Garr. He said Garr, who played second base, had terrible defensive skills and would never make it in the big leagues as a second baseman. He said if anyone drafted Garr, they would move him to the outfield. In fact, the Braves did position Garr in the outfield, but he had trouble fielding out there too. He didn't play a lot his first three years, and was sent back down to the minors. He came up only after one of the Braves' outfielders got hurt. Garr then became a big hitter for a few seasons, winning one batting title. He was very popular with the Braves' fans, and he was called the Roadrunner because of his speed. But his poor fielding finally caught up with him, and he bounced to a couple other teams before retiring. Everyone thought Grambling would win the NAIA tournament in 1967, but despite their record and despite winning the first two games of the series, they lost the next two to the eventual winner and runner-up.

The St. Joseph Telegraph, now defunct, in 1993 carried a story about the start of St. Joseph's Ukrainian Catholic Church in St. Joseph and reprinted a 1919 photo of members of that church. Grandpa Stefan is third from the left in the front row.

In the summer, we went swimming at the Hyde Park pool. Mary worked there as a lifeguard a few summers. Our favorite time to swim was on a Sunday morning, and we went after the 8 a.m. Mass. The pool on Sunday mornings was open for free to families whose parents had a business in the South End, and that was great because it wasn't as busy. During the week in the hot summer time, the pool was a mass of kids.

Sometimes we went swimming at Lake Contrary, an oxbow lake next the Missouri River in the South End. Like all oxbow lakes in Northwest Missouri, Lake Contrary was an extremely shallow and muddy body of water subject to filling in by silt over the years. Every so often the city would have to dredge the lake to keep it alive. And that wasn't all. A huge pump spilled water from the Missouri River into the lake to make sure it didn't dry up altogether, and sand was trucked in to build a beach. The sand had to be brought in periodically to restore the beach when the sand washed away into the muck of the bottom of the lake or blew away.

When my parents were young adults in St. Joseph, Lake Contrary was a very popular place. The lake had a dance hall built out over the water, and there was an amusement park nearby. By the 1950s, the dance hall was gone, and the amusement park had only a few rides left, one of them a roller coaster, a devil of a ride because it was made of wood and had aged. The roller coaster trembled and shook as if it would fall any moment, adding to the terror of the speed and rise and fall of the cars. The park also had a lover's water ride, little boats pulled through a canal that ran through a dark building that was decrepit by the time I was little. I only went on those rides a few times before they fell into disrepair and were dismantled. But we went to Lake Contrary sometimes to picnic under the huge cottonwoods in the park and swim in the lake.

Because Dad did business with Wyeth's, our family was invited to the annual fairs the company held at its St. Joe warehouse. Linda saved a memento from the 1967 fair, a photo from a booth operated by Behr-Manning, a division of Norton Co. based in Troy, NY.

In the winter, we used Hyde Park's hills to sled, although most of the time we just went across the street from our house on King Hill to sled. I forgot the family's name who had a boy Susan's age who lived there. But they let us sled their front yard. Their house was set back from the street, and it was a pretty good run down the slope from their house. We had to dig our toes into the snow at the bottom to keep from sliding into the street.

One time when I was about ten or so, the boy across the street got a chimpanzee from somewhere as a pet. He was showing it off on the sidewalk across from our house, and a bunch of kids were over there in a big circle looking at it. Susan and Mike were already there, and for some reason I wasn't. I crossed the street just as the kids all starting making monkey sounds and jumping up and down and laughing, which agitated the chimpanzee. I joined the circle walking right up to the boy and the chimp, and because the animal was frightened and confused, he jumped at me and bit me on the hand. The bite broke the skin, although I don't remember it bleeding a whole lot. Mom and Dad took me to the hospital where I received a tetanus shot, and the kid had to give up the chimpanzee.

One summer, the Tillmans, who lived next door to us, had a spider monkey. They had it on a leash, and the leash had a ring that was attached to their clothesline so the monkey could move about the back yard along the line. One day, I saw him catching grasshoppers to eat. Remembering my run-in with the chimpanzee, I was a little spooked, but he was small and cute, so I started catching grasshoppers and katydids and giving them to him. I never held him, but he always sat still and never lunged at me when I fed him. He was patient and composed.

The Pony Express statue in downtown St. Joseph. We grew up under its historical shadow and imagination.

Ronnie Tillman was a year or two older than I, and he was a big tall kid, very strong. One day, he and one of his friends were outside boxing – Ronnie had new boxing gloves – and Mike and I went over to watch. Ronnie asked me if I wanted to box his friend, who was slow and awkward. The friend was bigger than I was, but I was sure I could stay away from his big swings, and I did. I hit the kid several times pretty good and he never touched me. But then Ronnie said I had to box him. I didn't want to because Ronnie was one of those guys who was probably going to become a Marine or a Navy Seal. But he said he'd take it easy on me. He did for a while, and I was able to stay away from him, but that didn't last long. He hit me with a punch that landed square in my face, and I went down on my behind. I had seen cartoons of punched and knocked-out characters seeing stars circling their heads, and that's exactly what happened to me. These big bright stars were orbiting my head. Ronnie thought he had either killed me or pounded me into a vegetable because he kept saying you all right, you all right, and he put the gloves up. It took me a few minutes to stand up and walk home. I was wobbly for a while.

Mr. Reiser lived across the street from us. He was a lonely old man we hardly knew until Dad bought a big lot of stamps from someone. Somehow, Dad found out Mr. Reiser was an ardent philatelist. We got to know him then, and I started a collection of stamps from the United States. I went over to visit Mr. Reiser quite a few times to buy and trade stamps. He was a nice man, although he could be gruff, and he always wore a wife beater T-shirt and had bad BO.

Our house was only a mile or so from the city limits to the south, where there were a lot of farm fields and pastures. The area to the east of King Hill Avenue was very hilly, so a lot of

The poet Eugene Field, known best for the poem "Little Boy Blue," married a St. Joseph woman. After his marriage, he wrote a poem about a street in St. Joe named "Lover's Lane." This old postcard commemorates Field and the poem.

land was not covered with homes and development. We could slip into the woods behind John Webers' house, and lots of kids went up there to build forts and dig holes. Over the hill and down the other side was a cemetery and more woods that connected with Hyde Park. It was a great place to hike and explore. The cemetery supposedly had Civil War soldiers buried there; anyway that's what some people said. One night, a couple of guys went there to dig up a soldier expecting to find the body buried with his sword or some other valuable artifact. They got caught, of course. I don't think that there were actually any graves there that old, but that was the story.

King Hill Avenue was always busy since it was a main thoroughfare south out of town. But when we first moved there, it wasn't terribly busy as there weren't a lot of businesses south of us. Then Charlie Kovac, who at one time operated a little neighborhood grocery, built a big, new grocery store just a block north of us. He built the store with his son Paul, who took over soon after it was built. They had a grand opening probably when I was seven or eight, and the grandest thing about it was going there to cool off as it was one of the few places around that had air conditioning. The Kovacs also arranged the appearance of the supposedly "tallest man alive" at the time to come to their opening. He was more than seven feet tall, maybe eight. He'd let us kids come stand by him, and lots of people were taking photos, but we didn't have a camera with us.

The Kovacs' new store attracted a TG&Y, which opened up next to it, and Farmers State Bank had a new bank built on the same side of the street, so it created a little shopping center there. Mary and Mom both worked for the TG&Y at different times. The kindergarten where Susan had gone closed, and Dan Garvin built an insurance agency building there. Audrey worked for Dan when I met her.

But the big new store didn't end up being big enough for Paul Kovac. Several years later, he started a mall farther south down King Hill Avenue, just north of the Pitts' house, the house that Grandpa Zuptich built. Paul Kovac had another grocery store built with gas pumps, and he also had a row of stores constructed that he leased. The buildings included a Pizza Hut and a bowling alley was built behind there. The center increased traffic on King Hill Avenue in front of our house considerably. Paul Kovac thought he was going to revive the South End and turn around its commercial failings, which had been some time in coming. He became a big promoter of the South End and was elected a city councilor.

Looking across Mt. Olivet Cemetery in St. Joseph. The cemetery is off famous Lovers Lane, and my grandparents and parents, aunts and uncles are buried there.

But it was too little too late, not just for the South End, but the Downtown was in trouble economically too.

In the mid-1960s, the city began growing to the east where I-29 and the Belt Highway ran parallel to one another north to Omaha and south to Kansas City. The growth led to the abandoning of the traditional center of town as the buildings were aging and businesses were closing. East Hills Mall was built in 1965, and we went to the grand opening to see the new wonder. We'd never seen a mall before. My dad didn't like it. He said it was too far to drive six or seven miles. He said why would anyone drive six miles to get what they could get down the street. He didn't like driving out there to go to McDonald's, which had been there for several years already. Us kids liked going there for the 19-cent hamburgers and the delicious fries. Of course, my mom and dad didn't think it was real food. My mom made hamburgers like meatballs and put them on regular bread.

So St. Joseph merchants, following McDonald's lead, moved east to the Belt Highway. We watched our favorite stores close: S.S. Kresge's, Townsend Wyatt and Wall, Maid-Rite, United Department Store, The Paris, Eshelman's Music, Wyeth's Wholesale.

To try and stop the migration, St. Joseph, like many other US cities, started an urban renewal project. Initially, downtown St. Joseph's remake was highly touted a success. Interstate 229 was constructed to take traffic from I-29 west to the city's historical center. Some new businesses were recruited to take over and remake old buildings.

A walking mall was constructed along one of the major streets. The Missouri Theater was converted from a movie theater to a performing arts center. The once famous Robidoux Hotel was demolished along with other buildings across Francis Street to make way for businesses and a new Civic Center.

But the project ended in failure. The city continued to grow along the Belt Highway, and the Downtown continued to decay.

The two-year Missouri Western college abandoned its Downtown building, became a four-year school and the state built a new campus near the intersection of I-29 and Highway 36. Once beautiful Downtown buildings went empty, and many of them had to be demolished. In recent times, the city has continued developing further north along the Belt with Walmart, Lowe's, Home Depot, Sam's, Target and all the restaurant chains locating there.

The South End, where we grew up, suffered the same fate as the Downtown but to a worse degree. The packing houses started closing operations in the 1960s. Little by little, the old pens were abandoned and torn down. The huge complex of slaughterhouses turned empty, then were torn down. Only the Livestock Exchange remained, lonely and decaying. A few attempts were made to restore it, but it was a lost cause. The building still sits empty, with boarded windows and crumbling brick.

The businesses in The Valley and The Junction started closing too. Shoppers stopped patronizing the small business owners, went to the big retail stores. The clothing stores in the Valley closed. My uncle's television store closed.

My dad couldn't compete with Kmart, the king of retailers at the time. He stopped selling sporting equipment. He stopped selling bicycles and bicycle parts. Bill Hindery's hardware store closed. It became a bar. The only other grocery store besides Kovac's, a discount grocery on Lake Avenue, closed. Kovac's mall never filled up.

Paul Kovac died, and his children who inherited the grocery store ran it for several years, then gave up, sold it, and started a fireworks store and a small event center outside town.

We all left too. Bill left long ago, moving to Kansas City, Missouri, to work, and ended up in St. Louis for years. Kathy and Richard left for a suburb of Dallas in 1975, Mary for Tucson a few years after that. Susan and Farrell moved to Dallas and then moved back to live on East Joseph Street off Mason Road for a number of years. They had an electrical company before ending up in Kansas City, Kansas.

Audrey and I left in 1985 for Oklahoma. Mike moved to Tucson to be a firefighter. He met his wife, Mary, there before moving to the Denver area, where Mary's family lived. Linda moved to Charleston, SC, before returning to live and work in Kansas City, Missouri.

I took this photo in the mid-1970s of the back of Robert and Mary's apartment house on Illinois Avenue. Mom, Mike and Richard are on the back row. In the middle are Robert, Mary, Lynda, Bill and Kathy, with Dad, Rich and Jeff sitting on the front step. Steven is sitting in front of Dad.

| 3 |

14 East Hyde Park Avenue

The address of the first house I lived in was 14 East Hyde Park Avenue in St. Joseph, Missouri. I do not know how long my parents and older brother and sisters lived in it before I was born.

I do not have a lot of memories of this house because we moved to a small farm when I was five years old, but I do remember a few things.

The house was situated at the eastern edge of the Missouri River Valley, near the base of hills and bluffs running north and south. The house was a wood structure, built on a full concrete basement. The front and east sides of the house foundation were level with the yard, but west side and the back looked out at alleyways. The back yard was half yard, and it was half driveway and parking with an entrance into the basement. A retaining wall holding back the cut in the backyard slope gave our back yard two levels: the lower for the car, the higher for limited play.

The front and back yards were small, and though houses lined East Hyde Park eastward up the hill, our house was the first residential building east from King Hill Avenue. The west side of the house faced the Valley shopping area, which ran along King Hill. Our view to the Valley looked at the back of Bill Kenney's Pharmacy and across the street to a clothing store, Weiner's.

My childhood friend John Capps, second from right, lived two houses east of us. Here, I stand by John at his birthday party at his house. My sister Susan is at the left.

To the north of the house, across East Hyde Park, was a very high hill. It had been partially cut for the street, and the hill had horizontal strips of bare, light tan earth that showed pockets where children had dug out little caves. A boy my age John Capps, who lived a few houses east, told me that a few children died on the hill when the cave they were digging collapsed on them. I do not know if that is true. I heard it from other children too.

Bill, Kathy, Mary, Susan and me in the front yard of our Hyde Park Avenue house with the steeply cut bank across the street. Some children said the hill collapsed on children, killing them, as they dug caves into the hillside.

A few years after we moved from there, the highway department made East Hyde Park into a four-lane road. Across from our house, workers cut deeper into the side of the hill, slightly curving Hyde Park to the north so that instead of a quarter-block-long jog to Alabama Street to the west, Hyde Park flowed into it at a light-controlled intersection. Our house and two or three east of us ended up on a short street off the four-lane, though the isolated stretch was and is still known as East Hyde Park Avenue.

The living room window looked north, and the front door was on the east side of the house. The house was small: a living room, dining room and kitchen, with maybe three bedrooms.

The bathroom, a narrow room, was at the back of the house, and I remember being crowded in there with Susan and Mike standing beside me as we brushed our teeth before we went to bed.

I remember watching television in that house. The one show I remember watching was hosted by Milton Berle, who did many skits dressed like a woman. I remember that because Mom did not like it that he wore dresses for jokes. He always held a big cigar in his hand and waved it about. Mom didn't like cigars either.

Here I am wearing the Davy Crockett outfit I won at the Cowtown Drive-In drawing in 1955.

The Capps family lived up the street, and Kathy and Mary were friends with the older two Capps girls. I was at the Capps' house one time playing with John, and the second Capps girl was going up her basement steps when I was going down.

She grabbed me and kissed me. I remember that because afterwards, I told everyone at our dinner table, and Kathy and Mary said I was making it up, that the Capps girl wouldn't have done that. But she did. It was a simple kiss. It wasn't as if she molested me.

With the chick I won at an annual Easter Egg Hunt at Hyde Park.

My dad owned the shoe shop in the Valley. He only had to walk a couple blocks to get to his store. I don't remember going to the store much when I was little. I am sure that was because he didn't need a lot of children around when he was working. But I do remember going in the shop a few times. I remember the long line of bicycles at the front. That was when he used to stock, sell and repair a lot of bicycles.

There are photos of me wearing a Davy Crockett outfit out front of the East Hyde Park house. I won the outfit at the Cowtown Drive-In. The outfit was a promotion by the drive-in to entice people to see Walt Disney's *Davy Crockett: King of the Wild Frontier*, which came out in 1955 starring Fess Parker. Our ticket had the winning number, and my family promptly dressed me up like Davy, and posed me for photos. I was enraptured with Crockett for a number of years.

This photo was taken in our kitchen on East Hyde Park, Christmas 1954. Mike, held by Kathy, was born less than one month before.

I also have a photo of me standing in the back yard of the Hyde Park Street house holding a baby chick. The weather was cold as I have a jacket on, but it was probably early April just after Easter. I won the chick at the Easter egg hunt at Hyde Park. I don't remember what happened to my chick, but I don't think we had it very long. I do remember the excitement of picking up the sugared eggs wrapped in plastic and the silver egg that included the note stating that I had won the chick.

I remember one Christmas there very well. We went to Midnight Mass at St. James Catholic Church, where we regularly attended, and when we got home all the presents were out as if Santa Claus had come while we were away. Bill told me years later that he left church and returned home to set out the presents, then hurry back to church before we noticed he was gone. I received a battery-operated robot that year, one that simulated walking, but actually progressed on wheels. The robot made some noises. It didn't talk, I don't think. A week or so after Christmas, I took the robot apart because I wanted to see what made it go. Mom saw what I did, and I received a spanking for my curiosity.

I remember being jealous of Susan because she went to kindergarten. St. James didn't have an early program so she went to the one at Hosea Elementary, which was in a building separate from grades one through eight. It was set back a little off King Hill Avenue two or three blocks south of Dad's store. I did go with Susan to kindergarten one day. I don't remember if there were other younger brothers or sisters of students there, so I don't know if Susan took me as show and tell or it was some

This photo of Dad with Kathy, on left, and Mary, in front of Dad, was taken outside the front door of the East Hyde Park house probably in the spring of 1949.

promotion for next-year students. However, I lost my chance to go to kindergarten when Mom and Dad bought the farm south of town and we moved.

While we lived on East Hyde Park in the 1950s, Mom and Dad took in a few displaced person (DP) families. I don't remember that, but Bill, Kathy and Mary talked about it at times as we grew up. Mary said she remembered the funny smell from the basement as the Eastern European immigrants cooked ethnic food.

I'm standing in our back yard on East Hyde Park close to where Mary said she and Kathy buried their dead goldfish. The next-door neighbor's back porch is the back drop.

While I was a reporter for the Muskogee Phoenix, I received a note in the mail one day from a man in Eufaula, OK. He wrote that he had lived briefly in the basement of our house on East Hyde Park after coming to the United States. His short note stated that he was always thankful that my parents helped him out as he immigrated. After living years in Missouri, he had retired to Oklahoma. I meant to visit the man after receiving the note, but shortly after I received it, I misplaced it as the managing editor moved me from one desk to another. I have always regretted losing that note because I really wanted to visit him and talk with him.

I don't remember that basement very well, maybe because we didn't use it all that much. I don't remember playing down there either. It seems the washer was in the basement at the foot of very steep stairs. I do remember standing on the stairs watching my mother load the washer and take wet clothes out.

I have always had the impression that it was dark in that house, as if the house didn't have a lot of windows or there were heavy curtains on the ones that were there. My mother liked windows and lots of light, which makes me wonder why I have always remembered the house as being dark.

From my sister Mary

I was surprised by all the memories that came up from living on East Hyde Park. I was only nine years old when we moved to the farm, but I had many happy memories from living by the Valley.

It seems we took all our photos with other people's yards and houses in our background, not our house on East Hyde Park. It was well kept, though; our mother was not one to leave things lying about, nor did she let us do it.

Yes, David, the house was really small. But as usual, Dad was constantly redoing and adding to each house we moved into. I think Mom told me that Hyde Park was my first home and I was born in 1948. I remember having to sweat off the wallpaper from the walls and paint. And Corky Church came to sand and varnish the hardwood floors. Mom loved shiny wood floors, and we kids had a time learning how to walk on them. I remember Dad putting a piece of tape on the bottoms of our shoes so we wouldn't slip and fall. I don't remember how many bedrooms, but I think there was a larger room right beside the living room/dining room, so Dad built a closet in the middle of it. We could crawl through the closet to get from room to room. To tell you the truth, I don't remember where we all slept. Later, Dad added onto the back, the south side, of the house with a garage underneath.

Oh, David, I remember that basement! It was SO scary! The stairs to the basement were right off the back door on the porch. The stairs were steep and many of us, including me, fell down those stairs way too many times! At the bottom was the washing machine area, and where the DPs used to live. But the next room held the huge furnace. It had big arms coming out of the center of it, stretching from one end of the room to the other, and I know that it breathed. I think we called it the monster! Later, I found out that there was a little room behind that furnace, and we found boxes of love letters that Mom and Dad wrote to each other when he was in the service.

Since our family went to St James Church, Dad got to know Casper Erk, a single man who lived with and took care of his mother. Everyone loved Casper. He worked at the church keeping the old furnace running and cleaning the buildings. He helped Dad build nice kitchen cabinets for Mom.

When Susan and I crawled into the house a few years ago, some of those cabinets were still hanging on the wall. I think Casper ended up going down to the farm too and helped Dad build cabinets there, and rooms up in the attic.

My mother standing outside the basement/garage of our East Hyde Park house. She is facing an alley that separated our house from The Valley retail area.

As with most houses at the time, there was only one bathroom. And it had a terrible floor that Momma really hated. I remember she scrubbed it really good, painted the whole floor black, then sprinkled every color of paint she had and created a rainbow of colors on that floor. I think she was really happy with it.

Kathy and I played with Mary Agnes and Trudy Capps. Trudy was my best friend even though she was one year older than me. We would all walk to St. James every morning, and of course, pass by the donut shop to wave at Mr. Douglas. After school if he had leftover donuts, he would call us in to get a donut to eat. Boy were they delicious! We loved when Daddy would walk there first thing in the morning and bring home hot, mushy glazed donuts. What a treat.

A lot of our clothes and toys were hand-me-downs, but here's proof I received a new tricycle one Christmas. Dad had shoe and bike store, so we did get new bikes and trikes on occasion.

Kathy used to tease Mary Agnes a lot! I remember one time, she told Mary Agnes to open her mouth and shut her eyes, saying I have a treat for you. And Kathy stuffed a bunch of dandelions, the ones with the little flighty, feathery things, not the flowers, in Mary Agnes' mouth. Oh, she went home crying!

Trudy and I would make mud pies. We had little dishes for our dolls and sometimes we would even eat our cakes and pies. Not too smart. They tasted terrible.

And we would ride our tricycles and scooters up and down Hyde Park. I remember one year for Christmas we got a wagon, a tricycle and a scooter, and we all had to share. I'm sure we had lots of arguments, but I don't remember them. Another thing we did was roller skate. We would keep our skates attached to our shoes and wear our skate keys around our neck on a shoestring. We felt very important.

Oh, we had hollyhocks growing along the wall, and we would attach the flowers to strings and have a ballet over the back porch. We were so creative.

One thing Mom would buy us when we went downtown on the bus was a fish. But they never survived very long. Under that back porch, we had numerous little crosses marking where we had buried a fish in a matchbox.

Hyde Park, the park not the street, was where we went a lot as a family when we lived on Hyde Park Avenue. We would walk up there for sure on Sunday evenings because there was a band concert. Mom and Dad really loved music and did a lot of singing with us. Supposedly, I sang "You Are My Sunshine" one night at the concert on stage when I was

My proud mother dressing herself, Mary, and Kathy in matching coats and hats.

about four or five. I don't remember it, but I did know that song, and I loved singing it. We also went to every Easter Egg hunt as you said, David, and we went sledding there too in the wintertime. Also, they had great swings and three sliding boards, one larger than the other. We had lots of things to do there.

The other thing we did as a family was go to the Cowtown Drive-In. Right underneath the screen they had a playground, so before the movie we could play on them and later went back to the car. But we would bring lawn chairs and sit outside, because it was too crowded in the car. One summer we had a stroke of bad luck. Two or three Sundays in a row, we had a flat tire. Boy, Dad was mad!

| 4 |

God's Acres

In 1958, Dad and Mom bought twelve acres along King Hill Road about a mile or more outside town. They bought it mainly because of Mom. Her mom and dad had bought several acres near the city limits when she was young, built a house there, and had a garden and a little orchard and raised calves and pigs for butchering. Mom wanted to do the same thing. She thought we would be extremely happy living in the country away from the busy city and spending more time outside growing some of our own food and doing things together as a family.

This is an Easter photo of us from 1960 standing proudly in front of our farmhouse along King Hill Road.

I think most of us children were all excited about moving to the country. I know I was, but I don't think any of us thought how isolated we would be even though we were only a short drive from South St. Joe.

The twelve acres lay in a little valley formed by Contrary Creek. The creek flowed north from DeKalb toward St. Joseph, where at the city limits it turned west to meet the Missouri River in the river valley that was five or six miles across. Contrary Creek formed the west boundary of our property with King Hill Road forming the east boundary. A small creek that flowed west out of the hills next to Moore Road bounded the property on the south, and a neighbor's land to the north formed the north border.

The house was situated in the southeast corner of the property. A medium-sized red barn with a hip roof sat behind the house, and a pasture of about two or three acres ran north from the house and barn. The rest of the acreage to the west was cultivated in wheat, corn, or soybeans. Dad made deals with a local farmer who planted and harvested crops on our property and he shared profits from the sale of the grain.

Our King Hill Road house had four old-fashioned lightning rods on top. Lightning did strike and destroy an apple tree in the garden next to the house soon after we moved there. This photo was taken in October 1958, our first year there.

The hill across from us just to the north of Moore Road had a small cattle lot on it, and when it rained, water ran off Moore Road and the lot laid bare by the cattle. The rainwater swamped our front yard and garden, and the cattle manure it carried and deposited on our yard made it very fertile.

The water in the yard also made the basement under the house dank at times, but I don't remember it flooding. A few times while we lived there, and we were there only for a little more than three years, severe storms drove us into the basement, our storm shelter. Once a terrible storm went over, and the thunder and lightning seemed only worse from the confines of that dark concrete hole. We all cringed in a corner next to an old coal room. There was a terrible crash and boom, and we thought the house or part of it was surely gone, but after it quieted, Kathy went up to look around. She found that our apple tree had been knocked over. The tree was big and old, and it was a sad loss, but I remember the fun we had for a few days, playing in the tangle of branches on the ground before it was cut up and carried off.

Susan, Mary, Mike and I stand next to the washout of our driveway on the farm after a hard rain. It was probably the same ran that washed out the bridge at the intersection of King Hill and Turner roads one mile away.

Another time, Mom and Dad were gone, and we went the basement for a storm. Kathy was the oldest at home then as Bill had gone into the Army. After the storm passed, we thought we heard noises coming from upstairs, and we were sure somebody had broken into our house. Kathy went upstairs to check out the house, and I remember her coming back downstairs carrying a big butcher knife from the kitchen. She said she had gotten the knife for protection in case anyone had been up there. She said she crawled through the rooms checking them out with the knife between her teeth.

I remember there was a living room at the front of the house. But the front door actually led into a dining room which was set back a little from being in line with the living room. Opposite the dining room to the north were two bedrooms separated by a bath. Mom and Dad slept in one bedroom, the one closest to the living room, and Mike, Susan, and I slept in the other.

Bill, Mary, and Kathy slept in the attic, which was an open space when we first moved there. Eventually, Dad hired JR Thompson, a carpenter, to finish it out with a couple of bedrooms. Casper Erk, the maintenance man at St. James School, also helped with the attic bedrooms.

The dining room led to a kitchen, and at the back of the house, there were two stairways. One went up to the attic, and the other went down into the full basement. Besides the coal room, there was another room to the east where we stored potatoes and canned vegetables.

We had a big garden the first year. Mom and we children planted lots of potatoes. In spring we would dig up some of the small potatoes forming in the ground, and Mom cooked them with white gravy and peas, also from the garden,

Mike and I with Mom and Dad in front of the fireplace in the farmhouse living room. School photos of us kids line the mantel.

that we shelled out. We called the combination peas-zha-paw-zha. I have no idea if that was the food's Croatian name, or if we butchered the Croatian name, or if we made the name up.

We mostly grew the standard vegetables for that day, which were peas, carrots, beans and corn. I don't remember growing any zucchini, broccoli or cauliflower, and we didn't grow much lettuce. We did not eat salad often then, or at all, if I remember correctly.

Mom did grow cucumbers for dill and sweet pickles, and she liked pickled beets. We also had a stand of rhubarb. I don't know if Mom started it or if it came with the farm, but we had some. I do not remember eating rhubarb pie at the farm though, not until years later after we left. I don't think she grew sweet potatoes, but Mom made pumpkin pies with them. She never told us the pumpkin was actually sweet potatoes.

That first summer was busy and exciting, cleaning out the barn and chicken house, raising chicks, putting in a big garden. When the summer ended, Mom put me in Moore Elementary School across the street from us. St. James wouldn't let me in because I was just five, but Moore did.

Linda's first birthday in September 1959 in the farmhouse dining room. The living room is through the doorway on the right. Linda's baby bed is visible in the room to the left.

At the farm, we had a dog named Blackie, but the dog I am with here, definitely is not Blackie.

Mom sent me to school early as Mike was still at home, and she was pregnant with Linda.

Moore school was a country school, a one-room school that became a two-room school when after all 30 or so students recited the morning Pledge of Allegiance and the two teachers drew a curtain across half the one room to make it two. One teacher took charge of the seventh- and eighth-graders, and the other teacher the first- through sixth-graders. I was one of two first-graders, the other being a skinny blond girl. I was behind her on the slide when she started down the slide, fell off halfway down, and broke her arm.

I really enjoyed school there, but a couple of boys, eighth-graders, didn't. One weekend, in the spring of 1959, they broke into the school, overturning desks, breaking windows and dumping shelves of books. One was a tall, blond kid, the other a shorter, dark-haired boy that was a problem student. He wasn't allowed back in school while the blond boy was. One day after the tall blond boy came back, I asked him why he did it. He just shrugged his shoulders and said he didn't know why. He told me he knew afterwards it was a stupid idea. I guess his admission of guilt and stupidity got him back in school.

When Linda was born in September 1958, Mom let me invite all the students on my side of the school over for lunch and to see our new baby. Mom fixed snacks, and my schoolmates all ate in the dining room.

I think it was at the end of that year that we students at Moore school put on a program for our parents. We did a music and dance show that highlighted cultures around the world. My only first-grade partner and I dressed as a Dutch couple and did a little Dutch dance in wooden shoes. I don't know where my teacher got the shoes, but they were very uncomfortable and awkward.

Mike, Susan, and I played in the front yard of the farmhouse a lot. We ran through the pasture and the crop field too, although Dad got us after us for running through the field when the crops were in.

My mom in June 1960, standing in the front yard of our farm. An apple tree is at the right in our garden.

But I remember dashing through the field when it was planted with wheat and the stalks were shoulder high to us and the developing seed grains banged against our bare arms and faces. A few times, Kathy and Mary led us through the woods across Contrary Creek. I don't know whose property it was, but we walked around on the hillside as if we were explorers.

We had a few farm animals at different times. We had a cow, Dirty Face, who Kathy and Mary used to milk. We had a lamb, Dumbbell. I don't know why we had just one lamb, but it grew to a pretty good size, and Susan and I used to ride it. Inevitably, it would buck us off. Mike got on Dumbbell one time, and it promptly put Mike in a Dirty Face cowpie face first.

One of my birthdays at the farm. My cake has cowboys on horses on it.

Mom talked Dad into buying two pregnant sows. Susan and I claimed them as ours. Susan named hers Lollipop, and I named mine Stinkeroo. They had a slew of piglets, some of which died within a day or two, but Dad ended up with several to sell, and he sold the two sows afterward because they were a lot of trouble to take care of. If I remember correctly, they got out of their pens a few times.

Kathy talked Dad into buying her a horse, or maybe, he bought it for all of us. It was a big horse, named Duke. He was very headstrong, and no one rode him except Kathy. I don't remember how long we had him, but he got into the garden one day and foundered on the apples on the ground. I don't think anyone but Kathy missed him. I know Dad didn't like the horse. He was afraid of him, like the rest of us were.

We had a dog, too, a black dog named Blackie. I don't think he was exactly our dog. I think he actually belonged to a neighbor, but hung around our house quite a bit, and we fed him when he was there. But I don't remember playing with him a lot, or him following us around wherever we went. When we were moving back to town, I seem to remember Blackie was at the farm, and Dad told us that Blackie would be fine, that he would find a new home.

Christmas 1959 in the living room on our farm: Kathy, Mary, me, Susan, Mike, Linda and Mom. Mike and I received cowboy outfits and play guns. Susan looks pretty happy with her stuffed dog.

The excitement of living in the country didn't last for long after moving there. Bill left for the Army in the fall after we moved there. He went to enroll for Missouri Western State College, thinking tuition would be free because he had lived in the city for years and tuition was free for city students. But he discovered because we had moved outside the city limits, he didn't qualify anymore. He hated the farm because of all the work and not being close to his friends, so he immediately walked down the street from the state college to the service recruiting station and joined the Army.

I think we all eventually missed being close to friends. Whenever we wanted to go anywhere, for church or for entertainment, it was a long drive. I believe it was in the spring of 1960 when I was in second grade at St. James that a downpour sent floodwaters down the creek running on the north side of Turner Road. There was a wooden bridge crossing the creek along King Hill Road, and the bridge washed out. At that time, King Hill Road was the only road into town; the new road to DeKalb that ran alongside Contrary Creek wasn't built yet. So when Dad ran us into school in the morning and brought us home in the afternoon, he had to drive several miles out of the way east on Turner Road, then up Highway 371 to Mason Road, which led back down to King Hill Avenue and school. I don't know how long the bridge was out, but it was very inconvenient, and only added to our parents' growing annoyance at living outside town.

There was also a fire down the road one night. We could see the flames and smoke from our house, and we drove to see what it was. It turned out to be a big house that wasn't that old. The whole thing was ablaze and lots of other neighbors had come to watch the house burn down. Those were the days when there weren't rural fire companies. But someone called the city fire department and a truck did show up. But the house was so far gone, the firemen said there was nothing they could do and they only hung around to make sure the fire didn't spread. Afterward, we heard the owners of the house had a big bill from the city for the truck being called to the fire. I think it scared Mom to think that a house could catch fire in the country and not have a fire department around to put it out.

A big snow fell one year while we lived at the farm, but this doesn't look deep enough to be that year. Bill was home from the Army in this photo, and we were happy to see him. That's Mom, Dad and Mary in the back row with Bill, and Susan, I and Mike in the front. Kathy must have stayed in the house with Linda, who would have been only a few months old at this time.

Mom also developed some personal issues at the farm. After Linda was born, she suffered from depression and that cast a pale over the rest of our time there. The road to DeKalb also cut the property in half, and I don't remember if Dad sold the back half, the half without the house, before or after we sold the front part with the house. But a man bought the back six acres and started an organic garden there.

We had an interesting Christmas in the farmhouse the second year there. Bill was in the Army and had gone to South Korea for several months. He sent home a big crate, and it was marked from Japan. In it was a set of China dishes for Mom. She had them for many years after. Bill sent all the girls silky kimonos, and Mike and I got a huge package of Army men.

We had a huge snowstorm one year there too. I believe Dad called someone to clear our drive, and whoever did it pushed all the snow down our drive into the back yard where he left a giant pile of snow. It seems like it was six or seven feet tall, and we played on it for days afterward.

One winter, we went down to the farm of Z.D. Waller, who was also our rural mailman, to sled. He had a house and property on the hillside on the east side of King Hill Road just to the north of where we lived, but on the opposite side of the road. Z.D. had a pond too, and we slid around on its ice one cold winter.

In 2010, a St. Louis company published a novel of mine, "God's Acres," a fictionalized account of our time on the farm. The book won Oklahoma Center for the Book's Fiction Award in 2011.

When we first moved to the farm and when it rained, Mike, Susan and I would run around the front yard in our underwear, and if it was a hard rain, the water would wash down Moore Road into the yard where it was a few inches deep, and we would stomp and splash around. We seemed to have a lot of storms when we lived there. Another rainstorm gouged out a big part of our driveway that ran alongside a creek. Dad had to get the cut filled with rock and covered with soil again.

Our time on the farm always seemed to make a good story idea once I started writing, and a St. Louis publishing house published in 2010 a novella I wrote based on our time there. The farm was a good story because of the illusion it gave of an idyllic life that didn't turn out. And then Mom, from the first, had called our farm "God's Acres." She really thought it was going to be a perfect world and had a sign made with those words on it. She had Bill nail it to the barn, and I believe the sign was still there when we left – for a little while, until the next owner took it down.

| 5 |

6602 King Hill Avenue

It was sometime in 1961 that we moved back to South St. Joseph. Mom and Dad found a big, two-story house with a full attic on the corner of King Hill Avenue and Fulkerson Street. Several families from St. James Catholic Church, where we attended, lived in the neighborhood: the Miljavacs, Kovacs, Webers, Goucans, Mareks, Treus, and our cousins, the Hensleys.

Susan and Mom on the porch of the King Hill house. The ornamental evergreens on the left constantly were infected with bagworms, and after battling them for years, Dad had the trees and bushes removed.

I remember being excited as I had told my cousin Chuck Hensley at school that we were moving just up the street from him. Through the rest of grade school, Mike and I played with Chuck and his brother, Danny, more than any other neighborhood children. In summer, Mike and I would go over to the Hosea school and meet Chuck and Danny there. They didn't have far to go as the Hensley house backed up to the playground and field. It seemed like we always had it to ourselves except for a few kids roller skating or riding their bikes across the playground. There, Chuck, Danny, Mike and I would play baseball and football, the Hensleys against the Jurkiewiczes. I don't remember going to their house to play though. In winter, we only saw each other in school.

Our new house had a full front porch facing King Hill, and the front door opened into a little entranceway on the south side of the house. Walking into the house, the first thing anyone could see was the steep stairway that led up to the second floor. And just behind the door as it opened, we had a small table and that was where the phone jack and our rotary phone was. Anytime any of us had a conversation on the phone, anyone in the living room could hear what we were saying. The girls, when they talked to boyfriends or girlfriends, always sat as high up on the stairs as they could, stretching the phone cord and talking in low voices to try and keep their conversations as private as possible.

Upstairs there were three bedrooms, a full bath, and a small sunroom that became Mike's and my bedroom. Mike and I shared that room until I was in the sixth or seventh grade. Susan and Linda shared an adjoining room, and Kathy and Mary had their own rooms on the east side of the upstairs past the stairway to the attic. I guess it was after Kathy married Richard that Mike and I had separate bedrooms, and I stayed in the small sunroom.

Linda on the phone in the entryway that opened into the living room. Mom had new paneling put in the living room, but in this photo, carpet is still on the floor. Mom eventually had the carpet removed and the hardwood floor sanded and varnished.

The sunroom was about 14 or 15 feet long, but narrow, probably six or seven feet wide. It allowed just enough room to walk by the regular-sized bed I slept on. I had a desk and chair at the other end. One wall was along the inside of the house, with a door to Linda and Susan's room on one end and a door to the bathroom on the other end. The room could be a pain at times, because I had to go through either the bathroom or Linda and Susan's room to get out of it. Sometimes I had to wait a while in my room because Susan and Linda wouldn't let me through their room and someone was in the bathroom.

The other three walls, though, faced the outside and had a row of windows in them. The windows were short, starting about three and a half feet off the floor. The two short walls had only a couple of windows, but the long side had five or six.

This would have been taken in the back yard looking toward Fulkerson Street not long after we moved into the King Hill Avenue home.

A huge maple tree with a trunk about ten feet around was close to the house in the back yard. Its main branches reached up past the sunroom, and small branches with leaves were always scraping the windows and siding of the house in the wind, making noise at night. There was also a streetlight along Fulkerson that cast light and shadows up and into the room through the tree branches, so in the night the walls of the sunroom were usually moving and changing shape with any sort of wind. It could be artistically interesting, and in a storm, the wall could be disturbing as shadow and light moved and morphed with increased intensity. With lightning, the whole room burst into a flood of light, then descended into thick blackness before my eyes could adjust to the dark.

The sunroom was also just above Mom and Dad's bedroom, and the upstairs did not have forced heat delivered to it. Instead, the heat came up the stairwell and through open vents in the upstairs floor. One of the vents was near the bed in the sunroom. Mike and I could hear Mom and Dad talking at night and in the morning in their room. We could not hear their words clearly; we only heard muffled voices because the vent was not directly above them. It was off to one side in their room. Dad used to yell up the stairwell at us to settle down when we were making noise at night, but sometimes he yelled from his bed. We could hear him clearly then through the vent.

When Mary left for New York and the Peace Corps, her room became available for Susan, and then the youngest four of us all had our own room. Mary used to call about every Sunday morning from New York. She would call collect.

At one of Linda's birthdays, Susan talked a friend into bringing her pony for rides in our back yard. Mike is at the front on the left next to Robin and Melanie Hensley, our cousins. The friend is holding the horse. I am at the back left next to Susan and Linda.

One Sunday, I was the only one home, and I accepted the charges. Mary asked who was home, and I said me. She said why did I accept the charges if Mom or Dad weren't home. I said, "What? You don't want to talk to me?"

Mary, I seem to remember, had a lot of dates and went out with girlfriends a lot. Dad was pretty strict with Kathy and Mary and always told them he was locking the door at ten. If they showed up later than that, he wasn't going to let them in. Susan told me that Kathy came home a few minutes late one night and begged Dad to let her in, and he did. But Mary was ten minutes late one time, and Dad wouldn't let her in when she knocked. She slept outside on the porch swing.

Mary's and Kathy's rooms both had windows that looked out over the front porch roof. Kathy used to open her window and climb out on the porch roof and smoke. She also slipped away at night and climbed down the storm drain so Dad wouldn't know she had gone out. I don't know how many times she did that, and I don't know if she ever got caught either.

My eighth-grade graduation. I received a nice ribbon from St. James school, and Mom and Dad gave me a wristwatch.

Mom liked to dress Mike and I alike when we were young. Even our haircuts matched. The tree behind us was a huge silver maple tree with English ivy climbing around its trunk.

A few times Bill moved back in with us or came back temporarily. Whenever he came, he used Susan and Linda's room and they had to sleep with Mary or Kathy. One time, Bill visited when he was on leave from the Army. He came with a couple of friends.

It seems like their nicknames were French and Irish. Irish was a red-haired guy who was gross and vulgar, but he was memorable and interesting. He smoked constantly and blew smoke ring after smoke ring that drifted mesmerizingly into the air. Bill and his two buddies went out partying one night while they were in St. Joe, and they came back drunk very late. They woke every one of us up as they came up the stairs stomping and singing and talking loudly. Irish fell down the steps from halfway up, clunking as he hit the steps. Dad really yelled that night.

Bill lived with us for a while after the Army and also for a while after he returned from the Peace Corps later. He spent two years in Venezuela with the Peace Corps. After leaving the Army, he went to Missouri Western State College. I'm not sure what he took for classes, but he was in a comedic play that we all went to see. Bill played a drunk sheriff, and we were all so proud of him, except for Mom because Bill played a drunk; however, she admitted he did a good job. Bill had a lot of LP albums, and played them loud and long. They were mostly albums by folk music groups, such as Peter, Paul and Mary, and the Kingston Trio. I liked them and still know some of the songs.

This photo was taken at Ziph Photography in The Valley. Bill, middle at the back, had a hand-tinted copy made in Asia while he was in the Army. The copy hung in mom and dad's bedroom while we lived on King Hill Avenue.

When Bill came back from Venezuela, I was still in grade school, and he was in the house for a little while. He spent all his time in Linda's room typing. He said he was writing a novel based on his time in South America. Mom and Dad weren't as enthused about his writing as he was. They badgered him about getting a job. He wrote at least one chapter. I remember reading it as he left it lying on the desk. He shouldn't have because Mom might have read it, and it had some sexual stuff in it. Maybe she did. She could be snoopy when cleaning. Bill's desire to be a writer put thoughts in my head of becoming a writer. I remember taking a walk with Mom one day, and she asked me what I wanted to be when I grew up. I told her that I wanted to be a writer. She just sighed and told me to think about being a doctor.

After graduating high school, Kathy had a few jobs before marrying Richard.

Our nephews, Rich and Jeff, when they lived down Fulkerson Street just a little more than a block from us on King Hill Avenue.

One job she had that I remember was working for a blind man who bought and sold animals for zoos and people who were looking for exotic animals. Kathy told us that he had been bitten by cobras three times. We met him a few times, one time at Bean Lake. He seemed like a nice guy, and I think Kathy enjoyed working for him. But she was madly in love with Richard. She did an oil painting of Richard that was in her room for a long time of him in a New York Yankees uniform. Richard was a good ballplayer and played semi-pro ball. Kathy really got into art for a short time before she married, and she was pretty good. Susan, Mike and I found a painting Kathy hid in the attic during that time. It was a self-portrait of her nude.

Mom didn't like Richard at the first because he wasn't a Catholic, but he agreed to become one to marry Kathy.

They had a big Polish wedding. We called ourselves Ukrainian because that's what Grandpa said he was, but Polish wedding was the term for a big Eastern European or Slavic wedding. Mike and I were servers at the matrimonial Mass, and they had a their reception at the CIO Hall. The hall was just off Lake Avenue, where Gordon and Cherokee streets come together. Every couple who had a Polish wedding in South St. Joe then had a reception at the CIO Hall. The receptions were always held with lots of food and liquor, and a live band playing pop and polka music. Those receptions would last long after the couples left for their honeymoons, and about a fourth of the people who attended left drunk.

After Kathy and Richard married, they lived in an apartment uptown somewhere, but eventually they bought a little block house down the street from us. We all got to see Rich and Jeff grow up, and it was nice to have them so close to us. Rich and Jeff were like brothers to us, not nephews.

We saw Jeff and Rich a lot when they lived near us. They were like brothers, not nephews. I took the two photos of them when I was about 12 with a Kodak I bought. I learned to develop the negatives and make contact prints on photo paper.

The first floor of the King Hill house had a nice-sized living room, with three big, single-hung windows looking out on King Hill Avenue. The room was weird because it had a big closet with several sliding doors that ran under the stairs. I remember the closet mainly because Mom always said she wanted a fur coat. One day, Dad bought her one, which was quite a surprise. But Mom hardly ever wore it after complaining for years that she wanted one. Instead, the coat hung in that closet for years before she gave it away. I don't think she sold it.

> No man is an island,
> entire of itself;
> every man is a piece of the continent,
> a part of the main.
> If a clod be washed away by the sea,
> Europe is the less,
> as well as if a promontory were,
> as well if a manor of thy friend's
> or of thine own were.
> Any man's death diminishes me,
> because I am involved in mankind;
> and therefore never send to know
> for whom the bell tolls;
> it tolls for thee.
>
> by John Donne
> from Meditation XVII
> written December 1623

Bill wrote a few lines of Donne's Meditation 17 on the wall of our kitchen after the wallpaper was removed. It has always been oft quoted, but in the 1960s, its words were part of the ongoing cultural revolution. Part of the ending, "for whom the bell tolls," is famous because Ernest Hemingway titled that one of his books. Gary Cooper starred in the Hollywood movie, and Mom liked Gary Cooper's movies.

I remember the living room for something else. One time, Mike stuck a bobby pin in one of the electrical sockets. I swear it knocked him half way across the floor, and I did not put him up to it. I did something close to that. I took the battery-operated motor out of a little play car and stuck the wires in an electrical socket in the kitchen to see what would happen. I learned that something made for only a few volts did not perform well when supplied with 120 volts. The motor turned like a windmill in a hurricane for a brief moment, then flashed fire.

We weren't in the house very long before Mom had Dad hire a carpenter to put paneling on the walls. I remember Mom complaining to Dad about him. The guy was really slow, and it took him a long time. I think he may have been drinking too. The paneling wasn't dark, but a light tan, and she had the floor sanded and varnished. Corky Church and his brother, Sam, came and did the floors. Corky lived across the street behind the Webers. Corky was a nice guy, quiet. But Sam was a teenager then, and he was a loud, blustery guy, but a hard worker. Sam and Corky's sister, Aretta, married Audrey's uncle Clarence, but I didn't know Audrey then.

Mom redid the kitchen too, at least the walls. I don't remember if Bill helped take the yellowed wallpaper off or not, or just Mom and the girls, but Bill was there when it was off. He and his buddies started writing quotations and thoughts on the walls before they were repainted. One of the quotes Bill put on the wall was "No man is an island." I think he may have written several verses from John Donne's prose on the wall as well.

Bill's friends also wrote on the wall. Bill had several friends in his early adulthood, especially Arthur Treu and Dean Shepherd. They used to come around the house when he was there and play card games, mostly pitch and poker. Arthur's mom and dad lived nearby on Elizabeth Street on a big lot. They were really sweet people. I used to go down there. Arthur's mom had a garden and she would give me berries for pies. Mr. Kobzej and his family lived on West Hyde Park right behind Dad's shop, and he had a huge cherry tree in his front yard. It was loaded every year, and several years, Mr. Kobzej let me use his ladder and pick enough cherries for a pie. Mr. Kobzej was a displaced person who had been in a concentration camp in World War II. He complained about his legs hurting from the ill treatment he received in the camp.

A drawing I did in the 1990s of our house at 6602 King Hill Avenue. I did the drawing from memory when I discovered I couldn't find a photo of the entire house from when we lived in it.

Dad didn't help with the wallpapering. He told me, and that was the first time that I heard it, that Hitler had hung wallpaper for a job before becoming a politician and that was why he went crazy.

Mom and Dad's bedroom was just off the kitchen and accessed through the living room. They had a full bathroom in their room. They let us use their bathroom, so we went through their bedroom in the daytime. Mom was always neat and kept her house clean, so I don't think I ever saw her bed unmade. She made it right after she and Dad got up. It was at the King Hill house that Bill sent us from Korea a touched-up photograph of our family. It was a black-and-white one we had taken at Ed Ziph's studio in the Valley some time before, and the Koreans that Bill hired to enhance the photo had blown it up and put a little tinting to our faces. Mom was proud of it. But she kept it in her bedroom and not in the living room.

Like the second floor, the first floor had a sunroom at the back of the house, only the one on the first floor was bigger. It was a nice room past the kitchen, with two huge plate-glass windows. Each window had outside panes and insides panes.

Here we are acting silly for a photo. Mary, Susan and I, in back, and Mike and Linda in front. I don't remember the dog. We had a few dogs, but Mom didn't like them in the house, and we wouldn't have them for long.

The inside panes were locked into place by swivel clips. Every spring, Mom would have us take the inside windows out, and the girls would clean both inside and outside glass. The huge plate glass windows got dirty from condensation that built up between the panes when it was humid; plus, they did not fit perfectly tight and dust worked its way in.

We had some really nice holiday and Sunday dinners in that sunroom. We ate in that room almost every Christmas and Easter. Mom would make a ton of food, American and traditional Polish and Croatian food. We would buy Polish sausage and blood sausage from Gnat's or Walter Marek's. The table was always loaded, and we were always loud and laughing.

We had a few tense moments too. Bill came home from somewhere once, with a friend who sat down at the table with a tam or a beanie or a French painter's hat on his head, and Mom mistakenly asked Bill to pray. He started out, "God, if there is a God ..." and that was all it took to start a big fight. One time on a big event, somebody's birthday or a holiday, I said a cuss word. It wasn't a terrible word, but Mom took me into the kitchen and made me take a bite of soap. Then she sent me into her bedroom to sit and think about what I had just said. Mom didn't tolerate much cussing, although strangely enough she didn't see anything wrong with her saying chickenshit. One time Mike and I were shooting basketballs in our driveway. We had a backboard and basketball goal up on the garage. I made a long shot and Mike said, "You suck."

Mom and Linda stand next to a row of roses in our back yard on King Hill. The big backyard maple and the house are behind them. The roses died out, but Mom always planted marigolds and begonias in planters around the house.

Mom was outside and heard that, and she slapped Mike in the face. That was something we and other kids said all the time at school, but we couldn't say it at home.

The garage must have been made for a Model T as it was just barely wide enough for a 1950s or 1960s car. We never did very much in the garage besides park Mom and Dad's vehicles because of its small size. One time, Bill was home and accidentally hit the left side of the front of the garage, pushing it in and smashing a few boards. Dad had me help him fix it, and I remember him telling me that he hoped I didn't grow up to go out drinking and then come home and smash the garage.

We pose for an Easter photo in front of Mom's favorite tree, our flowering magnolia. Mike and I have identical suits, and Mom made dresses for Susan and Linda. I don't remember that hat that Kathy's wearing, but it is very stylish.

That reminds me of a story Aunt Anna told me about Dad once. She said she and Dad were coming home late one night when they were young, and he was driving. I don't think Aunt Anna ever drove. She said they were coming to a rail signal when it started flashing and the arm started its way down. She said that instead of slowing, Dad sped up and he hit the arm and broke it off as he went across the tracks beating the train that was coming. She told Dad he scared her and asked why did he do that. She said Dad said he didn't know why, he just did it.

Mom didn't drive until after Bill was born. I don't know if she took lessons or if Dad just showed her how. She said the first time she took the car out herself, she had Billy in the front seat and she drove up West Valley, where they lived, to the T-intersection with King Hill Avenue. She said she stopped at the stop sign, then started onto King Hill, and panicked. She couldn't get herself to do anything, especially take her foot off the accelerator, and she drove straight across the street and into the brick building on the other side. Mom said she wasn't going fast, so there was no damage to the car, or building, only a scrape on the front bumper. However, she said she did attract a lot of spectators.

My first baseball team was sponsored by Frosty-Treet. When our team won, we went to the ice cream drive-in for a free cone.

The garage on King Hill was memorable too because one time Mike found a pack of Camel cigarettes when we were eight and ten or so. We went out behind the garage to smoke them. We only smoked a couple cigarettes and got retching sick. I never could stand the smell of cigarette smoke after that, and I never smoked a cigarette again either.

On the back of the King Hill house, on the outside, was a door and a stairway to the basement. We entered the house through the basement frequently from the outside when it was wet or we were dirty. The washer and dryer were at the bottom of the steps near a shower head with a drain in the floor. We took showers there sometimes, but not very often because it was open. We never had a shower curtain up. There was another entrance to the basement from the kitchen, a door with a stairway that turned two times coming down. The basement was a low-ceilinged affair. Even before I was entering my teenage years, if I reached up, my hands hit the floor joists. A big furnace sat in the middle and took up most of the basement. But we had room for a pool table Dad got somewhere. We couldn't really play pool well, though, as the posts that held up the floors of the house were always in the way when we had to take shots at the balls. Mike and I had a dart board up on the inside door that led to the steps to the outside. Over the years, we missed the board and hit the door so much that one day it collapsed from all the holes we put in it.

Because the house was on a corner lot, the yard was fairly large. We had trash cans at the back of the yard, and Mike and I took the trash out and set it on fire in the days when that was still allowed. There was a flowering magnolia in the front yard next to our neighbor's house. The buds of the medium-sized tree usually froze each year in the spring with a late frost, but when it survived, it was full of blooms and beautiful. Mom loved that tree, and we took a lot of photos in front of it when it bloomed. The big maple in the back yard had a brick planter around it that was cracked and broken from roots, but we never put flowers in it. The planter grew ivy that wound its way up the trunk and a few of the big branches of the tree. Susan told me that years later after we left, a new owner had to cut the aging tree down. From the wood of that maple tree, the owner made nativity stables, and he gave Susan one of them. She was living on East Joseph Street in St. Joseph at that time, and he made a trip to her house to give her one. She told me she still has it.

The back yard along Fulkerson had hedge that ran parallel with the street. Each year, Dad would say we needed to go out and trim the bushes back. He would get us started then disappear. We used to laugh, and complain, about Dad doing that, starting a yard job with us and then disappearing and leaving us to finish.

When we moved to that house, it had a big Chinese elm on the right of way in front of the house. My senior year in high school, the tree died from Dutch elm disease and Dad had it cut down. I remember that because he had me go out with an ax and chop up the stump in the ground. It was a very hot day, and I took my T-shirt off. The sun burned my back and I was miserable for a couple of days. I remember lying in bed and the burn blisters popping and getting my bed wet from the blisters' leaking fluid.

Our Halloween costumes were pretty sad that year, but we seem to be happy.

We had cedar bushes, about four or so, by the front porch that we thought were nice when we moved there, but they became hated plantings. They would be covered in bagworms in the summer. Dad sprayed them and he sent us outside to pick the little larvae in their needle-covered bags off the bushes. No matter what we did, the bagworms always came back, and eventually, Dad had the bushes removed.

A circle of poppies, orange ones, came up each spring in the back yard. We all liked them, and sometimes we picked the seed pods and squeezed them just to see the small black seeds pop out and say we could make opium. One year a couple of rabbits hung around the poppies in the morning, and Mom was afraid the rabbits were eating them. Mike and I ran out trying to catch the rabbits, who had no trouble outrunning us. We even tried sneaking up on the bunnies with a dip net to no avail although we got close a time or two. Peonies came up in the yard too, and Mom liked to plant marigolds in a planter that ran around the sunroom. A crabapple tree, a big one and very old, grew at the back of the yard by the trash. We used to throw the little crabapples at one another when they set on. We tried cooking and mashing them once, but they were not very good.

Before we had air conditioning at that house, we sat on the porch together late nights in the summer talking and singing. The house had high ceilings and big windows, but hot air didn't seem to find its way out of the house, and humid northwest Missouri made the heat much, much worse. Even after we got air conditioning, we would sit out on the porch on cool evenings. Mom liked to sing "You Are my Sunshine" and "Those Faraway Places." Dad didn't sit out there as much as Mom. He liked to go to bed at ten o'clock. Besides, Dad's music preference was polkas. He loved "The Lawrence Welk Show," and he watched it religiously. He liked the "Beer Barrel Polka" and "She's Too Fat for Me Polka." We also sang a song I believe came from him, "My Gal's a Corker." It had multiple verses and you could make up verses to it because it lampooned a man's girlfriend whose physical characteristics were not very desirable. So a typical verse went, "My gal's a corker, she's a New Yorker, I buy her everything to keep her in style (which is repeated in every verse), She's got a pair of legs, just like two whiskey kegs, Hey, boys, that's where my money goes."

This photo is from 1966, before I entered high school in the fall. Susan, Kathy, Mom and Dad are in back, while Mike, I, Linda and Mary are in the front. I am not sure what I am proudly holding up.

Dad also, I believe, was behind Mary taking up the accordion and getting involved in a polka band, two guitars and a drum set, with the Dobosch boys. They played at weddings and a few other events. Mary was a very good accordionist, and one time when she was in high school, she took part in a music contest at the St. Joseph television studio out on the Belt Highway. I don't remember what she played, maybe "Lady of Spain," which I seem to remember she played a lot. She did well, but she only received second place. A young black man, who played the piano, came in first place. I remember somebody saying that the judges gave him first place because he needed the prize money more. I don't remember what the prize was, but that person said the pianist put his feet up on a chair at one point and displayed holes in the soles of his shoes to get sympathy from the judges. He had on an undersized black suit too. I doubt that's why he won. He played very well, but I heard it.

King Hill Avenue had a lot of traffic so there was car noise to put up with when we sat outside, but late at night, it wasn't quite as bad. Carl used to walk by a lot late at night and we would see him frequently. Carl, who was also called Banjo, was a mentally challenged person who seemed to eternally walk King Hill Avenue, up and down, all times of the day. He was fairly high functioning, but I don't think he worked. He just seemed to always be walking, and he walked with long strides at a very fast pace, as if he were agitated. He talked to himself, and sometimes he would stop to talk to us or other people, but I don't remember that he engaged in very long conversations. The poor guy always seemed to have cuts and bruises too. I'm not sure if he fell down sometimes or if he got in fights with bullies. I do know a couple of times that he was assaulted by degenerate toughs and beat up. Once, after being assaulted, the newspaper carried the story of the attack.

We had some interesting people who lived around us. Louie Marek grew up a few houses from us. He was much older than I was. He grew up to be a musician and had his own polka band that traveled a wide area. I think Dad would have liked for Mary to join his group. Louie married a very pretty woman who sang with him, but they had difficulty together. One day while traveling on the highway, she fell out of the back of the van and was killed. Police conducted an investigation into her death. The story was in the local newspaper, but the prosecutor didn't have any evidence that she was pushed. He ruled it an accident.

Linda with Kathy and her two boys, Rich and Jeff, on the front walk along King Hill Avenue. We had several years of good snows, and we either went across the street to sled down the hill in a neighbor's yard or walked up to Hyde Park to sled there.

Johnny Miljavac was a musician, too, a drummer. He was a very nice guy. All the Miljavacs were nice and polite. They lived two houses west on Fulkerson on the same side of the street as us. Mr. Miljavac, the father, was an electrician and died when Larry Miljavac, who was my age, was in the fifth grade. Mr. Miljavac had a heart attack at work one day. All the Miljavac boys grew up to be electricians. But when Johnny was about 15 or so, he was out with a BB gun and shot a blue jay in the crabapple tree in our back yard from the alleyway. I saw him do it, and he was sitting holding the dying bird in his hand. Johnny told me he saw it attacking a young robin fledging. He said he had seen blue jays kill other birds. That was why he shot it he said. But he said he really felt bad about killing the bird after he did it and was watching the blue jay die. Besides electrical work, Johnny played drums at a bar with exotic dancers on Frederick Avenue. I was there one night and saw him playing while a woman in skimpy clothing danced with a boa constrictor around her neck.

An old lady lived next to the Hensleys on Fulkerson who had a beautiful, fenced rose garden. It took up one entire lot. I don't remember her name or anything about her family situation, but Chuck and Danny always said she was a mean old woman. They said she wouldn't return their baseballs when they accidentally hit or threw them into her yard. I'm sure she didn't like kids traipsing around in her flower beds. I was always afraid of her when I was growing up and never talked to her. But when I was a sophomore, I believe, in high school, I had to do an insect collection for Biology. I was having trouble getting insects, and Mom told me I should go to that lady's house and see if she would let me catch some butterflies. Her yard was always filled with butterflies in the summer and fall. I didn't want to go ask her, but in the end, I did, and she turned out to be a really nice lady. She let me in the yard, and I caught all kinds of butterflies, grasshoppers and beetles. I had a nice collection for my project.

Some people commented how nice my collection was because we rode the bus all the way across town to high school. We caught the bus in the morning at 7:15 sharp on Fulkerson. We watched for it going down Fulkerson, where it made a little loop on Carnegie or Mack streets, and then came back up Fulkerson. We had to transfer to another bus at the downtown station, which was no more than a little blockhouse, but sometimes the bus drivers went in there and sat for a few minutes while we waited on them.

There was an overweight couple, sort of an antagonistic couple, who lived down King Hill Avenue too, who we really never knew. But we could hear them out playing in their above-ground swimming pool in the summer. One evening, about dark, the husband came driving down King Hill Avenue, and he was drunk. He turned late at the corner of Fulkerson and if we hadn't seen him coming, we would have gotten hit in the yard where we were playing. He ran over the stop sign on our corner and smacked it flat, then came into our yard. There wasn't much point in confronting him as he probably wouldn't have remembered what he had done the next day. But a few days later, Dad, Mike and I went fishing and one of us caught a big carp, probably 15 or 20 pounds. We took it home and I put it their swimming pool at night. We heard from a neighbor later that the guy asked why jokesters would put a big fish in their pool.

The Petro family lived across Fulkerson, on the opposite corner from us, for several years. The parents were a generation behind my parents, with two boys Rich and Jeff's age. The Petros were nice, friendly people, but the two boys were wild, and they drove fast once they started driving. One of the boys got into an accident not long after he turned 16 and died. We went to the funeral, and I heard Mrs. Petro telling someone she knew she spoiled her son, but she felt he lived life to its fullest while he was alive, which was all right with her. I couldn't understand how she could say that when he really didn't live very long.

The Brumleys lived there after the Petros left. They were an old, retired, nice couple. We had more interaction with them, and went over to their house to talk. Mr. Brumley was always puttering around in his yard and we would say hello to him. Dad bought an old-fashioned rocking chair from them. I ended up with the rocking chair, and Audrey and I had it for years, rocking our newborns in it. I gave it to Linda, and she had it in her house when her children were born.

The Cates family lived down Fulkerson about three houses from the corner. Nancy Cates, the wife, was a busy, energetic person and she and her husband had a couple little kids that Mary and Susan babysat. The Cates family lived in a big two-story house like ours, and they had a concrete Koi pond in the side yard. Mr. Cates would take his Koi inside to his basement fish tank in the winter. I remember spending one New Year's Eve in the Cates' house while the girls babysat and Mom and Dad went out for the evening.

Mom wanted color on our house, so she picked out apple green. Here Mom, me, Linda and Mike are with Kathy and Rich and Jeff, who was not cooperating.

Paul Kovac and his family lived down Fulkerson at the opposite end of our block. He and his wife had five or six children. Paul owned the major supermarket in our part of town. One of the children, a girl Susan's age, Jeannie, who went to LeBlond, died in a car accident on the Belt highway. She was with some kids from Benton, and she ran into the back of a vehicle in front of her. It was very tragic. She was a really pretty and sweet girl. Everybody liked her, and she was very popular at LeBlond. The yearbook that year and the next had tributes to her. We all wondered after that, if we happened to die while in high school whether they would even mention us in the yearbook since we weren't popular.

Scoop and his wife lived in the house just south of the Hensleys. Scoop was a vo-tech teacher, and a nice guy. I don't remember ever seeing him around his house or walking around the neighborhood. But he did come into the shoe shop a lot to sit and talk and drink coffee. He talked a lot about the students in his class, usually the worst and the best.

I mentioned the King Hill house had an attic. It was a full attic, but we never really used it for much, not even a lot of storage. I don't think anyone ever used it for sleeping because it was so hot up there in the summer and cold in the winter. But we used to go up there and play when it was tolerable. Mike and I pretended to be scientists for a while, and I painted the planets of the Solar System on a part of the ceiling that slanted with the slope of the roof. Susan stopped at the house years later when other people lived there and they showed her through the house. Susan said the planets were still up there; the lady said she didn't have the heart to paint over them when she thought about some kid painting them on the ceiling. I did my first artwork up there too, painting a daffodil in an impressionistic style.

That big old house with its creaky stairs, bright back sunroom, and my animated-at-night bedroom still appear in my dreams now sometimes, after all these years. I can still hear Mom get out of bed in the morning, get a skillet out of the cabinet and start frying bacon. I hear Dad yelling at us from his bedroom to keep it down when we were staying up late to watch a movie or were talking upstairs. I can see us sitting down in the evening in front of the television, Dad with his beer and potato chips and Mom with her sewing, watching "Bonanza" or "Gunsmoke," or Jacques Cousteau's "Undersea World" or a John Denver show or special.

In the spring of 1975, Mom and Dad sold the house. It was after Susan married Farrell McGinnis and she had the wedding in the back yard. She worried, of course, about the weather and the possibility of rain or cool weather, but it turned out to be a beautiful day. That would be our last big family event at that house.

Dad had bought a cabin at Sugar Lake sometime before, and Mom and Dad moved there briefly, through the summer of 1975, until they rented an apartment across from LeBlond High School. It was really strange to see them in that small apartment after all those years in that big house.

From my sister Linda

As far as your and Michael's bedroom goes, I remember we used to play this game where we would go between the springs and the mattress, crawling our way from one side to the other. Sort of a strange game, playing soldiers or something. I don't remember the mattress feeling heavy, as if it were going to smother me. We also would play some sort of "fort" game, and we would roll up our socks and throw them at each other and make a lot of noise. Dad really yelled when we did that. But we had a lot of fun and laughed a lot.

Wallpaper. That is a very funny story about Hitler from Dad. I remember Bill steaming the wallpaper from the kitchen walls. Boy, was he unhappy and complained the whole time. And unfortunately, I was present when Dad and Mom hung wallpaper in the upstairs bathroom. It was not pretty. It never happened again, either.

The CIO hall. Another moment of freedom as a child. While all of the adults were inside, enjoying the music, dancing and free drinks, us kids were allowed to disappear to our own devices outside the building, which frequently included scamming a drink or two as well, at least teenagers.

The attic. I still think of your painting of the solar system. I also remember that Kathy would hide cigarettes in the curtain rods. I found them at some point in my childhood. We also had some old fancy dresses up in the closets. They were full-length with lots of that stiff netting that made them stand out. But those closets were scary. I also remember loving looking out those windows. You could observe everyone on the streets without their knowing. Also, do you remember how skinny that staircase was up to the attic? And steep?

Linda was always ready to join in on being silly; Michael wasn't in the mood that day. I don't remember us ever using the picnic table in the back yard for eating. But it was our home base when we played a tag game called Monster.

One of my memories of Mom includes that attic. One night Mom, you, Michael and I came home from some event after dark. The lights were on in the house and Mom was sure she hadn't left them on. I'm sure she hadn't; we were so careful about turning off lights. So we went in to the house and she grabbed a butcher knife out of the kitchen drawer and she started stalking through the house with that knife raised, ready to pounce. Of course, all of us were following in line. We eventually got to the attic stairs, and I remember climbing up those in anticipation. Needless to say, there were no intruders. That story always perplexed me because Mom was always so sensitive and her feelings were always hurt so easily that I had difficulty putting my image of her with this mother who wielded a knife to claim her space. But I guess she was always brave when things were extremely tough.

That time you rammed heads with Danny Hensley, she was so calm, wiping the blood from your brow. Quite frightened, I was in the bathroom as she did it. When Michael was hit in the head by the baseball bat, she held it together. When we were at Dad's funeral, she didn't shed a tear. But boy, that was so not true when you hurt her feelings. I guess I got to the point that she really controlled herself in those intense moments of fear. And I suppose, parents do that to some degree with their children.

I love the story about putting the fish in that man's pool. I've never heard that one. Nor that you all almost got hit by his car.

The porch, a life on the porch. Remember how we would wave to anyone we knew that was driving by? Our arms were tired by the end of the night; we knew almost everyone.

Mom, Dad and Linda at the Sugar Lake cabin, where they lived the summer after selling the house on King Hill Avenue. This photo is from two years earlier, in 1973.

One night I heard a loud noise outside and went out onto the porch to find Mom and Dad, sitting on the swing, but the chains had broken, or pulled out of the screws, and they were on the porch floor, luckily with their legs sticking out in front of them. That was funny, but could have been bad. They must have been on an upswing!

I had a big closet in my room, which was under the attic stairs. Since we didn't have many clothes, it was easy to do other things in that closet. My friends and I used to have seances in there. That must have been during the Ouija board era.

As far as the back yard goes, I remember we had that small iron grate table. One night someone driving up Fulkerson veered into our yard. That table saved Mom and Dad's bedroom from being invaded by the errant car.

The poppy patch, so beautiful! One of my favorite memories was one time we had a "zoo." We took a whole bunch of cardboard boxes and cut out bars, stacked them all over in that part of the yard and put our stuffed animals in there. We might have even charged admission!

Music. I remember having that stereo on the landing on the second floor. Music was always blasting from that thing. My favorite memory is of Bill singing "The Great Mandela" by Peter, Paul and Mary. What a great song. And of course, the piano in the living room. I occasionally run across pictures of us playing music together. Those were fun moments.

The closet in the living room underneath the stairs. Mom kept one of her sewing tools in there. It was a yardstick that had a rubber ball and a container of white powder. It was used to mark a hem on a skirt. It was so fun to play with, although I suspect I made a big mess with it most of the time.

That's funny that you didn't go into the Hensley's house. Melanie and I spent pretty much every day together. I pretty much helped her with her dishes every night so that we could get outside to play faster. But we did do things inside their house too. Like one day we found Aunt Dorothy's falsies!

I feel like our childhood on that corner was in an era that was a gift for children. We had tremendous freedom. We were relatively safe. And I love my memories of being outdoors almost all of the time, roaming, biking, playing at the school grounds.

And I can still hear Mom's voice ring through the neighborhood, "David, Michael, Linda, it's getting dark; it's time to come home now."

Linda, Mary, Kathy, Mom, and Rich on the King Hill Avenue porch in the 1960s. While Rich is busy with a sucker, Kathy and Mom find something interesting off camera.

| 6 |

Stefan and Ahafia Jurkiewicz

Stefan and Ahafia were my paternal grandparents.
I did not know Ahafia. She died August 15, 1930, when my dad was 14 years old. I do not know what she died of.

This is a portrait of a young Grandma Ahafia, one that hung at Aunt Anna's house that we took photographs of. She and Grandpa Stefan came from the same village in Galicia, a territory of the Austro-Hungarian Empire in early 1900s.

They both were born in 1886 in Grodek Jagidonski, Dobrostany, Galicia. Galicia at that time straddled what is now the Polish/Ukrainian border and was part of the Austro-Hungarian Empire. After the empire fell apart, Galicians tried to nationalize the region, but fighting between Poles and Ukrainians who lived there, doomed the effort. The region was divided between Poland and the Ukraine, and the Ukraine was not a country, but a region within Russia.

Stefan's parents' names were Joseph and Anna. Aunt Anna, Dad's sister, who told me her grandparents' names, did not know what great-grandma's maiden name was.

Aunt Anna said Ahafia's whole name was Ahafia Chasi Milan, and her father's name was Nicholas Milan. Aunt Anna said Ahafia's mother "was not known."

My grandfather Stefan used to come into my dad's shoe shop occasionally and sit around and talk. He and Dad spoke Ukrainian to each other. Grandpa would come over and talk to me too, in English, but he had a very strong accent, and it was hard to understand him. He called me "Day," which I took was Dave. If he said David, he said "Davit," because in the language he spoke, a "d" at the end of a word is pronounced as a "t."

Grandpa told me that growing up, he lived in a small village, and his family was poor. He said they ate meat only twice a year, at Christmas and Easter. He said their house was a small house, only a few rooms. The house had two floors, a first floor built of stone with a dirt floor, and a second story of wood. Grandpa said that the animals lived in the bottom of the house, and his family lived on the top floor. They had some chickens for eggs, a pig or two for eating, and a horse for plowing and pulling a wagon.

Grandpa had an older brother, William. I don't know if he had any other brothers or sisters.

I believe Grandpa told me that his family raised sugar beets.

Grandpa Stefan was deaf in one ear, his left, I think. He said he was a young boy, and the Emperor of Austro-Hungary, Franz Josef, came to Dobrostany for a dedication of a new cathedral. He said his family traveled to see the emperor, who sat in his open carriage on the way to the cathedral. They also went to witness the big religious and military processions accompanying

A road and postal map of Galicia from 1900. I have approximately marked in blue present borders in Europe and the countries' names in black.

the emperor. Grandpa said that in Dobrostany, he wanted to see what was going on in the square near the cathedral, and he ran with some other boys with the same intent. Grandpa, however, made a wrong turn and ran too close in front of several cannons that were firing a salute for the celebration. The percussion from one of the cannons burst his ear drum and knocked him down.

Grandpa told me that he was sent away from home as a teen to learn to be a shoemaker. He served as an apprentice to a Polish shoemaker, living with his family for several years. I believe Grandpa ended up working as a shoemaker after his apprenticeship was done, but Grandpa told me that he, like many other young people he knew, wanted to immigrate to America. He said times were very hard at the turn of the century, and there was a lot of political unrest in Eastern Europe. He said he went to Austria to pick apples to earn enough money to buy passage to America.

From there, he said he went to Germany to board a ship for America. I am positive that Grandpa told me one time that the ship he boarded to travel to America was the Kaiser Wilhelm. However, the ship manifest with his name on it states he came over on the SS Gneisenau. Grandpa is listed as a laborer coming from Dobrostany and heading to Butler, PA. The ship left from Bremen on March 3, 1906, according to the manifest. Aunt Anna told me Grandpa came in 1904, but she told me that in the 1980s and certainly must have been mistaken. Grandpa was 19 years old when he left for the United States.

Grandpa told me that he, along with most everyone else on board, was sick for several days and that the immigrants quartered in the bottom of the ship, in steerage. He said there were more than a thousand people immigrating, and according to online records about the Gneisenau, built in

Stetlin, Germany, which is now a city of another name in Poland, the ship would hold 2,000 people in steerage. He said where they stayed at the bottom of the ship, it smelled of vomit, urine and human excrement. The Gneisenau arrived in New York at Ellis Island on March 16, 1906.

My dad stands with his mother and father, Ahafia and Stefan. Dad appears to be in his mid- to late teens, which would date this photo about mid-1930s.

Grandpa didn't say much about Ellis Island. He liked to tell the story that as he walked the streets of New York City after leaving Ellis Island, he saw a yellow fruit he had never seen before, so he bought one and tried it. He said it tasted awful and he spit it out, but later someone told him that if he peeled it first, it would taste much better.

Grandpa did not stay long in New York City; he went to Butler, PA, where he worked making railroad cars.

According to Aunt Anna, Ahafia came to the United States in 1907. Grandpa and Grandma, Aunt Anna said, were from the same village and engaged. But Ahafia went to the Chicago area and worked as a domestic. It wasn't until January 25, 1910, that Ahafia and Stefan married in Butler.

They moved Hammond, Indiana, soon after, and then to Gary, Indiana, where Joseph, their oldest child, was born Nov. 1, 1910. In 1911, Stefan and his family moved to St. Joseph, and Aunt Anna was born there on Sept. 2, 1913. Dad was born three years later in St. Joseph.

I'm not sure what all Grandpa did for a living, but I know that he worked as a shoe cobbler and as a tavern owner. According to the 1930 Census, he was a retail merchant in the grocery business, and the 1940 Census lists him as a tavern owner. He went in together with my dad to buy the shoe shop after my dad returned from service in World War II, but Grandpa didn't stay long. He would have been 54 years old then.

As long as I knew Grandpa Stefan, he lived with Aunt Anna and her family on Alabama Street. I do not remember him as a happy, loving, or joyful person. He seemed to be distant and harsh. He told only a few jokes, mostly about excrement. He would ask, what is the white stuff on chicken poop? The answer: Chicken poop too. He had a joke he played on me once. He said he could make a glass of water hang from the ceiling with a straw. So I took him a glass of water and a straw, and he stood on a chair holding the straw to the ceiling. He lifted the glass up to the straw, then he dropped the straw and asked me to pick it up for him. When I bent over to get the straw, he poured water from the glass onto my head and back. That was the joke, and he thought pouring water over someone was funny.

Grandpa, I understand from my dad, did send money to pay passage for his niece to the United States and St. Joseph. Dad said she came when he was still a baby, and that when Grandpa handed him, Dad, to "Kuma" – we called her Kuma because that means godmother – Dad, who was frightened by this unknown woman, bit her on the nose. Kuma's married name was Mrs. Plekan. She had three girls, Mrs. Miljavac, Mrs. Kovac and Mrs. Gomek. The Miljavacs and Kovacs lived on the same block as us. The Gomeks not far away.

Dad is seated far left, next to his mother, Ahafia, with Aunt Anna seated on her opposite side. Stefan is the man to the right of the groom, and Dad's brother, Joseph is at the far right. We do not know at whose wedding this photo was taken, and it would have been taken in the early 1920s.

None of us children knew our Uncle Joseph. When he was 16 years old, in 1926, he ran away from home. Aunt Anna told me that Joseph and Grandpa did not get along, and one night they had a long argument. That night, Joseph left. They never heard from him again. Grandpa told me once, regarding Joseph, that people told him he was too harsh on his son and that was why he ran away and was never heard from again. But Grandpa told me that they were wrong, he was only trying to be a good father to Joseph, but Joseph would not obey or listen to him.

Grandpa told me once too, that when Hitler came to power in the 1930s that he liked Hitler. He said that because there was a great deal of generational hatred between Ukrainians and Poles, and Hitler was tough on the Poles. Grandpa said he agreed with that policy. However, Grandpa said it turned out later that Hitler didn't care much for Ukrainians either, which made Grandpa later change his attitude toward the Third Reich and Hitler.

There is one other interesting story about Grandpa, and it is one that my mother told me. Grandpa and Dad went in together on the tavern, and Grandpa lived in the tavern in a second-floor apartment. During this time, Grandpa sent off for a mail order bride, getting a woman from New York to come to St. Joseph and marry him. Mom said that the woman was only with Grandpa for a couple weeks. The mail order bride had a drinking problem, and spent most of her time down in the tavern imbibing Dad and Grandpa's profits, and I believe, flirting with men too. It didn't take long for Grandpa to end the relationship. Mom said that early one morning, the mail order bride was downstairs drinking at a table, and Grandpa pulled her out of the chair and shoved her out the front door with an order and a warning, "Get out of here, and don't come back." She did not return.

Dad, Aunt Anna, and Grandpa, who was always a dapper dresser.

Grandpa developed lung cancer in his later years. He was hospitalized in the Sisters hospital in St. Joseph for an operation at one point. I don't think he was a good patient because we heard that he slapped one of the nuns. The story went that the nun came around to pray with him and give him a holy card, and he told her that he didn't need her God and hit her.

It may be that Grandpa was developing dementia, or getting cranky, or maybe became an atheist. I think Mom said that about him once. Or maybe he did what he did because he belonged to the Ukrainian Catholic Church, which was more Eastern Orthodox than Roman Catholic. He helped establish the St. Joseph Ukrainian Catholic Church, a small, wood structure on a red-brick lower floor in St. Joseph on Virginia Street. I'm not sure how religious he was, but Dad did go to church with Grandpa occasionally at the Ukrainian Catholic church.

There was a lot of tension between Poles and Ukrainians in the Old Country over a lot of things, but one of them was religion as the Poles were Roman Catholic and Ukrainians Eastern Orthodox and Ukrainian Catholics. Some of that tension carried over to America. Even when Dad was in the hospital dying in 1980, the priest at the Ukrainian Catholic Church got into a religious discussion with Mom and some of her extended family. The Ukrainian priest came to see Dad, and then sat with us in the waiting room. He was a young priest, maybe in his thirties, balding already, and a real talker and friendly, but he was very opinionated. He was one of the last full-time priests at the St. Joseph church because it lost so many parishioners that the head of the Ukrainian Catholic Church in the Midwest started giving priests split duty between congregations in Omaha, Nebraska, and St. Joseph. He came around to visit Dad in the shop because he knew Dad had grown up in the church and he asked Dad several times to attend there. Dad did once or twice.

In the mid-1960s, the Jurkiewiczes and Hameras had a get together at Aunt Anna and Grandpa's house on Alabama Street. Back row: Me, Richard Lamb, Linda, Kathy, Susan, Mike, John Hamera with his son James, wife Josephine, Wilfred Jung, James Brewer, Jeanie Hamera, Mary Hamera. Front row: Mary holding Rich, Mom with Jeff, Dad, Grandpa, Aunt Anna with John's son Stephen, Joanie (Hamera) Jung with her daughter Anne, Bernice (Hamera) Brewer, Barbara (Hamera) Liberty with John's daughter Karen.

I seem to remember it was Aunt Rosie who said something to the Ukrainian Catholic priest in the hospital that he really wasn't Catholic. That got a discussion going, and the priest delved into the religious nitty gritty, citing the Bible and church history, to defend Orthodox and Ukrainian Catholic beliefs, two of which centered around no three-dimensional objects of worship in church and allowing priests to marry. I don't think he was terribly offended by Aunt Rosie's comment because he probably heard that a lot, but he did give a comprehensive defense. We all gave a sigh of relief when he finally left because once he started talking, it was hard for him to stop and anyone else to get a word in. I wish I could remember his name. Audrey and I lived in a house on Virginia Street after we got married, and we would see him now and then and talk with him.

Besides the religious difference with Polish people, Grandpa resented that American officials constantly listed him as Polish because the area he came from was allotted to Poland after World

War I. One of the census records lists him as Polish, but it does note that he spoke Ukrainian. His United States naturalization certificate from March 1, 1926, also lists him as coming from Poland.

Though he said a few bad things about Poles to me, he got along all right with Polish people in South St. Joe. There were a lot of them, including another family with a similar sounding name, but it was spelled Yurkovich.

Grandpa died August 27, 1971. His funeral service was held in St. Joseph's Ukrainian Catholic Church. He was buried in Mt. Olivet Cemetery, ironically a Roman Catholic cemetery, but his grave is not next to Ahafia's. He was buried in the same row as Ahafia, but about ten plots farther to the south.

Joseph Jurkiewicz

Born Nov. 1, 1910, left home in 1926 and never heard from again

I have mentioned several things about Joseph in the story above about Grandpa. Joseph was the oldest child of Stefan and Ahafia, born in Gary, Indiana. He did not get along with Grandpa, and he left home in 1926, when he was 16 years old. At one time, I don't know when, maybe the 1950s, Dad paid to have someone try to locate Uncle Joe. The locator came up blank.

Grandpa talked to me about Uncle Joe one time when he came into the shop. I don't know what brought it on, but Grandpa said he received some criticism from friends and neighbors after Joe left. Grandpa said that they said he was too hard on his son. But Grandpa said he was only trying to make his son obey.

Steve Zanko, one of Dad's childhood friends, told me that years after Uncle Joe left, he was listening to a cops and robber show on the radio. He said the show described a shootout between several bank robbers and Detroit police, in which one of the bank robbers, a Joseph Jurkiewicz, was killed. Steve Zanko said he told Dad about the show years after he heard it. He didn't say anything at the time, he said, because he didn't want to upset Dad. But when he finally did tell Dad, Dad didn't believe Uncle Joe would have gotten involved with anything like that. The only thing that Dad said sounded reasonable is that his brother might have gone to Detroit because they lived there a few years when he was young and Grandpa's brother William and his family lived there.

Dad didn't talk much about his brother, but he must have liked him to have paid someone to try and locate him so many years later.

Anna (Jurkiewicz) Hamera

Born Sept. 2, 1913, died September 23, 1995

Aunt Anna was three years older than my father. She always told me that she raised Dad after their mother died, and took care of him. She married Russell Hamera and had six children: John, Joanie, Barbara, Bernice, Mary, and Jeanie. Jeanie was a year younger than I, and when she was young, Russell Hamera died from complications of diabetes. Aunt Anna went to work after his death, and raised those children on her own.

Dad with his sister, our aunt, Anna. I love the contrast of two well-dressed people standing by a little shed (outhouse?) with a wash bucket hanging on it.

She worked at The Bucket Shop in the kitchen for many years. She never drove a car. Aunt Anna's children were all good children, smart and good workers. John went into the Navy and was a career soldier, based in the San Francisco area when I was growing up. Mary was the same age as our Mary, and she was a very sweet person, as was Bernice. I always liked Bernice best. She was shorter and smaller than the other children, and she had a gravelly voice. Mary Hamera married Roger Wheeler, son of a farmer in the South End, and Mary and her family lived on Parker Road west of King Hill all their adult lives. Mary died of cancer in 2010, and Barbara and Bernice died sometime before. Jeanie married a man named Jack Wagers and they live in Wichita, KS, while Joanie still lives in St. Joseph.

My dad used to visit Aunt Anna, but Mom and we children didn't go see her much. I went several times, though, to her house there on Alabama when Audrey and I were living in St. Joseph in the mid-1980s. That was when she told me stories about Grandpa Stefan and the family.

From my brother Bill

In his old age, Grandpa dressed well. I think he usually wore a white shirt, sometimes a hat, and practiced good hygiene. I don't recall him smoking in the shop, but he may have been a part-time smoker. He had a heavy accent and was hard to understand. When he came into Dad's shop, he would usually sit on one of the two vinyl-covered chairs used by people trying on shoes and read a newspaper that was written in a foreign language. Ukrainian? Polish?

I think Dad and Grandpa went into the shoe repair business together with the shop in the South End. Where the money came from to buy the building and machinery, I have no idea. But they split up after a short period. Dad, I believe, said they didn't get along that well working together. Grandpa then started his own shoe shop in a building on Messanie Avenue, a few blocks south of 22nd Street. Grandpa's business lasted a few years. He was a hard man, opinionated, and not very polished, but he must have been somewhat progressive because his shoe repair business was located in a black section of St. Joseph. Most of his customers had to be African-Americans.

He liked women, played cards with them on a regular basis. Like you mentioned, David, as long as I can remember he lived with Aunt Anna on Alabama Street. So most of his card games occurred in that Slovakian neighborhood.

He didn't come to our parent's house often, but maybe he visited more when our family was living on East Hyde Park. I remember on one of his visits, he brought a pan of jelled pork fat mixed with garlic. I can't remember the name of this dish. It had an overpowering aroma, and Mom covered it and placed it in the refrigerator. When he left, she threw it out.

At least at one meal, he tried to entertain us, the kids. He began imitating a monkey, scratching his armpits, and making grunting sounds. I was probably only 10 or 11 years old, but I thought it looked stupid, not funny.

When he was very sick and dying from the cancer, Dad and I went to visit him in Aunt Anna's house. He was lying on a small bed in a small room and Dad sat on the bed next to him and held his hand. It was the first time, I believe, that I ever saw any intimacy between them. Not much was said and it seemed like we were there way too long and I was anxious to leave. When I suggested we leave, Dad turned to me and said, "Go on, son. He won't be with us much longer, and I want to spend some more time with him. But you can go."

The funeral was held in that little Ukrainian church not far from St. Stanislaus. What I recall was how somber and glum the music was, like the "Volga Boatmen," how dark it was inside, and the stifling amount of incense smoke that permeated the place. You could tell the people who were foreign to the church because they were the ones coughing. Lots of people had tears in their eyes, but maybe it was the smoke. But what I did take away from it was how appropriate the scene and mood was for a funeral. I've often said, that when I die, that's how I want the burial service to be, sad with everyone crying.

I don't think Grandpa left much money or property to his heirs. Maybe he had helped buy the house Aunt Anna was living in, so she was the recipient of that. What he did leave money for was a party to be held at a Ukrainian tavern. A lot of us drank too much. I don't remember what we had to eat, but I hope it wasn't that pork pie.

From my sister Mary

I remember Grandpa coming to East Hyde Park, and as Bill said, he pretended to be a monkey, eating a banana. Personally, I thought that was pretty funny. Also, I remember Grandpa came to babysit us at Hyde Park.

I believe Mom told me that Grandpa brought several women over that he thought would be his wife. He didn't care for any of them. But he did have a jar on the bar for people to donate to the cause of helping bring people from their country to the United States. One family in particular I remember living in our basement: Mary and Nufrey. It appears that people in the South End did help many people come to the US, even providing housing to them, until they could get on their feet. Quite a good thing.

I'm not familiar with that priest arguing with Aunt Rosie. But Mom did tell me that the Ukrainian church said that a couple was to be married in the man's church, and Mom and Dad married at St. James. I believe every time they ran into the pastor of the Ukrainian Catholic Church would tell Mom and Dad they were not rightfully married even after several children.

Grandpa had to be buried at the end of the row and not beside Ahafia because they could not afford two plots when she died. Daddy said he did the best he could.

A duplicate of Grandpa Stefan's naturalization certificate that he received in 1946, after he was naturalized 20 years earlier. Notice that the certificate states he is Polish, which Grandpa did not like as he was Ukrainian.

| 7 |

Phillip and Draga Zuptich

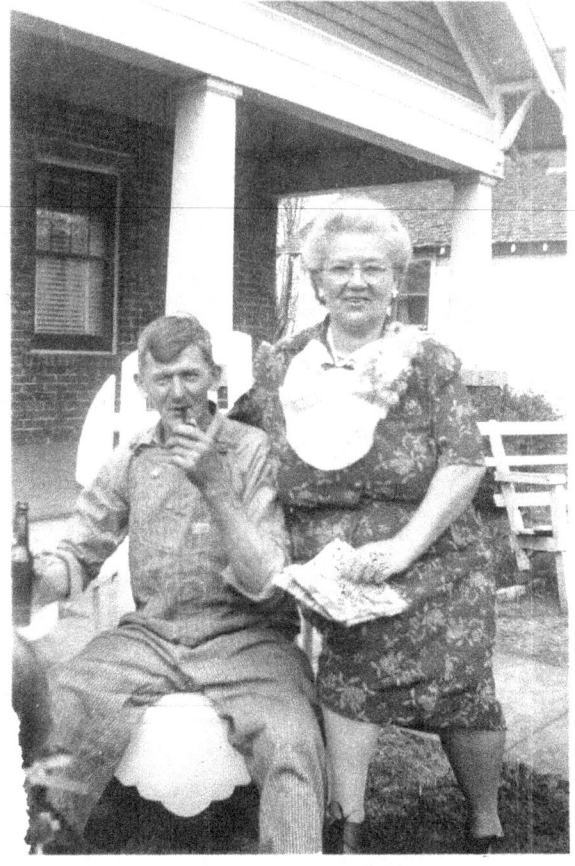

Grandpa Phillip and Grandma Draga outside their home on South King Hill Avenue. Both were from Croatia and immigrated in the early 1900s.

I did not know my maternal grandmother, Draga (Kuzmic). She died in early 1952 before I was born. But Aunt Katy, before she died, told Mary a few things about Grandma. She said that Draga was born Oct. 5, 1892, in Zagreb, Croatia, and her mother died giving birth to her. Her father was Ambrose Kuzmic, who was a fiddler, and following the death of her mother, Draga had three stepmothers. Aunt Katy did not say what happened that Draga had so many stepmothers, especially since Ambrose died thirteen years later. At the age of sixteen, Draga came to the United States. Passage cost her thirty-five dollars, and according to Aunt Katy, Draga rode in the hull of the ship and had to stand up all the way. She had a long stay for some reason at Ellis Island, according to Aunt Katy, although she did not think it was due to health reasons. Draga then went to Kansas City, Kansas, where she had some family, not sure who, and she lived with them for three years taking care of cattle. Aunt Katy said her mother was unhappy with the living situation, met Philip Zuptich and married him. She was naturalized a US citizen on March 29, 1948.

My cousin Gail Zuptich Row also gave me some information about Grandma Draga. Gail said Draga was born on Oct. 5, 1891, and died on Jan. 9, 1952. She came to the United States on May 27, 1907, and did not come through Ellis Island, but Boston, according to Gail. Draga was a passenger on the Laurentian, and came with a relative, a Katy Lister.

Gail said that when Draga arrived, she went from Boston to stay with an uncle Nika Kuzmic at 145 Main Street, Steelton, Pennsylvania. Draga worked there in a cigar factory. However, things did not work out, and she ended up moving to Kansas City, KS, where Nika had other family, perhaps a brother. There she met Philip, and they married on April 15, 1912. After marrying, they lived with Draga's sister in her boarding house. They had two boys, but they both died in 1918 during the Spanish flu epidemic, Gail said. She said that Aunt Rosie found documentation that the children were buried at Mt. Calvary Cemetery, but when she went there, she could not find the graves.

The Laurantian, the ship on which Draga immigrated to the United States. The ship normally carried 36 first-class and 1,000 third-class passengers. Photo used with permission of Norway-Heritage (www.norwayheritage.com).

I did not know my maternal grandfather very well. He died when I was five or six. He immigrated to the United States in 1904, according to a genealogical website.

According to Aunt Katy, her father, Phillip Zupetic (the spelling changed to Zuptich in the US), was born April 29, 1884. However, the website gives a birthdate of 1885, and that he was born in Selo Gorica, Ribnik, Croatia. We were told that Phillip was from Zagreb, the capital. If you look up Selo Gorica on a map today, you will see those two names appear as separate areas on either side of Zagreb; Ribnik is a small village about 50 southwest of Zagreb.

Gail said Grandpa came to the United States on July 24, 1904,o0 on the ship Brennen, which came out of Germany. On his immigration papers, he was listed as Hungarian Croatian.

According to the genealogical website, Phillip's parents were Roza Zeleznjak (b. 1853, Croatia) and Ivan Zupetic (born about 1850, Croatia). Phillip was number four among ten children, all born in Croatia: Michael, Feb. 6, 1875; Dora, Feb. 19, 1880; Helen, Dec. 14, 1882; Katherine, Nov. 25, 1889; Joseph, March 12, 1892; Barbara, about 1894; Apolona, about

Draga and Phillip met in Kansas City, Kansas, and they married there. After losing two boys in the Spanish flu epidemic, they moved to St. Joseph, Missouri.

1896; Mary, about 1899; and Ivan, about 1900. Dora, Helen, Phillip, Katherine and Joseph, all came to the United States, with Dora, Helen, Katherine and Joseph living and dying in Kansas City, Kansas.

A Zuptich family portrait taken about 1921 or 1922. Grandma and Grandpa with Uncle Phil standing, Mom below him, and Aunt Katy seated in front.

My mother said that Grandpa Phillip came to the United States as a conscientious objector before World War I, and Aunt Katy said the same thing. Aunt Katy said her father came from a wealthier family than Draga. His family owned a vineyard, but after coming to the US, he worked first in the steel mills in Pennsylvania. He moved to Kansas City, Kansas, however, because he had three aunts there. Aunt Katy said a younger brother, Joe, and a sister, Kathy Lister, came to America later. She said a brother in Croatia had a daughter named Anna Bucan who came to the United States and had two children, John and Anna, here.

Phillip and Draga were married in Kansas City, Kansas. They worked at the big KC stockyards in the Kansas River valley near the state line with Missouri. Those yards disappeared at the same time the stockyards in St. Joseph were disappearing. The KC basketball stadium, Kemper Arena, was built where the KC stockyards used to be. The arena is now called the Hy-Vee Arena. I don't know why Grandpa moved away from his brothers and sisters, and Aunt Katy said she didn't know why either. He did, however, move to St. Joseph, about sixty miles north, with his family. Their oldest son, Phillip, was born in Kansas City, Kansas, before they left.

When I was a child, we used to go to Kansas City to visit some of Mom's relations. Mom said her father would take his family to visit them quite often when she was a child. The relations lived in the Strawberry Hill District on the bluffs at the confluence of the Missouri and Kansas rivers. They attended St. John the Baptist Catholic Church, and part of the church's facilities are now the Strawberry Hill Museum and Center. A photograph of our grandparents is in the museum.

There is an interesting story about one of Mom's nieces. The niece was a quiet child and grew up to be a shy adult, but she found a man and the family put on a big Old Country wedding. Near the end of the reception, the bride and groom went off to their honeymoon suite not far away, and her parents cleaned up the hall and went home. They weren't home long when their daughter, dressed in her nightgown and crying, was knocking at the door. They let her in and she ran to her room. According to the story, the girl never did say what happened that she deserted her husband on their wedding night, and she lived with her parents the rest of her life.

Aunt Katy said that Phillip and Draga went to St. James Catholic Church upon arriving in St. Joseph, but they were not accepted as there was some discrimination toward "Black" or "Dark" Croats. She added that perhaps the family was unable to give money to the church as they were poor, and this may have been why they were unwelcome. Aunt Katy said she and her brothers and sisters attended St. James School, and they also were treated poorly by the sisters. Grandma and Grandpa Zuptich did not go to church until my mother was 16 years old, according to Aunt Katy.

I'm not sure when, but sometime after the first World War, Phillip wanted to return to Croatia, but according to my mother, her mother was an orphan, did not have any family there, and did not care to go back. But Grandpa still wanted to return and he was saving money in order to go back to Croatia. He kept the money in a box somewhere in their home, but didn't have near enough money. The story goes that one night, he went to a bar and met a couple of guys and he ended up sharing his desire to return to his homeland. Supposedly, the two guys were devious characters who assured Grandpa that they could double his money in some sort of investment. Grandpa fell for their story, went home, returned with his box, and when he showed it to the two guys, they banged him over the head and took the money he had saved. Another story went that someone broke into the home and stole the money box from under the bed. My mom said Grandpa never talked about going back home after that.

Grandma and Grandpa cultivated a large garden on their property with fruit and nut trees, and they raised chickens and a pig or a cow for meat, making and smoking their own sausage at times.

The 1920 US Census lists Phillip and Draga's address as 6019 Carnegie St. in St. Joseph, and they had a boarder living with them, a George Clemens, who came from Croatia in 1907 and worked at a packing house. According to the Census, Phillip could not read or write, but Draga could. Phillip is listed as a railroad shop worker. Oddly, the 1930 Census lists the couple's home country as Czechoslovakia, and the 1940 Census has them from Austria. In both the 1930 and 1940 censuses, Phillip is listed as a worker at a packing plant, with the 1940 Census stating he worked at Armour Co.

Grandpa and Grandma eventually bought property on either side of King Hill Avenue by Walter Lane near the city limits. They ended up with a few acres. They were a hardworking couple, gardening and canning, and raising a cow or pig on their property and butchering them and smoking the meat in their smokehouse at the back of the house. I remember seeing it when I was a child, but I don't know that Grandpa was making sausage then. Aunt Katy married, and she and her husband, Bob Pitts, moved in with Grandpa and took care of him till he died.

There is an awful story from their early time on King Hill Avenue. One day, Mom and Katy were playing outside and Grandma was doing some chores outside too, when a neighbor lady from across the street came running to their house shouting and screaming.

I believe this is after Aunt Dorothy's wedding in Grandma and Grandpa's house. Back row: Aunt Katy, Uncle Bob, Mom, Mary, Dad, Uncle Phil, Aunt Mildred, Uncle Sparky, Aunt Rosie, Aunt Dorothy, Uncle Charlie Hensley, Grandma, Grandpa, Uncle Charlie Zuptich. In front, Diana Pitts, Bill, Bobby Pitts, Kathy, Phyliss Ann Zuptich.

She was followed by her husband who was chasing her with an ax. Mom said Grandma scuttled her and her sister inside and closed the door before the lady could enter their home. The husband bludgeoned the wife to death on the porch. Mom said that Grandma was afraid to let the neighbor lady in because she feared the husband would break down the door and kill her and her children too. The man went to prison, but he was in only a few years because he killed his wife in a fit of passion and rage. Mom said when the man got out, he came to the door to apologize for killing his wife in front of the children and scaring them all. Grandma didn't let him in that time either. He apologized from the other side of a closed door.

When my family moved to 12 acres outside town on King Hill Road, Grandpa walked from his house inside the city limits to our house a couple of miles outside the city several times to visit. He stopped at a small grocery store along the way where Turner Road meets King Hill Road, and bought Hershey chocolate bars for us. I remember once pumping water for him to drink from our well at the back of the house. I don't remember him saying much. Mom would stop occasionally at Aunt Katy's to visit Grandpa. I don't remember him talking when we stopped to see him there. He was always in his room near his bed, and I think I just stared at him, and he stared at us.

Gail said that Grandpa Zuptich could not speak English and she could remember him visiting her family when she was young, bringing a gunny sack and giving her a Hershey bar. She said he would give her a nickel when he saw her, and on her birthdays, he would give her a silver dollar.

She said that the murder that occurred on Grandma and Grandpa's porch did occur on the house along King Hill Avenue, the house Grandpa built, when Anne was about 9 or 10 years old.

Linda stands in front of me with Mary, Susan and Mike at Mt. Olivet Cemetery in St. Joseph, where Grandma and Grandpa Zuptich are buried.

Grandpa died June 6, 1958, and he came to our farmhouse a few days or the day before he died. I remember Mom saying she felt guilty about his death because he had walked to see us.

I asked my dad once about mom's mom, Draga. He only said that she was a woman hard to get along with. I don't know how much of it was a mother-in-law/son-in-law thing or how much was real. If my mother took after her mother, then Grandma could have been somewhat temperamental. In fact, an example Dad gave of his mother-in-law was something my mother did often. Dad said after he and mom married, they would go visit her parents. I think he said they lived on West Valley then. He said they may have just visited mom's parents a few days before, but Grandma would say, "You haven't been here for a while to see me. I guess you don't love me." Mom was often like that, saying we must not love her when she had her feelings hurt over a perceived slight or insult, which leads me to write about my mom's brothers and sisters with the idea that their character and behavior might give some insight on their parents' character and behavior.

Before detailing the individual characters of my aunts and uncles though, there are two characterizations that are true of all Phillip and Draga's children:

First, they were all very hard workers. They had gardens, kept up their homes and yards, were successful blue-collar workers and/or business owners, and were active in their communities. They were also people who were proud of their diligence and work ethic. My mother liked to keep a list of things to do every day, even including mundane things such as washing her hair, and she scratched those items off one by one, often telling us during the day all the things she had accomplished. No doubt an element of pride found expression in her checklist, but she and my aunts and uncles came from a culture that stressed individual accountability at home and in the community.

Their recounting of all the things they accomplished was more an expression of their adherence to the standards of their cultural upbringing and place in society.

The second notable thing about all of Phillip and Draga's children was that they were all very loyal to the Roman Catholic Church. The families attended every Sunday and since all were married in the Catholic Church, all the spouses of the Zuptichs obviously converted to Catholicism. I once had a talk about religion with Aunt Dorothy and she said she had nothing against other Christian religions. However, she believed the Roman Catholic Church was established by St. Peter with the blessing and command of Jesus Christ. That is not a unique view for the era in which my aunts and uncles grew up, but it is notable all seven remained so faithful to their parents' religion given the membership losses the Catholic Church suffered in the 1960s and subsequent years.

The Zuptich family. Back row: Aunt Rosie; Aunt Katy; Uncle Charlie; my mom, Anne; Aunt Dorothy. Front row: Grandpa, Grandma, Uncle Phil. Mom and Aunt Katy were close because they were close in age, as were Aunt Rosie and Aunt Dorothy.

Phillip Joseph Zuptich, born March 19, 1916

Uncle Phil was a talker. He would come in Dad's shop every Saturday after dropping Aunt Mildred off at the hairdressers, and he loved to tell Dad and me all that he had done that week. He did all or most of the shopping for his family, and he would list the discounts he received at the different stores he went to in order to get the best bargains. He worked for Armour Swift his entire life and was a foreman when he retired. He did not go into the military in World War II because he had an accident in the packing house, slicing open one arm, I believe. He kept a big garden at his house, and Aunt Mildred would can all that his garden produced. Mom and Dad and Uncle Phil and Aunt Mildred liked to play cards, and we often went to their home.

Mike and I played with Jimmy, who was a year younger than I was and a year older than Mike. Linda and Mary Lou were the same age and got along well. Uncle Phil was always nice to Mike and I, and we stayed overnight at Uncle Phil's house quite a few times. He fed us very well, and Aunt Mildred was a good cook. Uncle Phil used to give me advice about stocks and bonds and putting money away for health reasons so I wouldn't have to purchase health insurance later in life. That was probably good advice when health costs were much less expensive than they are now.

I didn't take up his advice, partly because I never cared about stocks and bonds. But part of Uncle Phil's benefits at the packing plant were stock investments. I remember him mentioning he received Greyhound Bus stocks. Armour Swift owned the bus company and gave its employees stock in the bus company. Uncle Phil really started complaining about those stocks as they tanked when bus travel slacked off and as air travel increased. Uncle Phil died of cancer August 19, 1988.

Mom and Dad played cards with Aunt Mildred and Uncle Phil Zuptich frequently while we were growing up. Usually, we went to their house which was north off Mason Road. Phyliss Ann is the older Zuptich girl in the photo.

Catherine Pitts, born Feb. 11, 1920

Aunt Katy was two years younger than mom. She was a talker too, and loud, but she was a lovable loud. She had a quirky habit of telling you something that she thought was interesting or funny, then punch you in the shoulder and say, "Huh, huh?" as if to say, "What do you have to say to that?" Aunt Katy, like Uncle Phil and mom, had a garden and canned. She married Uncle Bob, who was from Pea Ridge, Arkansas, and was stationed at Rosecrans Field in St. Joseph. He was an airplane engine mechanic in the Air National Guard. Aunt Katy and Uncle Bob did some sausage making in her parents' smokehouse they inherited. If you went to Aunt Katy's house, you could not leave without eating. Aunt Katy would ask over and over, "Do you want something to eat? I've got some pierogi, some sausage, eggs, what do you want? I'll fix it." Even if you weren't hungry, in the end, you would end up saying, OK, fix me something.

Aunt Katy was hit by a car as a young woman when she was walking home one day from work. She had several teeth knocked out, but I never learned about it until I was almost an adult.

Uncle Bob Pitts, Aunt Katy's husband, who was an aircraft mechanic with the Missouri Air National Guard.

Aunt Katy's children were all about the same age as my mom's children, only Mom had seven, Katy six. One of Aunt Katy's kids, Patrick, had Down's Syndrome. He was high functioning, loved bowling, worked in the challenged workshop, and Aunt Katy and her family were very good to him, taking him to the special school, when there were special schools for the mentally disabled. Aunt Katy ended up being one of the most ardent community supporters for the disabled. This is what her obituary stated when she died Jan. 7, 2011: "Katy spearheaded the Committee for Developmentally Disabled Citizens that successfully campaigned for the creation of the Buchanan County Progressive Board for the Developmentally Disabled. The Progressive Board administers funds for group homes, a sheltered workshop, and other important support for the developmentally disabled. Katy served as the first chair of the Progressive Board. Katy also volunteered countless hours at Helen M. Davis Special Education School, Camp Wonderland, the Recreation Club for Special Citizens, the TOUCH Ministry and Special Olympics."

Charles Zuptich, born March 12, 1924

My mom and her brothers and sisters when they were much older. The photo probably was taken in the early 1980s, and my mother would have been 60-plus years old.

Uncle Charlie was also a talker. He didn't come into the shop as much as Uncle Phil, but when he came he had a lot to say about any topic that came up. Uncle Charlie talked politics, but I don't believe he ever ran for any political office. He also had a lot to say about social issues. I think he may have worked for the Democratic Party and supported labor unions, but I would be surprised to hear that he was a progressive on all issues. Uncle Charlie got my mother's ire when he married a divorcee, Aunt Margaret (Weese). But they were good for one another, and Uncle Charlie adored her. They had two girls, then four boys, one my age, Joe, who like his father is very friendly and sociable. Uncle Charlie worked at the packing house too, but as a clerk. He retired, then ran a tavern that I frequented when I was home from college. Charlie's

Tavern was on King Hill Avenue and was very popular in the 1970s with live bands and dancing. I do not remember Uncle Charlie gardening as I was growing up, but then he and his family lived in a house with a small yard on East Hyde Park. There was no room to garden there. But before moving, he had a big garden at his previous home, and after retiring and moving into a residential home for elderly, he gardened again and gave away a lot of produce. Gail said that her father would grow pumpkins that he gave to students in his grandsons' school classes. Uncle Charlie was a baseball coach for years; I was on one of his teams. He coached girls softball too. He died Dec. 2, 2007.

Rosemary Sparks, born July 10, 1927

Aunt Rosie liked to joke, and she laughed a lot.

However, she had some unfortunate things happen later in life. Her son, Jimmy, died in a football accident. Her son-in-law died in a car accident and a grandson died of cancer. So she had a sad side to her.

Aunt Rosie was probably the hardest worker of all her brothers and sisters, and that's saying something. She was always working on her house and doing things out in her garden and yard. Like Aunt Katy and Aunt Dorothy, she married a serviceman stationed in St. Joseph. Aunt Rosie's husband was from Georgia. His name was James Sparks Sr., but he was known as Sparky, and he was a barber. He was an affable guy, but Aunt Rosie was the engine of the family, and she had his concrete block barber shop torn down and a fancy barber shop built with a rental apartment on top. She had other barbers come in, and they promoted new hair products and cuts, something Uncle Sparky never tried. He basically cut hair in a few styles and never sold tubes of hair dressing or shampoo before Aunt Rosie started the new shop.

Uncle Sparky, Aunt Rosie's husband, cut hair at his barbershop in the South End. He was an affable man, friendly with everyone.

Aunt Rosie was my godmother, and from my early years, probably until I was 12, she would give me a card and five dollars on my birthday. She not only ran the barber shop, she also worked for years for Quaker Oats in St. Joseph. She had two girls besides her son. Andrea is the younger, and Valerie the older. I'll always remember Valerie for the support she gave me one time when I was running track, the half-mile, in high school. I was terribly slow, but I was in a meet at Benton where Valerie went to school. She practically ran beside me inside the track the whole way, encouraging me on. I felt I let her down when I got winded and only finished fifth. She was the same age as my sister Susan, and she died of cancer when she was 62 in 2013. Aunt Rosie was very good to her children and always proud of them, as was her brothers and sisters with their children. That was another family trait of the Zuptichs. Aunt Rosie died Sept. 26, 2011.

Dorothy Hensley, born July 14, 1931

Aunt Dorothy with her husband, Charlie, and her sister Katy. Aunt Dorothy was my den mother when I was in Cub Scouts.

Aunt Dorothy was my favorite of Mom's brothers and sisters. She was the most even tempered of them all, and the quietest, and probably the most thoughtful. Like Aunt Rosie, she liked to laugh, and Aunt Dorothy had a nice laugh, never loud or harsh, just a soft and amused laugh. I don't remember her being critical of other people. When Audrey and I were living in St. Joseph in 1980, Aunt Dorothy asked me to help her paint her house on Fulkerson, and I did. We had a good time for a week or more, and we talked about a lot of things. She had a good outlook on life, and she didn't complain. She taught me a few things about painting houses. One thing she taught me was that you could wrap a brush wet with water-based paint in a wet towel and put it inside a plastic bag overnight and use it the next day without having to clean it out every time. Aunt Dorothy married a serviceman stationed in St. Joseph, Charlie Hensley. He was from a little town in Tennessee and he had a strong hill accent. He was hard of hearing too, so he seemed to shout, which could intimidate someone who didn't know him well. But he had a good heart and was not a critical person. He learned how to fix radios and televisions either in the service or on the GI bill and started a television repair shop in the Valley. We bought a few TVs from him and he serviced them. Aunt Dorothy wasn't a big gardener, but she took care of her house and she helped run Uncle Charlie's television shop. He worked in the back, and she dealt most of the time with the customers and taking in sets for repair. She was my den mother when I was in Cub Scouts. I went to her house and our den did crafts in her basement. She had a group of eight or 10 boys, all cutting up and being rowdy, but she never got mad or upset, and she would lay out ahead of time all the pieces of our craft projects, whether it was making a kite or an art project with plaster of Paris. Her son Chuck was my age, and her other son, Daniel, was between Mike and I. Since they lived down the street five or six houses, we played together in the neighborhood all through grade school. I believe, Uncle Charlie and Aunt Dorothy were the first ones to buy a cabin at Lake Contrary, and they always invited us and the other Zuptich families for parties. Uncle Charlie had a boat and skis and he would pull all his nephews and nieces around the lake all day long. Eventually, TVs got where they weren't fixable, just throw-aways, and cheaper to buy at Kmart, so Uncle Charlie closed his shop. He started driving a semi and hauling freight, mostly from Kansas City to Dallas. Aunt Dorothy didn't seem to mind. She was a very independent person, and she went to work at a grocery along Lake Avenue in the South End. She died January 24, 2004.

This is a drawing I did of our parents from a photograph I took of them at their Sugar Lake cabin one summer.

Here is a formal photographic portrait of Mom and Dad which pictures the way they looked when I was a child.

| 8 |

William Bill Jurkiewicz

My father's full name was William Bill Jurkiewicz. That is what is stated on his birth certificate, redundancy and all.

Dad holding Susan and me. Dad didn't play with us a lot, and he didn't talk a lot, but he liked holding babies. He cradled children against his chest, holding them facing forward as he is holding me in this photo. Then he would sway back and forth, and babies were most always contented in his arms.

According to my dad, his father, a Ukrainian immigrant, could not speak English clearly, and when he was asked about naming his son by the person filling out the birth certificate, my grandfather replied, "William Jurkiewicz."

The certificate person didn't understand my grandfather, and asked again, "What name?" and my grandfather said, "William, William Bill," just to make it clear what he was saying. The certificate person then put William down for a first name and Bill for a middle name.

William Bill was born March 19, 1916, in St. Joseph. His father's name was Stefan, his mother's was Ahafia, and William had two siblings, an older sister, Anna, and an older brother, Joseph. Joseph was nine years older than my dad, and Anna was six years older.

My father's mother died when he was 14, and my dad's sister took care of him. Aunt Anna told me that she raised him mostly, and though they did not visit a lot in later years, I could tell when they did talk that they had a close relationship.

My dad said he was small as he grew up. He was not big as an adult, a little over five feet eleven and about 170 pounds.

I'm not sure when or where this photo was taken in St. Joseph, but it obviously was a dance hall with alcohol. My parents are seated together left of the two chums on the right. My father and mother loved music, and they liked to dance, although they didn't go out much after they married. But this may have been an early exception.

He never had a big belly and stayed trim even in his last years, all that despite drinking beer and eating potato chips almost every night. He had dark hair, and though it thinned, he did not start to bald much and his hair was still dark at his death.

I think he was a little bit of a dandy growing up and as a young man. He said when he was in his teenage years, he slicked his hair back with some sort of lard-like compound.

He was a good dancer. He loved to dance, and at weddings, he would dance with a lot of women, not just my mother. He said he used to go down to Lake Contrary, when there was a dance hall there. His music preference was pretty limited though. He liked old Big Band stuff and because of his upbringing, polkas. He loved *The Lawrence Welk Show* and would not miss it on a Saturday night. One time, Bill was visiting and he wanted to watch something else, though I think there was more to Bill's asking than he wanted to watch something else. Dad wouldn't switch channels, and Bill said, "You know that Lawrence Welk poops just like everyone else." Dad was pretty upset, and they had a short argument with Dad telling Bill that he did not pay the bills in the house nor did he own it.

Dad grew up in South St. Joseph, and he went to Hosea Elementary, a public school, not a parochial school. His father helped found the St. Joseph Ukrainian Catholic Church in the South

End, and that's where my father went to church before he married my mother. The church followed the old rites, and the services were conducted in Ukrainian. The church had a full-time pastor until the 1980s.

Dad's father came over to the United States from a small town in Eastern Europe, Grodek Jagidonski, and many people from the same village came over too. My father grew up with the children of people from that village.

My father second from left in the back row, in school in 1929. We also have a class photo of him from several years earlier, and he is at the left end of the back row in that photo as well, standing a little apart from the child next to him. It makes me wonder if he didn't get along well in school even though he was a friendly enough person as an adult.

Dad said they were picked on by the children of earlier immigrants, and especially the Irish. My father said since he was small, his friends would have him stand out in the open when the Irish boys came along and taunt them; then when they came after him, Dad's friends would come out from hiding and ambush the Irish. I really can't picture my father fighting. He was never an antagonistic person.

My father lived a short time in Detroit. My grandfather had an older brother, William, who came to the United States and settled in Detroit. I met him only a couple times. My grandfather moved his family to Detroit to be close to William for a few years. My dad told me that sometimes he would skip school and go to Detroit Tigers games.

They returned to St. Joseph. I don't think it was long after that my grandfather and his oldest son, Joseph, got into an argument. Dad said that Joseph and Stefan didn't get along, and one day they got into a big argument and Joseph, who was 16, ran off. That was in 1926. The family never heard from him again.

At one time, Dad paid someone to see if he couldn't track down Joseph, but no record of him was to be found anywhere. Dad was not an emotional or sentimental person, but the few times that he talked about his brother to me, he still seemed hurt and disturbed by his brother's departure. I think he was especially hurt that Joseph didn't bother to contact him after leaving, despite whatever feelings Joseph may have had toward their dad. Outwardly, Dad was a que-sera-que-sera type of person. He pretty much fatalistically accepted whatever happened.

Dad had a heart murmur and twice he was refused entry into the military after World War II started. On his third attempt to enlist, the doctor allowed him through, saying the military needed more soldiers.

My dad told me once that there used to be a small airport in the South End down by Lake Contrary, where small planes came into town and others were headquartered. He said he used to watch the planes, and he thought he would like to fly sometime. He said he kept bugging one of the local pilots to take him up, and one day the pilot told him to come the next day and he would oblige my father. My dad said he showed up, and he saw the man's plane in the air doing loops and flying upside down. Dad said he changed his mind and decided not to take up the pilot's offer.

Dad went to Benton High School for one or two years, then dropped out to go to work. I believe he must have been a popular student because even years later, he was invited to go to the reunions of what would have been his graduating class. I believe Uncle Phil and one of the Bazan brothers probably invited Dad to the reunion. He was the same age as Uncle Phil and, I think, Charlie Bazan.

Here, Dad walks down a Honolulu street with another sailor. Dad was stationed for most of his time in the Navy in Honolulu, but he didn't arrive until after the war started when the city was attacked.

Dad got a job as a meat cutter at one of the packing houses in St. Joseph. I don't know how long he worked there, but he said at one point he wanted to get away from home and St. Joseph. He said he and John Zanko moved to Fort Worth, Texas, for less than a year and worked as meat cutters there, living in an apartment. He said they both got homesick and returned to St. Joe.

I don't know where Dad met our mother, but he said he was attracted to her because she was quiet, not loud and talkative. He told me once that while they were dating, he had to do all the talking, but once they got married, my mother started doing all the talking.

At the start of World War II, my father wanted to go into the service, but he was not accepted because he had a heart murmur. He told me he went to the recruiter three times and was turned down twice. But the third time, later into the war, the doctor said it wasn't a serious heart murmur and the military needed all the soldiers they could get, so he was allowed in. My mother told me that she didn't want him to go, of course, especially as he left her on her own with a child.

Despite not having a background in the culinary arts, Dad was made a cook in the Navy. He said he didn't have to know much about cooking, as he mostly served stew for lunch and dinner, and a hash at breakfast.

Dad joined the Navy, and went to boot camp in Chicago at the Great Lakes training center. Dad said when his class graduated, he and some other Navy buddies went to an amusement park where they joined some women and went on rides with them. Dad said he rode the Scrambler with one of the ladies, a rather heavy lady, and he made the mistake of letting her sit on the inside. So when the Scrambler car jerked to the outside, her momentum carried her into Dad. He said she hit him so hard one time that he banged his side against the car and broke several ribs.

Dad was sent after graduation to Pearl Harbor. I'm not sure what he had been trained to do, but Dad said once he got there, the commanding officer pulled him and a few others in and asked them if any of them had experience as a cook. Dad said the others said they had no experience, but Dad said he knew how to fix an egg. The officer said good, you're the new cook.

Dad said that he mostly made stews and soups, and he was told to put a squirt of dish soap in each pot so that the sailors would have regular bowel movements.

Dad learned to play tennis at Pearl Harbor. We discovered that one day when we got on a tennis kick in late elementary school, and Dad went to the tennis courts with us. He could hit a wicked serve that wasn't fast, but would curve and bounce at an angle when it hit the ground. That was the only time he went to the courts with us.

Dad spent most of the war in Pearl Harbor, but he was shipped for several months to Palmyra Island, which is in the Palmyra Atoll about a thousand miles southwest of Hawaii. He said it was a small island only a few feet above sea level, and it was a staging area for sailors going to the front where the fighting was. He never had to go, but stayed on the island during his tour. He said several sailors who had orders for moving to the front shot their toes off in order to get out of active duty. He said one sailor in Chicago faked insanity by jumping out of a second-story dormitory window in the middle of the night into a pack of snow.

Dad didn't talk about his time in the service much. He really didn't talk a lot with us even though he could be quite talkative with his friends and customers in his shoe store. He was a friendly man. He did not, however, like discussing politics or sensitive topics with anyone.

He did tell me once that I should always vote Democratic because he believed the party stood for the little guy, and he was a little guy who owned a small business. He said the Republicans only represented rich people.

He didn't talk about women much either. He started to explain the birds and the bees to me once when I was about 15 years old, but he became embarrassed and then asked me if I already knew about it. I said yes, and he said OK and said no more. He did tell me once that if I married to be sure and pick a woman with thin ankles. He said if she had thin ankles then even if she got heavy as she aged, she had the ability to lose weight. But if she had thick ankles then she was doomed to being fat. He warned me to be careful about how much a woman talked, but even if she was quiet while dating that was no indication that she would be a quiet woman later on after getting married. It was a clear reference to our mother.

Dad made Eagle Scout as a teenager. He is the scout on the left at the front.

Susan said Dad was pretty strict with the girls, which I don't remember. To me, it seemed like he favored them. But Susan said Dad had a strict curfew of 10 o'clock for Kathy and Mary, and Kathy came home a few minutes late one time and she had to beg Dad to let her in. Mary was Dad's favorite, but Susan said Mary came home ten minutes late one time and he wouldn't let her in. He was at the door, and he said she could just sleep on the porch, which she did. She slept in the porch swing there.

Dad loved Western television shows. *Bonanza* and *Gunsmoke* were his favorites. He liked Western movies too, and Mary said that one time when Dad was dating Mom, Mom wanted to go to a romantic movie, but Dad wanted to see a Western that was showing. When they couldn't agree, and neither would give in, Dad took Mom home and they went to no movie.

He had several friends with whom he went duck hunting when I was very young, two of them the Bazan brothers, Raymond and Charles, who had six other brothers. I believe Dad also went with Bill Pflugradt, a salesman for Wyeth Co. who stopped by the store once a week at least. But Dad stopped going probably when I was seven or eight because his family demanded more time, but he also told me he couldn't stand sitting in a blind in the cold wet weather anymore. He especially hated cold water.

He was not a scientific man and did not read much. He read the newspaper, but I believe he only read two books in his life. One was a book on shoe repair, mostly about fixing orthopedic shoes. I remember the book lying around the store early on.

The other book he read was *Paper Moon*. He read it because when the book was being made into a movie, his Model A was used in the filming. I was in college at Columbia, Missouri, at the time, but the St. Joseph News-Press ran an announcement that Peter Bogdanovich, the director, was looking for early 20th-Century vehicles and extras during the shooting in the St. Joseph area. Dad sent in photos of his 1931 Model A and himself and was selected.

Dad bought the Model A while I was finishing high school, and a few times I helped as the antique car was being restored with the help of Harold Grimes, a St. Joseph fireman. Harold was a big guy, not fat, but sturdy and strong, and he did the body work on the vehicle. Harold had a very obese wife who we saw rarely, but came out a few times in a loose house dress and she seemed very slow mentally, but Harold was sharp and smart, and he knew about cars.

Paper Moon was filmed in the fall of 1972, mostly in Kansas, and Dad's Model A was parked on the streets of White Cloud, Kansas, during one shoot. I'm not sure how many places he took the vehicle for filming. Dad said he was selected as an extra a couple of times and dressed as a farmer, but did not end up being used. He said he sat down next to Ryan O'Neal, the movie

Dad was baptized at St. Stanislav Catholic Church, a Polish church in the South End, as a child. This certificate of baptism probably was needed for him to marry Mom in St. James Church as the date is 1940. The document lists Dad's name as Wasyl, which is a Ukrainian name, but it does not translate to William.

star, during lunch one day on the set, and talked to him. Dad was a sociable person and not bashful. He said that O'Neal was a nice guy, not conceited or standoffish, but that Tatum O'Neal, his daughter, probably 9 or 10 then, used foul language around the set.

Thanksgiving that year, I came home and we all went to Downtown St. Joe, where some of the last of the film was being shot around the St. Charles Hotel. We only watched. Dad was not in any of the scenes nor was his car used in the shoot that day.

I was teaching at St. James school, and I believe it was the fall of 1976, that I was called to the school office, and a worker from the heat and air store across the street from the shoe store was on the phone. He knew me and that I worked at the school. He said that Dad had come across the street after suffering a stroke. The man said Dad was pretty much unable to speak and he was having difficulty walking. The man had called for an ambulance.

I ran to the Valley from the school. It was only four or five blocks. Dad was there sitting in the chair, and he had a distant look, and he didn't really want to look at me. I asked him a few questions, but he couldn't speak. He mumbled something one time, but I told him that was OK, not to answer. I held his hand as we waited for the ambulance, but after about ten minutes, it never came. So the heat and air guy helped me get Dad in his car. As I was driving to the hospital up King Hill Avenue, I had to stop for a light, and I stopped behind a police car. I ran up to the policeman and told him that my dad was ill and I needed to get him to the hospital right away. The policeman said to follow him. He turned on his lights and siren, and we went through several traffic lights and we drove into the emergency entrance of the hospital.

This is the last photo I took of Dad. He and Mom visited Audrey and me in New York in May 1980, and we went fishing. He caught this big carp in the Genesee River. He died a few months later.

Medical workers put Dad on a stretcher and took him into an ER staging area, not a room. I waited there with him for about 20 minutes and no one ever came to look at him. Finally, I went to the desk and asked a nurse about the situation, and she said that there was nothing that could be done for a stroke immediately to alleviate the condition, and that they would get Dad to a room as soon as they could. Other than that she told me that I should be patient.

Dad recovered fairly quickly, but he had trouble finding words for several months and he had trouble with the pronunciation of some words. According to the doctor, Dad had a blockage in his heart, and a blood clot broke away and subsequently blocked blood to his brain causing temporary paralysis to his left side. He took blood thinners after that.

Audrey and I moved to Castile, New York, in 1979, and Mom and Dad visited in the spring of 1980 to see Jessica who was about six months old. It wasn't long after that, that I got a call from home that Dad had another stroke. I had some friends over that night and we were playing cards. It was nice that they were there, and I was distracted from what was going on back home. But in the morning, I got another call that Dad wasn't expected to live and I caught a plane home. Dad actually had a heart attack. He had stopped taking his medication, and it caught up with him. That was on a Friday. The doctors said that there was no brain activity and he should be taken off life support. However, the law dictated that they had to wait 24 hours before they could do it, and that would mean we would go into the weekend when the doctors would not be available to take him off the machines. So we had to wait until Monday morning before the doctors came back. It was Labor Day, but they did work that day, which was officially the day that Dad died, Sept. 1, 1980.

The Shoe Shop

When Dad came home from the Navy, he went back to work as a meat cutter, but he didn't like working at the packing house. He and his father bought a tavern together, and they ran that a while, but Dad, and especially Mom, didn't like the tavern business. But I don't know if that was before the war or after. But definitely after, Dad and his dad bought a shoe repair business on King Hill Avenue in what was called the Valley Business District.

Billy and Dad outside the entrance to Dad's shoe shop. This is the entrance as it was when he bought it, and before thieves broke windows to get in. Dad was forced to make the front less inviting. This photo was taken in the mid-1960s.

Grandpa Stefan had learned to make shoes in the old country, and he taught Dad what he knew about shoes. However, Grandpa had learned to make shoes by hand, and he did not like the machinery that came with the store and would not use it. Eventually, Dad bought Grandpa out. The man who Dad bought the shop from was also named Bill, and I think his last name was Stevens. His shop was Bill's Shoe and Bicycle Repair, so Dad didn't have to change the name or sign out front, and that Bill also showed Dad how to use the machinery. Dad said the shoe repairman he bought the store from worked with him for about a month.

Besides fixing shoes and bicycles, Dad also sold new shoes and bikes. But Dad would not sell women's shoes. He said he couldn't take women trying on several pairs and not being able to make up their minds. He also carried sporting goods equipment, which he purchased wholesale from Wyeth Co. and the salesman Bill Plugradt. Bill Plugradt used to tease me with nonsense talk. He was very good at it, and I always fell for it.

Dad did fairly well with carrying sporting goods until the mid- to late 1960s when Kmart became popular, and Dad could not compete with its prices. Over a number of years, Dad let his stock dwindle down, until he stopped carrying sporting goods and bicycles, though he continued to make bicycle repairs. He could make pretty good money on the labor charge.

I started working on Saturdays in the store when I was eight years old, and Dad paid me $1 a day. I'm sure I didn't do much to start with. I mostly polished shoes and took worn-out heels off shoes and boots. At that time, Dad had a pinball machine at the front of the shop, and after school and on weekends, there were a lot of high school and younger aged kids hanging around the shop to play on the machine. They were noisy and rowdy sometimes, and Dad didn't like it. However, he put up with it because he received a good percentage of the money by having the machine there.

One day, some big kids were messing around by the machine, and one kid was swinging a baseball bat from the store and accidentally hit the gumball machine breaking it. Gumballs went everywhere. It had just been filled. It wasn't long after that Dad had the pinball machine removed. I picked up the gumballs off the floor and put them in an empty shoebox. I had gumballs to chew for a long time afterward.

When his sporting goods business was slipping away and even when shoe sales took a dive because of cheaper shoes at discount stores, Dad began dealing in antiques. That would have been about the mid-1960s. He knew a lot of people from being in business so long, and I guess his antique business started when the wife of a man that Dad knew died, and the widow told Dad she had some things to sell. Of course, antique stores were coming into fashion then too. All of sudden, he had old beds and dressers, wardrobes, and vases, oil lamps and carnival glass dishes in his store. I know he bought from estates after people died because I went with

Dad sitting outside the back of his shop. I took this photo before Mike and I put new siding on the building, and we turned the back half of the shop into an apartment in 1974.

him several times to old houses out in the countryside to look at stuff and cart it home. We went several times into the hills south of town down around Rushville and DeKalb.

Dad always said if he could turn a dollar on something, he would sell it rather than hold it in the store for long. But he did pretty good, I think, despite selling at low profit margins; he was shrewd enough to know when he had something good and not sell too cheap. His antique business did well. He began to get a name for having nice antiques, and even buyers from California and other places out west used to stop by as they traveled the Midwest looking for merchandise to resell back in their shops.

He bought a stamp collection from a widow one time that was a huge collection. There was one stamp in it, a Vatican City stamp, with a book value of $1,000. Dad held onto it for a long time, but, of course, couldn't get $1,000 because in St. Joseph, he couldn't find a buyer, nor could he find one anywhere else. There was no Internet marketplaces in those days. I'm not sure what he did get for it. A man across the street from our house on King Hill, Mr. Reiser, was a collector who Dad consulted about stamp prices. I believe Dad may have eventually sold it to him.

Dad also made some money on duck stamps, and he asked his customers to turn in their old stamps. I helped Dad put together two or three complete sets and he was able to sell them for several hundred dollars to collectors. I know he sold the first one for $100, and he got more as time went on. We mounted the stamps that went from 1934 to the year we put them together on poster board and framed them.

Dad had a little bit of a fascination with guns, but probably more so because they were such great sellers and in demand. He had quite a collection for sale at one time.

Dad out front of his shop in March 1974. Dad bought the shop and shoe repair equipment in the late 1940s, and though the shop changed, he never replaced any of the equipment.

But thieves broke in the shoe shop, busting out the front glass window, and took a dozen or more guns. He didn't deal in as many after that and was careful about how he displayed them. He kept a lot in a cabinet or stored away and only brought them out if someone came in asking for them specifically. He had a .38 or .45 caliber handgun one time that had "Jesse James" stamped in the metal below the hammer. It also had four or five notches on the inside of the grip. Dad consulted a gun historian who came and looked at it. The expert said it could have been a gun owned by Jesse James. Dad had no documentation though, so it was mainly an interesting piece, not of great value. Dad took Mike and I out into the countryside one weekend, and we shot at cans with it. None of us could hit anything.

Dad also used to loan people money, and he would allow men to buy work shoes on time. Dad never charged interest on the shoes. He kept track of those accounts on ledger sheets torn from a small invoice book. We'd mark down the date and amount paid each time someone came in, and sometimes it took a customer six months or longer to pay off a $40 or $50 pair of shoes. I am sure that Dad charged interest on money he loaned out, but he never talked about it with me. He was quiet about that.

This is a faded copy of a photo clipped from the St. Joseph News-Press. The caption reads, "With the current bicycle craze it seems that 'everybody's doing it,' however Bill Jurkiewicz, shown above on his ten-speeder, has been riding for transportation and pleasure since his navy days in World War II." We don't know when this appeared in the paper or if it was accompanied by a bicycle story.

The one loan I knew about was to Jim Testerman, a Southwestern Bell lineman who came into the store a lot. He lived in a little community outside St. Joseph, I believe Agency, and he had a big family, seven or eight children. He needed money one time and Dad loaned it to him. Jim came in regularly every couple weeks, and it was a long time before I figured it out that Jim was bringing Dad payments. I never saw the money being handed over. Jim was forever grateful to Dad for the loan as he wasn't able to get a loan from a bank. When I worked at Table Rock State Park in the summer of 1972, Jim Testerman loaned Dad the use of his truck and camper to come pick me up when the summer was over. Dad, Mom and Linda drove down, and we went to Silver Dollar City and Roaring River State Park before going back home to St. Joe. Mom didn't like the camper, but Dad enjoyed it, especially just sitting outside at a campsite and relaxing. We used to fish together, and the only kind of fishing Dad would do was sitting in a lawn chair and waiting for a carp or a catfish to come along and take his bait. Somebody came in the shop once told him to add a few drops of banana oil to carp bait, and after that, Dad swore by the concoction. It did seem to work.

A lot of regulars came into the shop to visit, drink coffee and talk, though Dad complained he really didn't have time to talk. The guys stood near the back of the shop where the work area was and talked or sat up near the front in the chairs for trying on shoes. Mom's oldest brother, Uncle

Phil, always came in on Saturdays when he took Aunt Mildred in for her weekly hairdo. Mom's younger brother, Uncle Charlie, came in infrequently. He liked to talk politics and social issues, mostly work and business related.

A fellow named Scoop used to come in quite a lot. He lived down the street from us and was a wood workshop teacher at a technical school. He talked about the problem students sent his way, and he told me once that while he was in the war, he captured a whole company of German soldiers by himself. It turns out the war was ending and the Germans wanted to surrender to Americans, not Russians. Scoop said he was in a Jeep on a joy ride by himself and happened to come across the German soldiers who all laid down their guns and put their hands in the air.

Dad always wanted to take a trip to Honolulu and see how it changed since he was there in World War II. He finally bought tickets for himself and Mom sometime in the mid-1970s. Before he left, he said, "If anything happens to anyone at home, just put them on ice. I don't want my vacation interrupted."

A quiet, very slight, little man, I think his name was Clarence, used to come in the first few years I worked at the shop. He was an auto mechanic and had his own shop down near Lake Avenue. He told me he once fixed Bonnie and Clyde's car as they came through St. Joseph. He said he suspected it was them when they stopped late one afternoon and said they needed their car fixed immediately. He did it, and then saw they were in a shootout with police the next day south of town toward Kansas City. He recognized them from the pictures in the paper.

Harold Grimes, the fireman, and Bill Plugradt, the Wyeth Co. salesman, came in a lot. Another salesman who came in frequently was Mr. Wilson. He sold shoe materials for a Kansas City company, but then ran for judge in Buchanan County and won somehow. He was a dour guy, thin and sallow. I think he was probably a hard judge. He was replaced at the shoe materials company by a tall, talkative man named Joe, who was missing the four fingers on his right hand. He said he had the fingers cut off in a farming accident. He was right-handed and could still hold a pencil between his thumb and the stub of his index finger.

As I said, our dad was a nice guy and he didn't mind helping people out if he could. There are two instances I remember that he did something for people that was out of the ordinary.

One time a farmer from south of St. Joe came in at closing time who had spent most of the day at the Fin and Feather Tavern down the street. He didn't know where he was and he was stumbling around and said he needed to use the bathroom. However, I don't think he needed the toilet too much because he had wet himself all down his pants. Dad knew him and where he lived. I sat with the guy while Dad went home and got the car, and Dad took him home.

Another time, another drunk, not quite as drunk, came running in the shop. He had been in a fight at Kodrak's Tavern, and he was bleeding from the nose and mouth. He said the police were after him. He asked if he couldn't stay there a little bit. Dad let him go into the bathroom and clean himself up a little; then Dad let him slip out the back door. I don't know if police were really after him or if he imagined it because we never saw police out the front window as Kodrak's was right across the street.

From my sister Mary

Now this is something that Mom told me about Dad. Yes, he was a ladies' man. He dressed cool (whatever that might look like) and would stand around with cool guys and check out the girls. Mom said when she saw him the first time, she was really attracted to him and even told her sister Katy that she was going to marry that guy! I wonder if maybe they saw each other at the packing house, but I can't imagine people being well dressed there.

I agree with you that Dad was a pretty easy-going guy, didn't push his own agenda or was the talker. But one time when he and Mom were going out, early in their relationship, Dad wanted to go to a ball game or maybe something else and Mom wanted to go to a movie, probably a love story, so when she told him she didn't want to do what he was planning and wanted to go to a movie, he took her back home!

I thought that Uncle Bill and Aunt Shtrena lived on East Valley and we would visit them. The house smelled like sauerkraut, a really bad smell. Mom and Dad told us we had to go inside and say hello. So we would take a deep breath of clean air, run in and say hello and run out real quick. We were so rude. But when we were younger, the adults would always visit and play cards. We kids would go to another area of the house or outside and do our own thing. We didn't interact with the adults. Uncle Phil and Aunt Mildred came over a lot and they played pinochle. If we went to Uncle Phil's we all had to play in the basement so we wouldn't get Aunt Mildred's house dirty.

Dad poses with mom's youngest sisters, Aunt Rosie and Aunt Dorothy. As a young man, he obviously dressed neatly, complete with tie clasp and watch fob chain, which evidently impressed the ladies.

Mom and Dad first lived in a little house on East Valley that they paid $500 for. When Dad went to the war, they were living in that big, two-story house on King Hill, close by the Kovac store, which was not there then. So Mom and Bill moved back in with Grandma and Grandpa until he came back home. I guess Mom was pregnant with Kathy then because I think I was really the first kid as a baby with Dad around. I was told I was always his favorite. Ha!

I remember Dad bringing home a cardboard box of dead ducks after hunting. Those poor ducks were lying in the box with their heads hanging over the sides. We girls sat on the floor by that box and petted those dead ducks and asked Dad, "How can you kill such pretty birds? That is so cruel."

Dad faithfully read the paper every day, but he was not as good about other reading opportunities. He said he read only two books in his life: a book about orthopedic shoe repair and the novel "Paper Moon."

Maybe he quit because we said that to him. Also, where he hunted was on Mud Lake on John Rupp's property. Didn't Dirty John live there and take care of the place? And once a year, Dirty John would go visit his daughter. He would get cleaned up, buy all new clothes and go to see her. Then he didn't wash or wear clean clothes again! I remember him showing up at St. James Church on occasion. He would stand in the back of church.

I didn't know that you went to the shop and took him to the hospital during his first stroke. I was in Columbia then. I drove up that night and a friend let me into the hospital. It had to be 10 or 11 pm. She let me see Daddy. I was surprised to find him awake, and he seemed happy to see me. It was the first time I remember him telling me he loved me.

I remember the shop having a fire. We could see the flames from a window on Hyde Park. When we moved to the farm, Kathy, Susan and I had to ride into town with him each morning. We either walked to school or rode the bus. And then after school we stayed in the shop until he closed it at five. So we did homework there every night, and of course, we would stand around the pinball machine and watch the big boys play. We girls were boy crazy, and I'm sure Dad didn't like them looking at us. Also, Mom kept telling him not to let us stand there and watch that terrible game and be close to those big boys. That's probably why he took it out.

Yes, I remember all the men who came into the shop to visit with Dad. The funny thing was he always had a pot of coffee on and the guys would drink coffee. When Betty in the Wander In Café heard that Dad was giving free coffee, she told him she was going to call the health department on him. The pot was really nasty as were the cups. They were just rinsed out in the bathroom that was even nastier. (That's one thing I did do there. I always cleaned up the bathroom and washed the coffee pot and cups.) Betty was mad because they didn't come and buy coffee from her. Dad would go back and forth having coffee, then telling her he got rid of the pot, and they would come over and buy from her.

Remember the Wander In Café was initially right next door to him; then she moved up closer to the clothing store, and on the other side was the Salvation Army. We got comic books and puzzles regularly from there.

From my brother Bill

Our father worked at either Swift or Armour packing houses (not in the stockyards) both before and after he was in the Navy. I think both Mom and Dad worked as meat cutters in the packing plants before the war and maybe that is how they first met. I believe he worked a short time in the packing houses when he returned from World War II, but hated working there. He had a job for a short time as a butcher in a store in The Valley but that place is no longer there. I'm pretty sure about that because he nearly cut off his finger one day cutting meat. Trauma always enhances a person's memory of events.

Somehow, he and Grandpa Jurkiewicz decided to go into business together and bought out the shoe shop in the Valley. I'm guessing that would have been in the late forties before Mary was born. I'm also guessing they both learned their trade on the job. Grandpa was always an entrepreneur – had owned and operated a grocery store and then the bar on Alabama Street. So probably the bulk of the money came from our grandfather, although Dad may have had some mustering out pay from the military.

We have few photos of Dad working inside his store, and this one is not very good. But here he has the finishing machine on, and he's sanding off the excess material on a new shoe sole he has put on.

As I recall Dad telling me, he and grandpa did not get along very well working together. So he ended up buying out Grandpa's share. How he was able to do that and when, I don't know. But Grandpa ended up having a shoe repair shop of his own uptown on Missouri Boulevard, I think, in a predominantly black neighborhood. Grandpa maybe had that shoe shop for four or five years, and I remember he would come down to the Valley store on occasion to talk shop with dad and maybe even get dad to repair some of the more difficult shoe problems for him. Maybe our dad was the only one that had certain machinery. Anyway, their problem with working with one another did not have a lasting impact on their relationship.

When Grandpa was sick and dying, lying in a bed in Aunt Anna Hamera's house on Alabama, Dad and I went to visit with him. I was surprised when Dad took his hand and held it. Nothing much was said by either of them. Grandpa either couldn't talk or would not, and as you know, our father was not exactly garrulous. After a while I got antsy and was ready to leave. Dad said, "He won't be with us much longer, Billy. Please stay with us."

I was probably 10 or 11 before I began helping Dad in the shoe shop. David and Michael probably started working at about the same age. I worked a couple hours almost every day after school at the shop and put in a full day on Saturday. If I recall correctly, I was paid $5 a week.

Our father was very piqued at the changes that took place in the materials and craftsmanship that went into modern-day footwear. I think the big store on the south side of King Hill Road between the Valley stores and St. James Church was first created as a Payless Shoe Store. Or at one time in its existence, it was a Payless store, and just like the cobbler in the poem, Dad would tell a customer bringing in a cheap pair of shoes from Payless that it was impossible to repair them.

My memory is failing, but I think the rim around the bottom edge of a shoe is called a welt and the sole on the shoe is sewn onto the welt. One of the features missing on the Payless shoes was a welt so Dad couldn't replace the worn-out sole with a half-sole. And half-soles were his bread and butter.

One of my strongest images remaining of our father is of him standing behind his workbench, hammer in hand, nails between his lips and ready to attach a new set of rubber heels to a pair of shoes. Maybe whacking the bottoms of those shoes was a form of therapy for him.

Mom and Dad's tour group on their trip to Hawaii. Mom said Dad, who was not a bashful person, went around Honolulu talking to everyone and telling them what the city looked like 30 years earlier when he was stationed there. Mom said she was embarrassed, and she knew the people Dad talked to were only listening politely to him. But Dad was not deterred. Mom and Dad are the third couple from the left.

| 9 |

Anne Marie Jurkiewicz

My mother, Anne Marie Jurkiewicz, was born August 19, 1919, in St. Joseph. She was the second child of six and the oldest girl. My mother said she grew up speaking Croatian because her parents spoke Croatian. However, she said when she started going to school, where everyone spoke English, she told her parents they were in America and they should speak English. I never heard her or her brothers or sisters speak Croatian except for a few words related to ethnic food.

We do not have many photos of Mom as a child. Her parents were poor, so they probably didn't have a camera. But she posed a lot for photos as a proud young wife and mother. Here she is with her first child, Billy.

My mother said her family was poor as her brothers and sisters were growing up. She had a couple of stories about that. She said they were so poor that her parents couldn't afford toys, and all she and her brothers and sisters had to play with was a rubber ball. They took turns bouncing it off the side of the house.

She said that once she graduated from grade school, her parents expected her to go to work, so she never went to high school. I think it was a sore point with Mom that her brothers and sisters finished twelfth grade, but she didn't. I don't know this for a fact, but knowing my mother, I believe she would have thought it was her duty to help out at home, and it was probably as much her decision to drop out and go to work as it was her parents' decision.

She said she went to work first in the strawberry and tomato fields for ten cents an hour, and she worked 10 or 12 hours a day. Linda said she thought Mom earned only five cents an hour. Mom would have been 14 years old when she dropped out of school in 1933, right at the start of the Great Depression. *The Handbook of Labor*

Statistics from 1936 states that the hourly entrance wage for common workers in the United States was 5 cents in 1933 and 10 cents in 1934. In the Central U.S., according to the handbook, the wage was a little more, 10 cents in 1933 and 18 cents in 1934. No matter what year or salary you consider, Mom didn't make a lot of money, and she shared her wages with her family during that time.

Eventually, she went to work at the Swift packing house. The 1940 Census shows that she was employed there and still living at home. She would have been 20 by that time. She said she worked cleaning out animal intestines which were used in sausage making. She said the intestines came in big drums, and she would pull them out one by one and wash out the feces with a water hose. Mom was short, only five feet two inches tall, so she said once she emptied the barrel about halfway, her arms weren't long enough to reach the intestines at the bottom. She would have to lean over into the barrel to get them out. She said she was ready to get married in order to get out of the packing house. She married my father on May 4, 1940.

I don't remember my mother talking a lot about her teenage years or dating any boys or men. She occasionally would say an actor or singer on television was handsome – she really liked John Denver, watched all his specials – so I don't believe she grew up "man crazy" like some teenage girls. I do remember her really lik-

This is a pose by my mother that is very uncharacteristic of her. She must have been feeling very relaxed or brassy that day.

ing the movie *Dr. Zhivago*, and her commenting how handsome Omar Sharif, the male star, was. She didn't say that often about male actors. However, she was a big Spencer Tracy fan, and I remember her talking about the movie *Guess Who's Coming to Dinner?* after she saw it. She didn't like it. I'm sure the racial focus of the movie was something hard for her to deal with. She believed in equality, but not matrimonial mixing.

I am sure she was a chaste person as she was very religious, and she would not let us go to any B or C movies. B and C movies were movies designated by the Catholic Church's Legion of Decency as unfit for Catholic audiences. C were condemned movies, and B were morally offensive movies. When the James Bond films came out, they were rated B by the legion, and Mom would not let us see them although other children at school talked about going to them.

Someone we knew let her kids go to *Goldfinger*, and Mom asked her why she did that as the movie was rated unfit. The lady said she called Monsignor at St. James and he asked where the movie was showing. The lady said at the Missouri Theater, and Monsignor said, "Well, if it's at the

Missouri, then I'm sure it's OK to watch," which shows how out of touch Monsignor was with the world.

My parents' wedding party. Aunt Anna and Aunt Katy are to the left of mom. Aunt Dorothy is the flower girl on the left. John Zanko is Dad's best man, and Uncle Russell is next to John Zanko. I don't remember either Mom or Dad talking very much about their wedding day.

Mike and I got into big trouble one time when we went to the Dex Theater on Illinois Avenue to see *What Did You Do in the War, Daddy?* That movie came out in 1966. It was risqué and suggestive, but not offensive; still it was rated B. Mom didn't realize it was B until later. Then she was upset and asked me if there was anything in it that was bad. I told her no, just ladies running around in their underwear. She told me that I should have taken my little brother's hand and gotten both of us out of there.

If Mom had any fantasies, they involved travel. She always said she wanted to go to New York City, but Dad never took her there. She wanted to go to the Big Apple when we went to Brockport, New York, to see Mary in college, but Dad only agreed to go to Washington, DC. Mom was thrilled when Dad decided he wanted to go to Hawaii. Mom was as happy as I had ever seen her about that. I think she had a good time there too, even though when they went, they weren't on the best terms as she seemed irritated by him and all of us then. But the only thing she complained about was that Dad went around telling Hawaiians how everything had changed since he had been there, and he kept saying that this is where such and such was when he was there and now it was gone. She said Dad's constant references to his Navy days irritated her and she told him to stop because, of course, he had not been there in thirty years, and Honolulu was bound to have changed.

It's interesting to see a family member in a setting you normally don't see them. That's the case here with Mom with a travel group in the Holy Land. She is third from left. She was not comfortable in large groups, so traveling with these other tourists must have been hard for her.

After Dad died, she went with a travel group to Rome and the Holy Land. I believe it was a trip sponsored by Catholics in northwest Missouri and led by a priest who had been there before. Mom didn't know how to use a camera – she was terrible with electronics and machines – but she bought some commercial slides in Israel and brought them back. We all looked at them, and she gave them to me afterwards. That was a big moment for her because she really didn't travel a lot in her life, although she and Linda also went to Mexico City after that. I remember she had a postcard of the cloak worn by the Mexican peasant who had a vision of the Virgin Mary.

Just to highlight her distaste of electronics and machinery, and I think it points to her timidity to change, she didn't learn to drive until after she was married and she had to learn to drive to get herself and her kids places they needed to go. She said the first time she took the car out herself, she had baby Billy with her and drove up West Valley Street where it makes a tee with King Hill Avenue. She got to the stop, panicked, and couldn't turn the car when she pulled out. She said she drove straight across King Hill, across the sidewalk, and hit the side of the building there. She said she was crying and people came up asking if she or her son were hurt. She didn't like driving, and when we got old enough to drive, she let us drive and she was content to be a passenger.

Mom always lamented that she had to go to work after eighth grade and was not able to attend high school. But she finally took night classes and earned her GED in 1974. She didn't ask for much help from us, but worked through the study guides on her own. She was 55 years old when she received the certificate.

She had another accident with Bill, which she could laugh at and I didn't hear until I was a teenager. It seems before she could drive, she went places in the Valley by pulling a wagon with baby Billy in it. One time, she walked several blocks from home before she looked back, and Billy wasn't in the wagon. She ran back the way she had come and a few houses from their home, Billy was lying in a yard and crying. Before she could get to Billy, a lady going by picked him up. Mom said she was embarrassed to explain to the woman that Billy had fallen out of the wagon without her noticing, and she said the lady gave her a look as if she was the worst mother in the world.

Mom liked to read, but I don't remember what novels she read. I don't think she was big on historical books or great books of literature. I don't remember us ever discussing any works of literature except for a couple. One was *Wuthering Heights*. We talked some about it after a movie of it came out, and she had read the book. The other was *The Old Man and the Sea*, and again we talked about that because of the movie with Spencer Tracy. I couldn't tell you who her favorite author was. She read a lot of religious books, especially later in life. She talked about Thomas Merton, a Trappist monk who was a popular writer in the 1970s, and I remember seeing his books in her apartment in the building where she lived in downtown St. Joseph.

This is an interesting photo of Mom and her sister Katy at one of our Zuptich family reunions at Aunt Rosie's lake cottage. Both are wearing a reunion t-shirt, of course, but they are wearing similar earrings and necklaces with crosses. I am sure they didn't coordinate their attire for the day.

She was very devoted to the Roman Catholic Church. She belonged to the Altar Society at St. James Church all of her life, and not just belonged to it, but helped as the name implies with providing things for the altar and church. I don't think Dad was especially concerned that we went to Catholic schools, but Mom insisted on it, and all of us went to parochial schools through high school. Private schools were not as expensive then as they are today, but I'm sure sending us to St. James and the Catholic high schools was a hardship as there were would have been five or six of us going at one time. She did without things in order to pay for our education.

Mom had a love/hate relationship with education as she had with everything. She wanted us to be educated, encouraged us to do well in school, and encouraged us to read and learn about new places and people. However, she did not help us with homework very often, if at all, even though she reminded us it needed to be done. The one thing she did for me in school occurred in the first grade when I was going to Moore school. We had a Better Breakfast Competition among all the students. I've always thought it was a presidential challenge, but it may have just been something that originated locally. In the contest, we all received points for eating breakfast and for eating certain foods. Over the course of a week or two, we also were supposed to eat a variety of foods. I told Mom that I wanted to win as the prize for winning was the heart of the watermelon that was going to be the center of the party at the end of the competition. Mom went out of her way to see that my breakfasts were more than just bowls of cereal in the morning and varied. I ended up tying for the win with another girl. The teacher of the 7th and 8th grades cut a big middle piece out of a huge watermelon that was near frozen, and it was delicious. Oddly, I think we had cake too, but it seems we played in celebration all afternoon.

Mom really got after me one time when I received a D on one of my St. James school report cards. She sat me down at the table and pulled out that grade card. She laid it open on the table and put her finger on the D and talked to me about how that was not acceptable because I was smarter than that. She said there was going to be worse consequences if I came home with one again.

But Mom also often complained about people being too smart for their own good. As we got older and went to college, she was jealous of us, but she also complained we were too educated and she was concerned we would get lazy. College was only worthwhile to her if it helped you get a good job. I don't think she believed college had the ability to make you a better person.

She was a worker. I don't know that she loved work; she simply was raised by her parents to be a hard worker and she had a religious notion that hard labor was more noble than ideas and creative arts. I think all the work she did on the farm in canning, cleaning, sewing, taking care of animals, teens and young kids wore her down and made her more susceptible to depression and even a worse mental condition. She had to be hospitalized twice in her life for that, and she received electroconvulsive therapy. I remember her being gone and receiving treatment while we lived on King Hill Avenue and Fulkerson Street. When she came back from the St. Joseph mental hospital, she was very complacent as if she were drugged, and she couldn't remember things very well. She had a vague look in her eyes and asked the same questions over and over. That lasted for a few months. But it was not permanent. She eventually fell back into depression, feelings of inferiority, and being persecuted.

She made us work when we were young. The girls cleaned the house on weekends and did the dishes, and Bill, Mike and I took care of the yard and took out the trash. We helped her with dinner sometimes, and usually, we all made pierogis when we made them. We made one hundred when we made them, and folding the potato filling into the soft, floury shells seemed to take forever. I doubt we did half of them, as Mom was fast with her hands. She could fold several in the time it took us younger children to do one, and she picked up a lot of ours and pinched them again to make sure they didn't come apart in the boiling water. Of course, a few of ours always fell apart because Mom had the water roiling in the pan. There was no need for that because all the dough had to do was soak up a little water and become dumpling like, which can be done in a few minutes in heated, not boiling, water. But Mom liked to get things done. She wasn't one to waste time. When she fried bacon, it sizzled and popped grease over the stove. Her fried eggs had hard edges from the very hot grease. And when she boiled water, the bubbles coming off the bottom of the pan were big and turbulent.

Mom was a good cook, but her food repertoire was limited to the old standards of meat, potatoes and one of three vegetables: corn, peas or green beans. Here she is in the kitchen on King Hill Avenue that led into a sun room on the back of the house.

Mom liked for things to be neat and orderly. We had to pick up things in our bedroom and make our beds in the morning. She also didn't like clutter, so if there were things that she didn't need or want anymore, she got rid of them. And if we weren't using something, then it had be put away. She didn't get sentimental over a lot of things, although Mike and I did get a spanking for knocking a painted plaster bust of Jesus with a crown of thorns off a cabinet and chipping it in several places. When I went to college, I left baseball cards at home in a shoebox, and when I didn't ask about them for a year, she tossed them out. There were cards of many big name players in there from the late 1950s and into the 1960s. She threw them all away.

She did save the letters that I wrote home, and maybe after my second year in college, she gave me the letters bundled by a rubber band. She said I could have them back. When I was in West Texas and it was my twenty-first birthday, she sent me an envelope with some holy cards I had as a youth. I don't believe she saved them all that time looking for the perfect moment to make them a gift. She probably came across them in box I put somewhere and only returned them because they were holy. If they had been baseball cards, she would have tossed them.

I usually say about my mom that she didn't have a sense of humor, but this 1961 photo proves otherwise. Her even getting close to a Jeep is ridiculous, and her sitting in this one was only for fun. She was a cautious driver, but not a good one.

Mom didn't have a sharp sense of humor. She didn't tell jokes, and she didn't like a lot of the popular comedians on television. She didn't like George Burns because his humor involved making Gracie Allen a silly woman, and Burns smoked cigars. She didn't like Jackie Gleason because he yelled at his television wife all the time, and he portrayed a drunk in some skits. She didn't like men dressing up like women as Milton Berle did. And she didn't like slapstick humor, the antics of the Three Stooges. That was just stupid to her.

But she did like to laugh; she had a sense for comedic irony in life. For instance, she found the madcap adventures in *It's a Mad, Mad, Mad, Mad World* without humor, but she did find amusing the turn of events and human failings that landed characters in situations they actually wanted to avoid. She thought it was fair that in the end, none of the characters got the treasure, and they all ended up in the hospital because of their lack of self control.

She didn't like us getting carried away by silliness and the gross humor that kids find interesting. One night at the supper table, Kathy, Mary and Susan started laughing at something, and whatever it was tickled them so much that they started snorting. Mom kept saying stop that, stop that, but of course, they didn't. They began laughing and snorting more, and Susan slapped the table, hitting the edge of her plate so that the piece of meat on it flipped into the air and came down in her glass of milk. We all found the steak in the milk quite amusing, but Mom didn't appreciate it nor that kind of behavior.

She liked variety shows, singing and dancing, which is one of the reasons she liked John Denver. But if she watched TV, she sewed, crocheted or embroidered while she watched. She could not sit and do nothing or just sit and watch television. She crocheted doilies to put under lamps and on table tops, she embroidered flower, birds and other designs on kitchen T-towels and pillows, she crocheted a few afghans, and because of her frugal upbringing, she patched the knees of jeans and the toes and heels of socks when they had holes. I remember disliking patched socks because where Mom bound them, the material was doubled over and it hurt to walk on those knots. But that's the way she was; she had a hard time throwing away something that had a fundamental utility in life and could be repaired.

She was a big gardener and canner when we lived on the farm. She put up everything from apple butter and applesauce to peas, pickles and tomatoes. But she was not big on salads or zucchini. She grew up on potatoes and turnips, and her food preferences were old-fashioned. She never made a real pizza. She rolled out those eight biscuits in a can, covered them with ketchup, and put on a few pieces of pepperoni and Velveeta cheese, then baked them as little pizzas. She made spaghetti sometimes, but her tomato sauce was more like gravy, even brown. We never ate meat on Fridays. It was always cheese sandwiches, fish sticks, salmon patties maybe, or tuna and noodles. On Sundays, she pan fried chicken or fixed a roast or a ham with mashed potatoes or potatoes roasted with the

Here's bit of tomfoolery that Mom took part in early in her marriage that she wouldn't have when we were children. Mom and Dad took a vacation, to Colorado apparently, and took turns sitting on an ugly white horse to give views of both ends. My mother turned toward the adverse end.

meat. We didn't eat baked potatoes very often, but she liked to make twice-baked potatoes. After we moved from the farm to King Hill and Fulkerson, she tried to garden a little in our back yard, but that ended after a couple years. She still liked to put out flowers in a brick planter at the back of our house. Her favorites were begonias and marigolds. She usually bought an Easter lily too, and put it in the ground somewhere after it was done blooming.

Mom's religious notions meant that a person did things for others out of moral duty. That's not to say she didn't have a good heart. She felt compassion for people. She worked for a soup kitchen in south St. Joe for several years. She worked with a Catholic organization that assisted unwed mothers with things they would need for their babies. She gave money to several Catholic relief agencies. We received a lot of pleas from them in the mail at our home. But relief aid and work were points of conflict for her too as she believed in a strong work ethic. When she donated her time or money, she feared her aid was making people lazy and dependent. She often made comments that they were only taking advantage of people's goodwill, and it was personal too, if she got to know them. For instance, she sometimes complained about the people seeking aid at the food kitchen or the unwed mothers she got to know from working with the Catholic aid agency. She sometimes had a hard time balancing her generosity with her abhorrence of the sin they had committed. In her mind, they had done something wrong for which they were being rewarded, and if Mom sensed any expectancy in a client for the help the group offered, Mom couldn't but help say something to us about it. She wouldn't say anything to them, but she would complain to us.

Mom believed in discipline. She disciplined us if we did something wrong, especially at school. Susan, Mike and I joke about the heavy flyswatter she bought with the big sunflower on the back.

Mom had a vision of the perfect family which didn't make room for the pressures and conflicts that Twentieth-century life put on families. But we had some good moments with her, as we did here apparently at a little get-together in 1976: back row, Farrell, Robert, me holding Matthew; middle row, Dad, Susan, Mary, Audrey; and front, Mom, Shane, Angela, and Linda.

She'd take us downstairs at the farm and beat our bare butts with the flyswatter, and she hit hard, knocking petals off that swatter. We laughed afterwards, and sometimes even while Mom was beating us, which made her hit harder. Then we'd laugh even harder, but that thing hurt. As we grew older, she didn't spank us anymore, and we weren't terrible children or teenagers. But when we wanted something, clothing or a toy or game, she would tell us that she didn't have those things growing up, our family didn't have that kind of money, we needed to work to get things on our own, and things wouldn't make us happy. But at the same time, sometimes she would give in and get us what we wanted. She and Dad said I had to pay for my own college, and I did, but Mom would give me ten or twenty dollars sometimes when I came home to visit. A few times, she sent me money.

She talked Dad into loaning me money for my first vehicle, a Karmann Ghia. After that quit, they loaned me money for a Volkswagen beetle. She probable did the same for my siblings.

She felt sorry for us too if something disappointed us. I wanted to go to Colorado the summer after my first college year, but I didn't have money or a car. She made a deal with me that we'd go together in her car, but I had to pay for the gas and a repair, if something went wrong with the car. She said she would pay for food and attractions that we would go to. Mary and Linda went along with us. So we took off, and sure enough, halfway across Kansas, the car engine began slipping gears and finally quit. The engine was running, but not engaging the wheels. It turned out the transmission fluid leaked out when a seal wore out. It cost about $300 to fix, and Mom said a deal was a deal. She felt bad about it though because she mentioned several times that she was sorry about my bad luck. I didn't have that much money, so she paid for it at the time, and I started paying her back that summer as I was working at college in the wildlife department. I paid her back about $200 and then she told me that was good.

Mom was a generous person with her money and time. Here she received an award for helping a housing organization that reached out to the elderly, disabled and low-income families in St. Joseph.

After most of us children had left home, she wanted to go back to work, or thought she would like to go back to work. I wasn't there for that, so I'm not sure what all jobs she had. But I do know she worked a while at Wire Rope, an electrical company. She didn't need the money, and I think she did it just for the adventure, to get out of the house, and the opportunity to meet different people.

She was a quiet person, not one to start talking to people on the street a lot or start a conversation with strangers while on vacation. Dad did that, but if someone started talking to Mom or she felt some sort of connection with someone, she was very friendly. I don't remember her having many friends that she did things with while we were growing up. She was too busy then, but after we left, she seemed to have a few lady friends. I don't remember them because I wasn't around, but she talked about a lady who lived just east of Noyes Boulevard and north of Frederick Avenue. I believe her name was Jean. I remember Mom talking about this lady because she too had a son named David. He was older than I and had a history of mental troubles. Mom talked a lot about her and him, but I never met them. She also became friends with a lady who had been married to a US ambassador and lived in Cameron. I went with Mom to visit her once, and the lady knew the people I would work for in a Houston restaurant one summer. And Mom became friends with Audrey's Aunt Glady when Mom and Dad lived on Terrace Avenue for a few years. Aunt Glady and Uncle Harold lived along King Hill Avenue about a block away. Mom and Aunt Glady would meet once a week for Bible study and lunch.

Mom was a healthy person apart from the depression she experienced. I don't remember her ever being down from a cold or flu or having to go in for some unexpected medical condition. She did have knee replacements in her old age, and she seemed to get through those operations well.

She was living at the high-rise apartment in downtown St. Joseph when she exhibited the first signs of forgetfulness. Susan eventually took care of Mom, finding her an apartment on Alabama Street, before taking her into her home in Overland Park. Because Mom was in such good health, she lived for a number of years with Alzheimer's. She finally passed away May 29, 2005.

From my sister Mary

I believe that Mom told me that Grandma lost her first two babies. I think they were miscarriages months before they were full term. Also, Mom told me that she only spoke Croatian when she went to school and she was punished at St. James when she spoke that. The nuns would hit her hands with a ruler. She was left-handed, and they hit her for that too. She had to write with her right hand.

Mary baked and decorated a cake for Mom for one of her birthdays. The arc of flowers is similar to a pattern Mom might have embroidered onto the corner of a T-towel or pillow case.

So Mom was ambidextrous. I would see her write with both hands at different times, and her left arm was much stronger. I don't remember her saying she told her mom to speak English. From what I know, Grandma spoke very little English, and Grandpa spoke even less, and he couldn't sign his name. He would just make an X on legal papers. I learned about this when I went home for Christmas one year after I was taking classes at the University of Arizona. I was telling Mom about my bilingual and multicultural classes, and then I found out Grandma didn't know English either. And when I told her, "You know Grandpa scared me as he always sat on the back porch smoking a pipe and he never spoke to me." She said he didn't know English!

Do you remember Grandpa talking to you when he came to visit? I don't. But I do remember he would walk up to Hyde Park and bring wine that he made in their basement. And he would sit at the kitchen table and drink wine. We had to play outside.

Yes, they were poor. I have no idea how much Grandpa made at the packing house, but they were never hungry during the Depression.

They had a big garden, a cow for milk, and chickens, besides raising and butchering a pig each year.

Mom was very unhappy that she couldn't go to high school, but her mother told her she didn't need an education. She would only get married and have babies, but her brothers needed to go to school and they needed clothes and shoes. So Mom had to give all her money she earned to her parents for her brothers. I used to tell this story to my students trying to let them understand what a gift an education was.

I remember having to check the Catholic Digest to see how each movie was rated before we could go see it. And Mom monitored what we read. I can't remember what author she found among Bill's books, but she made him take it back to the library. Maybe Kurt Vonnegut? Also, Kathy gave me *Marjorie Morningstar*, a racy young woman's book by Herman Wouk when I was in high school, and Mom was so upset when she found out we had read it.

Yes, Mom was devoted to the Catholic Church. And she did all kinds of volunteer work. She won the volunteer award of the year in St. Joseph. I think she was volunteering at the hospital at that time. But she was always finding a cheap refrigerator or stove or clothes to give to the poor. At her funeral, a young woman came up to me; she never told me her name, but she said, "Your mother was a wonderful woman. When I came to town, I had nothing, and she helped me out. I am indebted to her."

She also got involved with a charismatic group of Catholics who used to meet over at a church between 22nd and 28th streets. It was when I lived on Maurice Drive. I think it was in an old movie theater. Anyway, it was way out there, people speaking in tongues and laying hands on each other. I was surprised that Mom was involved with that, but I think there were some nuns who invited her. Although I participated in a group, on occasion, that was charismatic, it was led by a group of women. The retreats were a lot of singing and waving of flags and hands and bodies. I felt uncomfortable with that. But at the end of the day, their husbands would come and these three or four ladies would pray over us one by one and lay their hands on us, and boom, we would have hit the floor if one of the husbands weren't standing behind us to catch us.

She didn't like clutter, and she knew how to keep things neat. For years she told me I needed to come get my box of childhood mementos in the attic on King Hill. She tossed them before I got them. I felt bad I didn't get at least one of my swimming trophies. Oh well, they say keep the memories not the stuff, right?

I forgot if you said it or maybe Bill, that Mom didn't have much of a sense of humor, or she wasn't into jokes. Here's a funny story when Mom was a little girl.

When Mom was little there was a cherry tree in the front yard of Grandma and Grandpa's house, and I remember it too when I was little. Anyway, Mom said that her mom, our Grandma, didn't pit the cherries, just served them with the pits. So Mom said when they were little and Grandma served cherries for dessert, they would spit the pits at each other at the dinner table. Of course, they got in trouble, but she remembered how they all laughed and had fun doing it. It's hard to imagine them doing that, but maybe they needed some humor and laughter in their lives.

I seem to remember singing a lot of funny songs when we were growing up. Do you remember singing "My Guy's a Corker?" I seem to remember Daddy had a lot of songs he learned in the service. We all liked to sing, especially in church. Daddy was in the choir. And of course, we always watched "Hit Parade" on Saturday nights. Was that before or after the Saturday night fights? And Dad would have a beer on Saturday, and we all asked for a sip and then we would say, "Uck! That's nasty. How can you drink that?" So he never got to drink a whole beer.

Here's a great story I have told people over the years about our mother. When the incident happened, I was very embarrassed, but then I realized Mom was just telling the truth! Now I find it really amusing.

Hazel Elliott became my accordion teacher when I was 12 or 13 years old. She was a big bosomed woman who always garbed herself in professional dresses or suits with nylons and heels. She had a comical laugh and usually had a linen hanky in her hand or pocket, and she would constantly wipe her brow or wave it to help cool herself. She terrified me.

One hot summer day, Mom couldn't find a close parking space to the music studio, so Mom and I had to lug that big old accordion three blocks uphill to my class that day. It was very hot, and we both worked up a sweat by the time we reached the office. Mom sat down to enjoy the cool, air-conditioned office and catch her breath.

Mrs. Elliott came out and greeted Mom as she always did and asked how she was dealing with the heat. Mom said fine. At that time our house did not have AC, nor did the car, so we were used to the heat. Hazel said she was not doing so well. The heat was just too much for her. She said, "I'm fine at home because the house is air conditioned and so is my car and office. But I get so hot walking from the house to the car, and from the car to the studio."

I believe, as Bill states, that Mom was happiest early in her marriage, but then as children kept coming, she saw her ambitions and dreams slipping away. She always talked about traveling, and I believe she really would have liked to devote herself to some cause, religious or social, but she didn't end up with money enough to do either. Nor did she get an education in order to be a leader and felt she would always be stuck on the bottom rung of any endeavor.

Mom looked at her and said very calmly with a straight face, "Well, Hazel, I guess you could put a popsicle up your you-know-what from the house to the car and from the car to the office to keep yourself cool."

Hazel, stunned, looked at Mom, unbelieving, then broke out into a comical laugh and shook that hanky as fast as she could. "Ohhh, Mrs. Jurkiewicz, ho, ho, ho ..."

I was so embarrassed at the time! I couldn't believe my mom would say something like that to my music teacher.

I don't remember Mom working at Wire Rope. I do know that she worked at TG&Y, and she bought way too much material. And she worked at the donut shop, which was nice because she brought home donuts.

I was fortunate with being in the Peace Corps program in New York that I received free tuition, but Dr. Crandall, our coordinator, helped us get Work Study jobs to help with living expenses. Then I got a few loans, but that amounted to only a few thousand dollars. Like you, David, when I came home for a visit, Dad would even ask if I wanted the car for an evening and then quietly handed me a $10 bill, and Mom would quietly hand me another $10. They were generous.

From my brother Bill

I'm sorry Mom threw away your baseball cards. You could probably be living in a penthouse now if she hadn't disposed of your original Honus Wagner card. Or even a good Stan Musial card from his early career would be worth a lot now.

> **The Blue Skirt Waltz**
>
> I dream of that night with you,
> O Lady, when first we met.
> We danced in a world of blue.
> How can my heart forget.
>
> Blue were your eyes
> And blue were the skies
> Just like the blue dress you wore
> Come back, Oh Lady, come back,
> And don't be blue anymore.
>
> The Blue Skirt Waltz was a popular tune in 1944, when it originated in Prague. Frankie Yankovic and his band popularized it in the US in 1949.

Bill remembered that Mom liked this song and used to sing it.

If it's any consolation, Mom trashed everything I stowed away in the attic as well. She probably figured she was doing God's work when she threw out my collection of *Playboy* magazines. Unfortunately, one of those issues was an early one which had Marilyn Monroe as a centerfold. It's a collector's item now, too, with a value that would be significant in a down payment on a jet airplane.

Mom was a hard woman, mostly hard on herself. She had high standards in regard to morality and behavior. I don't think she felt she ever measured up to the ideals associated with her beliefs. It's hard to understand how entrenched she was in the Catholic religion, especially since, as you pointed out, her parents were not regular church-goers. But her beliefs, and her failures to always comply with them, cast a shadow on everything she did and on what we became and accomplished as well. It's more than conceivable that part of her guilt complex came from what she felt that she failed to do in raising us.

Like you pointed out, David, she was a strong proponent of education, and all of her children graduated from higher learning institutions. But she also blamed our educations on leading us away from religion. The problem of learning about history, facts, science, is that they are usually not consistent with religious beliefs.

She was a compassionate woman, nonetheless, and she loved us a lot, devoted her middle years to raising us as best she could. When I was small, an adolescent, we would take Sunday car rides around St. Joseph and we would sing together. *Gonna Take a Sentimental Journey* still rings in my ears and mind. When you, Susan, and Mike were small, and I was still around, she would hold you in her arms and rock you to sleep. One of her favorite songs was the Irish lullaby, *Over in Killarney*, and I would warble, "Too-ra-loo-ra-loo-ral" along with her in the hush and darkness of the night. And as the first verse ends, "I would give the world if she could sing that song to me again."

From my sister Susan

You all made Mom smile today! I agree with all comments. She was a tough but loving mother. She was our mom and I believe we all know we can't pick our mothers. Just ask our kids!

A couple things to share though. Remember how she would keep her allowance money Dad would give her in the kitchen drawer, maybe $100? I'm amazed to say how she always made it work no matter what happened, and I'm sure there were unexpected expenses.

Mom in one of her apartments in her old age, with an angel to watch over her.

But just think how we were being taught accountability and honesty. Yes, going to the store with cash and a list was a given, and she knew exactly what change you should bring back, but many times that nickel spent for a candy bar was overlooked. And I remember at the clothing room she would buy new underwear for people because she said, "No one should have to wear someone else's underwear."

She gave our stuff away but she also gave away her own stuff. I remember going to her apartment and the couch or chair would be gone, and she would say, "Oh, they needed one."

My best memory is when I was sick and got to stay home from school. Of course, we didn't get sick together so that ended up being "my mom time." She would let me lie in her bed and she would make a Vicks vaporizing tent so I could breathe easier – and get meals in bed! My senses are always heightened by Vicks, and rubber cement glue because Dad used that in the shop!

And if you think about it, Mom had three babies in three years and under at one time.

I often think of and hope that Mom had happy times. Along with her disappointments maybe during those 15-minute naps she was at peace.

Susan with Mom at a dinner, and an art show, it appears. I don't remember the lady on the left of Mom, but Wanda Mason is on her right. Mom and Wanda were close friends in youth I believe, and Wanda had a few children our ages too.

I am not sure when Mom and Dad went to Yosemite, but here she is overlooking Vernal Falls.

My sisters, brothers, and Mom during a get together in south central Missouri in the mid-1980s.

A hilltop view of the Contrary Creek Valley south of St. Joseph, where we lived on a 12-acre farm for three years when I was just starting grade school.

| 10 |

Accidents and Injuries

The first injury in our extended family that I remember happened to our cousin Bobby Pitts. He was riding his bicycle down King Hill Avenue and a passing car caught one of his pedals. Bobby broke an arm and got skinned up pretty good. I remember Mom and Dad talking about whose fault it was, but I don't remember if the driver was ticketed or if the police put the blame on Bobby.

In our immediate family the first accident that I remember happened to either Mike or Mary. I don't remember which one occurred first, but I think Mike.

***

Mike's first was not a serious one, but it looked bad. He asked Kathy if she would take him for a ride on her bicycle in the front yard of the farm on King Hill Road. She said yes, and he sat on the back fender of the bike, and the two of them went bouncing on the grassy yard. Mike wasn't on there a minute and one of his ankles went into the spokes of the back wheel and took some skin off his shin. He didn't go to the doctor, but it became raw and swollen.

***

Mary broke her arm in a fall at a skating arena in St. Joseph. I seem to remember a phone call home that it had happened, some discussion, and then she came home with her arm in a cast.

***

Something stupid happened to me when I was small that I was teased about for a long time afterward. Susan and I were playing on top of a stack of hay bales in the barn one day on the farm. It was a nice day, and the rest of the family was outside or in the barn doing things. I don't remember why we were all out there, but I went too close to the edge and fell off the stack, landing on my head on a brick. The fall didn't knock me out, but I was wobbly as I got up. Mom came running when Susan called out that I had fallen. Mom caught me up in her arms and promptly dunked my head in the horse trough. I don't remember how far I fell, but it seems the stack was seven or eight feet high. Mom and Dad didn't take me to a doctor, though I seem to remember some discussion about a possible concussion. The joke about the accident was that when I landed on my head, I landed on the brick and the brick broke, not my skull.

***

Mike broke his collarbone, or more correctly I broke it, while we lived on the farm. It was a warm, sunny day, and Susan, Mike and I were playing outside in the front yard as we often did. Mike and I wrestled a lot, and it often got us in trouble. Once we were bouncing on Mom and Dad's bed in their bedroom next to a big cabinet with shelves on top and drawers in the bottom half. Somehow, we went off the bed and knocked the cabinet over. The thing would have killed us, but the top hit the foot of the bed as it fell. We survived in the triangular space the end of the bed made as it held up the cabinet. But the day Mike broke his collarbone, we were outside and I was swinging Mike around making him dizzy. He liked it. I swung him a little too hard one time, and he went flying, then tumbling, and came up crying his shoulder hurt. It turned out his collarbone was broken, and Susan told Mom, "David did it," which was true. But as I said, Mike kept asking me to fling him around – until he got hurt.

***

I don't want to bring up things that are sore points in people's lives, but one incident became notable, yet avoided in our conversations, in our family life. Poor Bill was in high school at Christian Brothers, and Mom and Dad let him take the truck to school one day. After school, a bunch of guys asked Bill for a ride, and they all jumped in the back of the pickup. As Bill was driving from school, the truck overturned as he rounded a corner. One boy hit his head pretty hard so that he was in the hospital several days. Fortunately, he recovered fully. Years and years after this happened, we were at the house of one of our aunts visiting, and the aunt brought up the accident. Out of the blue, she said something like, "Remember when you turned that truck over, Billy, and almost killed that kid?" Then she went to a cabinet and pulled out the newspaper story about the accident and passed it around to everyone to read. I know Bill was horrified at the mention of the incident years later.

***

Susan was the first one to have a cut sewed up by Dr. Christ, I believe. She got her cut at St. James Parochial School one day. Somehow Susan was hit in the head by a swing seat, which in those days was a thick, heavy slab of wood. My class was on the playground at the same time as hers so I was there. Or maybe it was after school and we were waiting for a ride home to the farm. Whenever it was, it seems as if a lot of kids were outside, and there was a collective gasp by everyone who saw it happen. Susan put her hand to her head, and it wasn't long before blood was running down her hand. Dr. Christ had an office in the Valley, and that's where we went for minor injuries. I think Dr. Christ put five stitches above one of Susan's eyes.

***

Kathy got a nasty burn one time. I don't remember this very well, probably because Kathy was trying to keep it from Mom and Dad. She had a boyfriend who had a motorcycle, and Dad told Kathy not to get on it with him. Dad and Mom considered motorcycles dangerous, and they were afraid she would get hurt. But Kathy did it anyway, and while she was riding with her friend, she bumped her bare leg, as she was wearing shorts, against the motorcycle's exhaust. Susan said Kathy was wearing long pants for a while after that, and when Susan asked Kathy about it, she pulled up her pants leg to reveal a very nasty burn. Susan said it looked awful, but Kathy didn't seek medical attention for it.

* * *

Bill came home from the Army on crutches one time when we lived on the farm. He sprained one of his ankles badly. He didn't break it. I remember Bill saying he was with one of his buddies who was driving a vehicle and crashed it. Although Bill was a passenger, he reacted automatically by stomping his foot as if he were the driver. Bill thought his false braking added to the injury to his ankle.

* * *

When Mike was just starting junior football, he broke his arm in a game. This was after we moved to the house on King Hill Avenue. I was working at the shoe shop that Saturday when the phone rang. I had a premonition that something happened to Mike, and when I answered the phone, one of my sisters said, "Let me talk to Dad. Mike broke his arm." The premonition would happen again later when Mike got hurt a second time. I'm not big on ESP, but Mike and I slept together in a bed for years, until I was 12 or so and he was 10. I think that formed some sort of psychological link between us. I felt sorry for Mike when he broke his arm, but that didn't last long. We still slept together, and he groaned all night long, and as he always did, he ground his teeth while he groaned. His groaning and grinding didn't stop him from sleeping, but it did me. I didn't get a good night's sleep the whole time he was in that cast.

* * *

Dad was injured while taking part in a silly activity at Hyde Park Pool. We used to go swimming there on Sunday mornings in the summer. One day, the pool put on a dad watermelon battle. Watermelons were placed in the deep end of the pool, and the dads were supposed to jump off the side and race and fight to get a watermelon and carry or push it back to the other side. Somehow in the melee, Dad and Mr. Marr banged heads, and Dad got a cut above one of his eyes. He had to get a few stitches, but I don't believe he went to Dr. Christ because the office was closed on Sundays.

* * *

Dr. Christ was open or came in late when the same sort of accident happened to me later. Mike and I were playing football at Hosea school with a group of guys from the neighborhood. Danny Hensley and I ran into each other and bumped heads. The top of Danny's head caught me right on the ridge above my right eye, and the pressure on the bone split the skin over my eyebrow. Danny and I collided pretty good and I was dizzy afterwards. But I felt blood spurt down my face running onto my shirt. After I steadied myself enough, I started running for home, and I yelled, "I'm bleeding." I ran to Fulkerson Street from Hosea's south entrance, then the block east to our house. I remember a car stopping as I neared home. The people in the car had horrid looks on their faces because the wound bloodied my face and the whole front of my shirt. Mom was pretty distraught when she saw me because she couldn't see where the blood had come from, just that it covered my face and torso. But she took me in the bathroom and cleaned me up. With the blood off my forehead, she said, "Oh, you just have a cut above your eye." Dr. Christ put seven stitches in my head. Aunt Dorothy came to the house to check on me afterward. She said I shouldn't have picked on Danny's head to have a collision with because he was hard-headed. However, I remember bumping heads with Danny when we lived on the farm. The Hensley's came to visit and Danny, Chuck, Mike and I were bouncing on our bed. Danny and I collided, and he went crying to his mother. She didn't say he had a hard head then. I got in trouble for not being more careful and making a guest in our house cry.

* * *

I went back to Dr. Christ maybe a year or two later when Hugh McCullough ran into me on the playground at St. James school. It was the afternoon recess, and the playground was full of kids as St. James had a lot of students in those years. My class was playing kickball, and Hugh, who was in the class behind me, was playing football with some other boys. While he was going out for a pass, he ran into the back of me, his face hitting the back of my head. Hugh ended up with a cut above his eye. I had blood on my head and figured it was Hugh's blood, so I went into the bathroom to wash it off, but I kept getting blood on the towels trying to dry my hair. I said something to another boy in the bathroom that Hugh sure left a lot of blood in my hair, and the boy looked at the back of my head and told me I had a cut too. I ended up with four stitches from that collision.

* * *

Richie suffered a split eyebrow when he was little. Kathy and Richard were living in the little block house down the street from us, and we were able to watch Richie and Jeff grow up there. Richie couldn't have been but three or four, and he and Jeff were pretending to be ghosts, putting sheets over their heads and running around the house. Richie banged into the footboard of his mom and dad's bed and received a cut over his eye that required several stitches. I remember Richie saying, "I'll never play ghosters again."

* * *

I don't know what years the accidents happened involving Aunt Katy and Uncle Phil. They just happened years before I was born, and I remember Mom telling us about them as we were growing up. That's why I put them here.

When Aunt Katy was a young, unmarried woman, she was walking along King Hill Avenue facing traffic as she should. I believe Mom said Aunt Katy was walking to work, when a man driving his car in the other lane, in the same direction as Aunt Katy, crossed lanes and ran into the back of her. I don't know all the injuries she suffered, but the one Mom mentioned was that Aunt Katy lost most of her teeth in the accident and had to get dentures as a young lady.

* * *

Uncle Phil's accident is a tragic story. His occurred after he was married to Aunt Mildred and was driving home from work one day. A little boy ran out between parked cars right into the path of Uncle Phil's vehicle. The boy was in the hospital for several days, I believe, before he died. Mom said even though it wasn't Uncle Phil's fault as he had no time to stop and he wasn't speeding, he still paid for the boy's hospitalization. Uncle Phil talked a lot, but I never heard him say anything about the accident.

***

Mike received a split lip in a neighborhood accident when he was about ten that could have ended very tragically, but thankfully did not. We were outside playing with other neighbor kids along King Hill Avenue in front of the Marek's house, when John Weber, who lived across the street, came outside. He carried what looked like a fireplace poker only it was made of shiny metal, had a wooden handle, and didn't have a hook on the end. It was just a straight metal rod with a point at one end and a wooden handle on the other. We were running, chasing each other, when John Weber, who was a golfer said something about practicing his swing. We stopped to watch him take a couple of swings, and he promptly lost his grip on the thing. It went flying and spinning away from him and right at Mike who was in the line of fire. The thing could have skewered Mike. Fortunately, it didn't, but the metal point caught Mike's lip as it spun upwards, splitting it open. Poor Mike had to get three stitches, and the doctor said he couldn't sedate Mike's lip because sedating a lip is difficult and anesthetizing a lip sometimes causes disfigurement.

***

When I was twelve years old, I made the all-star baseball team for the South End. I was playing on a team sponsored by a plumbing shop and managed by Mr. Murphy. He was a really nice man, and I liked him a lot, especially after playing two years for Mr. Pummell, who didn't like me and hardly ever let me in the games. But Mr. Murphy selected me as an all-star from our team. I went as a catcher, and I started the first all-star game in the tournament. Russ Tischner was the pitcher that day. He was a lefty, and threw the ball really hard. The game was just in the second or third inning, when a batter fouled a ball that hit the top of my catcher's mitt and caught the middle finger of my right hand, my throwing hand. My finger hurt, and I shook my hand, then retrieved the ball at the backstop, and threw it back to Russ. He looked at the ball funny and said something about blood being on the ball. I looked at my hand and my right middle finger was broken open at the first joint and blood was spurting out. I don't remember who the all-star manager was, but he sent in another player, and Mr. Marr, who was there, put ice in a bag on my finger. I don't know why, but I got nauseous and light-headed, and when I said something, Mr. Marr and another man each grabbed one of my legs and told me to put my arms over their shoulders. They carried me to a car, which embarrassed me to no end, and somebody took me to the hospital. Dad met us at the hospital, where I got an X-ray. My finger wasn't broken, but a tendon in my finger snapped. The doctor gave me a local anesthetic, and I watched him used forceps to grab and reattach the tendon and sew up my finger with five stitches. I didn't get to play but a couple innings on the all-star team. I didn't even bat.

***

While we were in high school, Mary and Susan had car accidents. Mary's wasn't her fault. She wasn't even in her car when someone drove into it. She parked her vehicle out front of our house on King Hill, which happened to have a slight curve there at our house. Someone wasn't paying attention and rear-ended her car. I remember her crying in the house after it happened.

***

Susan, unfortunately, was driving when she rear-ended someone. I mention this because she had a pretty yellow Mustang and the accident disclosed something interesting. I don't think she had the car very long when she came to a stop behind someone on I-229 and US 36. The person driving in front of Susan made a move to turn right, but then stopped. Susan thought the person had traveled on through the light, and gave her Mustang the gas, only to ram the car in front of her in the back end. The motor in Susan's car came off the motor mounts and had to be towed to a shop. Obviously, a former owner either worked on it or had it worked on, and the bolts to some of the motor mounts were not inserted. Eventually, Susan would have had problems with the car, but the accident gave away the issue early.

***

Richard Lamb broke his foot while we were playing basketball on the Hosea school playground one day. Mary and Robert were at the house along with Kathy and Richard and their two boys, and they and Susan, Mike, Linda and I went over to the school to play. We were having a good time, and Richard, who was quite athletic in his prime, went in for a layup. He made it, but he came down all wrong and twisted his foot. We laughed about it, and Richard tried to continue playing, but he said he couldn't put much weight on it. He walked back to our house, but went to the hospital later. He broke a few little bones in his foot.

***

I broke my left wrist in an accident on Hosea's playground as a result of acting wild and an oversight in putting a Moped together. Dad bought a couple of Mopeds, which are small, low-powered motorcycles with a step-through frame. Harold Grimes, a fireman who came in the shop often and knew a lot about cars and motorcycles, said when they ran that they sounded like someone farting in a bathtub. I seem to think Dad's Mopeds were made in Europe, but maybe they came from Asia. Dad had me put them together, as they came in slender boxes with the handlebars off and hanging to the side of the frame. He bought them to sell in the store, but he let us ride one of them around on the playground and grassy area of Hosea school. We only did it one time, because I ruined it for us. I began racing around in big circles, and carelessly got too close to the chainlink fence that bordered the playground. The left side of the handlebar caught the fence, and that jerked the bike into the fence and me off onto the ground. The bike wasn't damaged, except for a few scratches, but my left wrist immediately swelled. I could move my hand and wrist, but the pain was bad. I didn't want to go to the hospital, but after an hour or so, I couldn't take the pain anymore. Dad took me for an

X-ray, and the larger bone in my wrist had a green tree fracture. That fracture is one in which the bone does not snap in half, but cracks halfway through and splits partway up the length of the bone either direction. I didn't need a cast. I only had to wear a sling for a while and keep from using that hand for several weeks until the break healed. After the accident, Harold looked at the Moped and discovered I had put a U-bolt on wrong, which limited the turning radius of the handlebars.

* * *

Our family was fortunate that we did not have much sickness and many accidents. The worst that happened was bad, but it turned out as best could be expected for us. In Mike's freshman year at Christian Brothers High School, he was standing outside with other students viewing an intramural softball game. CB conducted intramural sports over lunchtime, and my class was playing softball with another class on one part of the football field. I was still in the lunchroom, when I saw Brother Dennis come in the door at the opposite end of the room. He looked all around, and stopped at a few tables asking students something. I had the feeling, just like I had with the phone call years before when Mike broke his arm, that something had happened to Mike. Sure enough, someone pointed me out, and Brother Dennis came up to me and told me to come with him. He led me into the gym and one of the locker rooms. He said Mike had gotten hurt. Mike was sitting on a table with a cold compress to his head, on the right side toward the front. Brother Dennis said Mike had been hit in the head with a ball bat, but didn't say anymore. He said a couple of the brothers were going to take him to the hospital and wanted me to go with them. Mike wasn't talking. He was pale and trembling, but he seemed alert. When we got to the hospital, the medical people took Mike to an emergency room, and I was left outside. Mom and Dad came soon, and they told me to go back to school, and I went back with the brothers. When I returned to my class, some of the students and brothers asked me how Mike was, but all I could tell them was I really didn't know. I heard then that Mike was standing along the third base line when Mike Jackson, a kid in some of my classes, was batting. He was a tall, very pale teen, who was a joker. They said Jackson made a big swing and lost hold of the bat. They said boys parted to get out of the way, but Mike was talking to someone and never saw the bat coming. The barrel end of the bat hit him right in the head. When school ended, I had football practice, but I called the hospital first, and I talked to Mom. She said Mike had been given an X-ray and he had a skull fracture. She said they took Mike in for surgery, and they were concerned about a blood clot. I left school and went to the hospital.

I believe it was the next day, they took Mike in for a second surgery because of the clot and pressure building in his brain. We were devastated, and Mike didn't look good. He was in a coma and unresponsive. Aunts and uncles came to visit, and we were all very somber. I think the priest from St. James came and gave Mike the Last Rites. Thankfully, Mike pulled through. He came home with a big arcing line of stitches across his shaved head, and we were told to be careful around him and that he might be forgetful and slow in thought and movement. But he did really well, and went back to school quickly. He even played baseball his junior and senior years after CB closed and the male students began attending LeBlond High School.

* * *

I've written about Linda's broken foot in the account of the trip to Minnesota. Here's a brief summary again: Mom, Dad, Linda and I went to St. Peter to fish at the resort of one of Dad's old friends. One night midweek, Linda and I were walking down a slope to the lake and a community building when Linda stepped into a hole and twisted her ankle, we thought. She cried all night, and in the morning, Dad and Mom took Linda for medical attention. It turned out she broke some bones in her foot, and the doctors in Minnesota set her foot in a cast. Linda complained that her foot hurt the rest of the week, and when we got home, a doctor in St. Joseph said her foot was set incorrectly and it had to be reset.

***

The worst tragedy in our extended family occurred in 1976. Jimmy Sparks, Uncle Sparky and Aunt Rosie's son, was playing in a regular season football game for Benton High School one evening. Jimmy was a defensive back, a good one, who previously made the All-City team. This one night, on a typical play, he made a tackle, got up, but then collapsed on the field as he walked back toward the huddle. He was taken to the hospital, and doctors diagnosed him with a severed brain stem from the impact of the collision on the field. He died a few days later when doctors took him off life support. I didn't know Jimmy well, but he was well-liked by his high school classmates and teachers. They said he was studious and thoughtful. He must have made a deep impression on people because the school changed the name of the football stadium to honor him. The stadium is still known as the James Sparks Stadium.

| 11 |

The Day Kennedy Was Shot

I wrote this on April 8, 2021, after my grandson Heston recited a presentation to me on John F. Kennedy that he did at school the day before. Students in Heston's class were to find five things that represented the life of the thirty-fifth president, show them to the class, and tell how they were important in Kennedy's life.

John F. Kennedy's official photo from his time in presidential office, from the National Archives.

At the time, Heston was in the fourth grade at Marquette Catholic School, Tulsa. He told me that his class was learning about Kennedy, and he knew quite a bit about JFK's life. Heston seemed especially intrigued by Jack Ruby, who murdered the suspect in JFK's death, Lee Harvey Oswald, while Dallas police looked on.

Heston's retelling of JFK's life brought back all the memories of those terrible days in late November 1963. The event is one that everyone remembers what they were doing when it happened.

I was in the sixth grade at St. James Parochial School, and my birthday had been the day before, Nov. 21. On Friday, Nov. 22, my class had just eaten lunch, and all the boys in school who were altar boys had gone to the school basement to listen to the principal, Sister Mary Michael, review our responsibilities in assisting the priests in the Mass. Another sister was standing with Sister Mary Michael at the front. I don't remember who she was, but she and Sister Mary Michael had their backs to the entry to the basement room. All of us altar boys could see the corridor leading into the room, and Sister Mary Michael had just started her talk when we saw Mrs. Fry, the school cook, coming down the corridor crying. She had a towel to her face, and she was hurrying toward the two nuns. The sister whose name I don't remember heard Mrs. Fry's steps and met her before she got into the room. Mrs. Fry whispered something to her, and a horrid look came over the sister's face. Then Mrs. Fry whispered her message to Sister Mary Michael, and Mrs. Fry rushed back out of the room, sobbing harder than when she came in.

Sister Mary Michael's face never showed any change of emotion. She was a tough old lady, though I'm sure she was devastated. Like all Catholics at that time, we were proud of President Kennedy, and he could do no wrong. Sister Mary Michael told us to stand as we were going to say a prayer for our president because "He has been shot." Sister Mary Michael then sent us to our rooms, and it wasn't long before we were sent home early from school. I can't remember if we knew when we left school that Kennedy had died, which had been announced on TV at about 1:30 PM that day or if we learned that at home. We had the television on constantly the entire weekend once we got home from school. It wasn't long before we learned a suspect, Lee Harvey Oswald, had been captured and that he had killed a policeman, Officer Tippit, before being arrested in the Texas Theatre.

Home was a somber place. My mother was a huge Kennedy fan. We all were. We had watched Jackie give her tour of the renovated White House on television the year before. We had listened to the "First Family Album," a lighthearted parody on the Kennedys that had come out the year before too, but parts of which had been played on radio programs for a long time afterward. We all read "Profiles in Courage," JFK's book about Americans who had stood firm against bigotry, hatred, or conventional wisdom and showed exceptional resolution in the face of adversity. Then there was the allusion to the JFK administration as the embodiment of Camelot, the perfect kingdom. And, of course, JFK was our first Catholic president. We were Catholic. We loved him.

President John F. Kennedy's motorcade in Dallas on the day he was assassinated there. National Archives.

It was a flurry of news that night. Lyndon Johnson was sworn in as the next president, and JFK's body was flown to Washington, DC. The next day, we mostly watched TV, only taking breaks from the dire news to play outside with friends. With either TV or friends, the talk was all JFK and his death, and we all wondered if Lee Harvey Oswald was the real assassin, and if he was, who put him up to it. Some people said it was Castro. Some said the Russians were behind it. Some said The Mob was behind the assassination. And some said Lyndon Johnson had Kennedy killed just so he could be president.

But none of it made sense. Why would anyone want to shoot John F. Kennedy, a man who came into the White House with youthful vigor and high ideals; a man who was rich, but showed compassion for the poor; a man who had a vision for the future, not someone content with the way things were?

There were also comparisons of John F. Kennedy to Abraham Lincoln. They were both assassinated on a Friday. Lincoln's secretary was named Kennedy; Kennedy's secretary was named Lincoln. They both were followed in office by a Johnson. They both had seven letters in their last names. There were more coincidences. I don't remember them all.

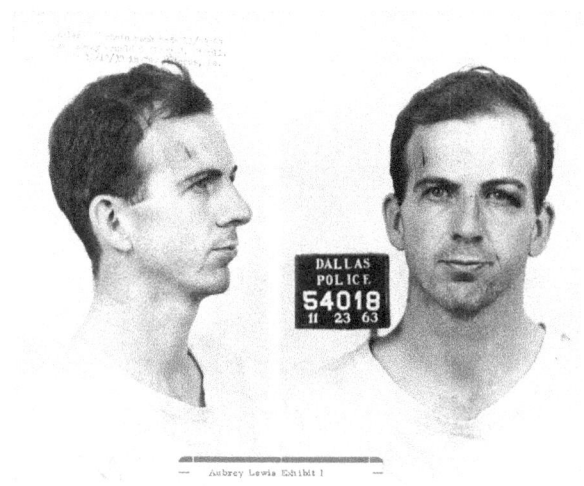

Lee Harvey Oswald mugshot after his arrest for the murder of JFK. National Archives.

On Sunday, we watched as the casket with Kennedy's body was moved into the US Capitol Rotunda to lie in state. People filed in all day long to see the closed casket. President Johnson brought a wreath to place by it. Four or five soldiers from the different military branches stood at the corners and ends of the casket immovable, like the stone statues in the Capitol building. I said something about what if they itch. My brother Bill, who had been in the Army, said the soldiers couldn't scratch; they would be court-martialed.

Later, we heard that Oswald was going to be moved from the Dallas City Jail to the Dallas County Jail just after lunch. Mike and I didn't stay inside to watch. We went outside to play with friends along King Hill Avenue. Suddenly, John Weber came running out of his house across the street and yelled, "Oswald's been shot. Oswald's been shot. I saw it on TV. It was on TV!" Then Mike and I were disappointed that we had left the television, and missed that bizarre twist to an incomprehensible event.

We stayed home for John F. Kennedy's funeral the next day, watched the procession, the whole sad affair on TV. The assassination was the first big tragedy to temporarily stop all regular television programming. In those days, there were no DVRs, no movie videotapes, no movie rentals, no computers with Internet, no readily available cable TV channels. There were only three networks, and they only showed one thing. There were no other viewing options. If you watched the television those four days, you watched continuous coverage of JFK's assassination and burial. And when the eternal flame had been lit, when the three networks finally stopped replaying little John Kennedy saluting his father's casket, when the Warren Commission was appointed by Johnson a week after that miserable and disgraceful day, nothing still seemed normal.

John F. Kennedy was not perfect. We knew it then. We know it now, even more than then. He had grown up in a family that accumulated its wealth illegally and sought power and privilege. JFK, like other men in his family, craved sex so much he used women for his own ends. JFK was only too human.

But JFK expressed the hopes and dreams of our nation better than anyone had done in its history. He was a talented speaker and a politician who pushed for equality, something the US said it stood for but had not achieved. He asked for people to enter public service, and he advocated for the arts. He sought to alleviate poverty and raise the economic standards of third-world countries. He believed Americans had a duty to help others, and he wasn't afraid to make that claim.

Linda saved this Santa photo of us from Christmas 1960. I guess Bill and Kathy were too big to visit Santa by this time.

| 12 |

The Valley

Kodrak's

Directly east across King Hill Avenue from Dad's shop was Kodrak's bar. I think the real name of it was Hyde Valley Tavern and Café, and it was run by Francie Kodrak. I believe her husband, John, established it, and they went to St. James Church. I went in the tavern a couple of times. Once, Dad sent me over there, and I was pretty young, probably not ten, to take Francie something, a pair of shoes, I think. I just remember that it was dark in there, and I didn't know what Francie Kodrak looked like and Dad acted as if I should know. Walking across the street, I had an image of her looking like Miss Kitty in the Longbranch Saloon in *Gunsmoke*. When I got there, she did sort of look like an aging Miss Kitty with her dark dyed hair, bright red lipstick, drawn on eyebrows, and skinny face.

Woods Supermarket

Across King Hill Avenue and south to opposite corner was a grocery store, Woods Supermarket. It was a small neighborhood grocery, old and grimy looking, with a low ceiling and narrow, crowded aisles. I used to go in there a lot because Dad sent me down there when I was working at the shop to buy his cigarettes, Camels. Eventually, Dad stopped smoking. We kids badgered him to stop, and he did it pretty easily about the third or fourth try.

When Dad had his teeth pulled and was waiting for his dentures to be made, he sent us to the grocery to buy the sugar drinks that were in miniature wax bottles. The little bottles of wax, about a couple inches tall, if that much, were made to look just like a soda six pack that in those days came in a lightweight cardboard carrying case with a handle. Dad let us drink the sugary solution inside; then he chewed on the wax to toughen up his gums. He said the doctor told him to do that. It seems like it took several weeks to a month to get his dentures.

Farmer's State Bank

Farmer's was on the northeast corner of King Hill Avenue and East Valley Street. The brick bank had an angled front door that mimicked the curve of the corner, and inside it had a big walk-in safe with its door visible in the lobby. When I was eight and I started working for my dad, I opened a savings account there. I think my initial deposit was five dollars, which took me five weeks to earn because Dad only paid me one dollar each Saturday I worked.

I was sure proud of that savings account book. In those days, a person took his or her account book in with them each time, and the bank clerk would write in the deposit and stamp the book with the date. I was even prouder of myself when I turned 12, and I made a withdrawal to purchase a football helmet to play in the youth football league. Dad started paying me five dollars a day a few years after I started, so I had several hundred dollars in my account by the time I graduated from high school. I remember taking out $300 for college in Columbia in 1970. I closed the account soon after that. I think the most I ever had in the bank account wasn't much more than $300.

Valley Poultry Market

Next to or near to Uncle Charlie's shop was a slaughterhouse. It was a remnant of another time, but it lasted into my childhood.

Mom used to go there to buy chickens, whole chickens. The business bought them, killed them, plucked them, gutted them, and sold them. It was a smelly place, and I remember the hooks hanging from the ceiling and chickens in a showcase.

Audrey's grandfather used to raise chickens. Audrey told me that she went there with her Grandpa Roy, who took the chickens he raised to be butchered.

Fox and Weiner's department stores

There were two clothing stores in The Valley, owned by two separate families. Mom almost always shopped at Weiner's. She hardly ever went into Fox, which was more expensive. There may have been other issues, but it seemed Weiner's served more common folk.

There was a lady who worked at Weiner's who was very friendly and waited on us a lot. Her name was Goldie. She was a nice-looking lady with blond, almost golden, hair, but who it seemed wore too much makeup and had several rings on her fingers before it was vogue. She called everyone kid. She would say, "Here, kid, try this one," or "Oh, kid, you look good in that." She called my Mom, my Dad, me, everyone, kid.

The thing that turned my mom and a lot people off Fox occurred when old man Fox died and his son took over. The son changed the name to Fox's Emporium and started carrying drug paraphernalia. People went to see it and they all were shocked. He had all kinds of pipes and tubes and things that we didn't know what they even were for, only that they were for drug use.

The Donut Shop

We were very disappointed in the early 1960s when the little donut store north of Fox Department Store closed. A short, rotund man with a chubby face ran the store and made the most delicious glazed donuts ever. I don't remember him making many different kinds of donuts. He wore white pants, a white short-sleeved shirt, a white apron, and a little round white hat.

Our family stopped frequently, and often Mom or Dad sent a couple of us down to purchase a dozen or more which went into a white paper bag. We always seemed to be eating only the round glazed donuts with the hole. Even before we got home, the bag was nearly soaked in grease. Of course, we went early to get the freshest donuts. The donut-maker was a nice man, always friendly, and he would give us extras or ones right out of the fryer to eat while on our way. Linda said that she used to take in glass bottles that she found on the street, which were worth five cents each on return to a grocery store then, and the baker would give her a donut for the bottle.

Marty's Hardware Store

Marty was a small, skinny man, and he never did a lot to keep up his store. The floor was old well-worn wood, the ceiling had water spots, and when it rained, he and his workers just put pots and pans out to catch the water. I'm sure at one point, he had to have the roof fixed, but I don't remember it. I only remember pots and pans.

I think Dad got along all right with Marty, but Marty did complain when Dad started carrying seeds and vegetable plants in the spring. Dad only did that a few years because it was a lot of trouble helping customers with filling the little packets and sacks with seeds. Dad hated it when someone came in and couldn't make up their mind about which seeds to buy and how much.

Marty's Hardware also served as the Post Office for the Valley. So Dad and I went over there a lot, mailing payments for bills, and Mom would give us mail to take there too.

When I was a teenager, Marty, for some reason, had a couple of small alligators that he kept in a round watering trough in the middle of the store. They were there several years, and lots of people went in just to see them.

Sparky's Barbershop

Besides my father's shoe store, one of the other Valley businesses I frequented a lot was Uncle Sparky's Barbershop.

Uncle Sparky was a nice guy, friendly, and he cut Bill's, Mike's and my hair, and the hair of all my male cousins, for nothing all the years we were growing up.

I don't think Mom or Dad paid him that we didn't know about because a lot of times I went in, there would be several guys waiting and even if I got there first, I had to wait until he had cut the paying customers' hair before he cut mine because it was a freebie. A couple of times, a customer would point to me and say, "That boy was here before me," and Uncle Sparky would say, "He's my nephew. He doesn't pay; he can wait."

It wasn't said in remorse, but the honest truth. And Uncle Sparky only asked me to do something for him one time. He asked me to shovel the walk out front of his shop after a snow. That was the old barber shop, before Aunt Rosie had the new one built and Uncle Sparky worked with other barbers. I only went to the new shop a few times. After I went to high school, I didn't get my hair cut as often.

But like I said, Uncle Sparky only asked me to do something for him that one time, and now I feel guilty that I didn't offer to help him because that was a generous thing to do for all his nephews.

Looking back, he didn't have to cut our hair for free. Dad didn't give out free shoes or shoe repair to our cousins. But you know it's funny. I don't remember Uncle Sparky, Uncle Charley Hensley or Uncle Bob ever coming in the shoe shop very much. Of course, I only worked there on Saturdays growing up and then during the week in the summers for a couple years in high school. Uncle Phil and Uncle Charlie Zuptich came in to talk, but I don't remember them buying much, maybe a ball glove or bat for their sons a few times. Uncle Phil bought seeds when Dad sold seeds a few years.

But back to Uncle Sparky and the barber shop. The times I went for haircuts and sat and waited, I learned a great deal. Usually several customers were there waiting, and they were all bantering back and forth with Uncle Sparky, talking sports, making friendly wagers, telling stories – frequently dirty stories – cussing, and I guess what has now become known as, having "a locker room talk."

One time, Uncle Sparky was making bets with his buddies on an upcoming college football games and after they left and he was cutting my hair, he asked me if I was interested in college football. I said I followed how the Missouri Tigers were doing. He asked me if I thought they would do well that week. I said something about not knowing enough to be able to predict the score of a game beforehand, and Uncle Sparky said he could tell me the score of the game before it started.

I told him that I didn't think he could, and Uncle Sparky said he would bet me five dollars that he could tell me the score of the Missouri game that week beforehand. I thought that would be an easy five dollars and we shook on it.

And Uncle Sparky said, "I predict the score of the game before will be zero to zero. You owe me five dollars."

Well, he was correct, of course, and I protested, saying that he tricked me, that that's not what I meant by predicting the score, but as nice as Uncle Sparky was, he said a bet was a bet and I owed him five dollars. I think I was only twelve or so, and I didn't have five dollars and I told Uncle Sparky that I would have to go get the money and bring it back to him. He said instead of the money, I could pay it by sweeping up inside and outside the shop. So that's what I did, which only took about 15 or 20 minutes, but Uncle Sparky told me that I should really think it over before I ever made a bet again. I thought after I left that I needed to really think it over before I made a bet with him.

The barbershop could be a place for raw stories, not that that happened all the time. Uncle Sparky and the customers mostly talked sports, football, Uncle Sparky's favorite topic. But sometimes the language became really raunchy, and I remember a few times Uncle Sparky having to say to the customers, "Hey, there are kids in here."

But sometimes when those men got going, they could get downright dirty. Our mother would have had a conniption fit if she knew some of the things we heard there. I wasn't a saint, but I had a religious conscience more sensitive than other people because of our mother's dedication to the Catholic Church. I felt as if I needed confession sometimes after I went there, at least until I was 14 or 15, and I started hearing that kind of talk in high school. Then it became sort of normal because I heard it from other guys at Christian Brothers.

But that kind of talk went on quite a lot at Uncle Sparky's old shop, not much after the new one was built, though. The new shop was more a hair stylist shop, a step up from the old-fashioned men's barber shop.

Uncle Charlie's Television Shop

Uncle Charlie had his television shop on the east side of King Hill Avenue in a block of buildings near Uncle Sparky's barber shop. It was in a light brown brick building that was two stories tall.

Aunt Dorothy handled customers at the front and Uncle Charlie worked in back. He was a like a magician to me around all those huge old televisions and radios and all the tubes and replacement parts sitting around.

Uncle Charlie didn't inspire me to buy a crystal radio set and build it. But I know as I was doing it, I thought of him around all those sets, diagnostic equipment, and manufacturers' repair books. I thought I would have to go to him for advice when my set wouldn't work, but eventually I put a longer receiving wire on it and found a place in the house where it worked best without bothering him.

Uncle Charlie came to our house a few times to diagnose and repair our sets when they were too big to haul around easily. As TVs got smaller, we had to take them in to him for repair.

In was in 1965 or 1966, our family was visiting the Hensley's at their home that we saw our first color television set. Uncle Charlie and Aunt Dorothy had one, and we were there eating with them, and I think some of the other Zuptich families were there too. They were watching football, the annual game between the University of Oklahoma and Oklahoma State University. Usually, OU beat up on OSU, but in those two years, OSU upset OU. I suspect it was 1965 because it was a big deal that OSU won, and it was in 1965 that TV broadcasters switched to color broadcasts on a big scale, and by the next year all prime time shows were in color.

Whichever year it was, soon after going to the Hensley house, Dad and Mom went to Uncle Charlie's shop and bought our first color set. The next year when "The Wizard of Oz" came on at Easter, we actually saw Oz in color for the first time at home. We didn't have to say to each other, "You know, this part is actually in color."

Uncle Charlie turned to trucking when televisions and radios became solid state and throw-away devices. He did both, truck driving and repairing sets, for a while. Eventually, he and Aunt Dorothy dissolved the business and Uncle Charlie turned solely to trucking.

Bill Kenney's Drug Store

Bill Kenney had an old-fashioned drugstore on the southeast corner of East Hyde Park and King Hill Avenue. But though it was old-fashioned, I don't remember it having a soda fountain. This was before corporate pharmacies took over. He sold a lot of things other than pharmaceuticals. He had candy and toys, jewelry and knick-knacks, snacks and drinks. It was always a very clean store, and everything was always neat and in order despite having a lot of customers passing through. He didn't have any competition in the far South End, except for Helen Wrinkle, who had a similar store in the Junction.

Bill Kenney was a bachelor for years. He ended up marrying a woman 20 years younger than he was. As far as I know, it worked out.

Audrey worked for Bill Kenney for a short time, and she said what everyone said about him: He was a nice guy.

Hindery's Hardware

Bill Hindery was a nice man, and he had a very nice hardware store, one he kept up, unlike Marty, who didn't spend much money on capital improvements.

However, Mr. Hindery's store which took up two buildings on the south side of my dad's store caught fire one evening. The fire department put out the fire, but it pretty much destroyed the half of the building connected to my dad's store, which also suffered some smoke and water damage.

Bill Hindery ended up tearing down the burned-out building, and he kept open the other one for a few years before selling out. He had a son my age, William, who we called Pat. We went to school together. Pat took part in track in high school, and he was good. He was a cross country runner, and I believe he set some city records.

When Bill Hindery sold out, the building went through several owners. One operated a slot toy car racing operation. He set up a track, and kids would buy these cars three or four inches long that ran around tracks powered by electricity. The kids operated their car with a little controller that tied into the track that had three or four lanes on it. We would race in heats with the winner of each heat advancing to the next, until there were only two racers left.

I did it for a while, but I was terrible at it. I lost every time, and it cost a few dollar to enter the races.

The Salvation Army

The Salvation Army had a thrift store next to Dad on the north side. Unlike most of the buildings in the Valley, they were not attached. There was a space of about three feet between the two. I hated mowing between those buildings because a lot of trash collected there.

As Mary pointed out, we bought books and puzzles there. I don't remember if we shopped there very often or bought a great deal, but I remember going in and looking around to see what they had, and I remember when the building came down.

Because it belonged to a nonprofit for many years, it didn't get much care. In fact, in the early 1970s, it was empty and falling apart. I was working with Dad when the city, I believe, hired a demolition business to tear the building down. They crew was not made up of careful workers. They were rather sloppy, and several times I heard and felt boards, posts and beams hitting the side of Dad's shop.

I complained to the workers and to the guy who ran the business. He would come and supervise every so often. He was a big, heavy guy who wore brand new jeans, pressed cowboy shirt, and cowboy hat. He was never dirty, and when I said something to him about his workers, he gave me a look of contempt.

One day, the workers were using a small dozer to knock down sections of the wall. Instead, they inadvertently pushed over most of the back of the building on top of two workers. Even inside Dad's shop, I could hear them screaming and calling help, help. I called for an ambulance as did some of the demolition workers, and before long, emergency workers and police were there. The arrogant demolition owner showed up, and he was standing and laughing with police as a few of the workers raised a wall freeing the two trapped coworkers. They were OK except for a few non-serious nail punctures.

I walked over to the policeman and the owner. I was upset, and I told the policeman that the whole operation was done poorly and I had complained to the cowboy there beside him that something like this was going to happen as they hit my dad's building several times.

The policeman looked at me and said, "Well, opinions are like assholes. Everybody has one."

The policeman and his cowboy friend had a good laugh at my expense. When I related that story to Dad and other people, they told me, "What do you expect? Police deal with criminals all the time, and some of the cops get to be pretty good friends with the criminals."

Billiards and rock shop

When I was about 12 or 13, the building across West Valley from the Salvation Army became a pool hall. Dad worried that it was going to attract all kinds of rogues and late-night shenanigans. It didn't turn out as bad as Dad thought, but there were some odd characters hanging around and a lot of noise on the corner with vehicles parked everywhere.

But Mike and I went over there, too, some. Playing wasn't very expensive then, and of course, we never played for money with anyone, and I never saw anyone betting on games. We weren't there late at night though.

The pool hall didn't last very long, only a few years, and then a rock shop moved in. That didn't last long either, but I had a geode from somewhere out West that I had brought home and never opened. The guy in the rock shop had a stone cutter and cut it for me for a dollar. I still have that geode, which was not a spectacular one, but nice.

Betty's Cafeteria

Betty was a woman in her mid-forties or early fifties when I was growing up, who had a coffee shop next to Ed Ziph and Fox's. She did a good business serving breakfast and lunch even though it was a long but very narrow building that had only five or six booths and a short counter to eat at. She was a pleasant lady, and a good businesswoman.

Dad usually kept a coffee pot going for himself and customers, but for short periods of time, he didn't. Then he sent us kids to Betty's to buy coffee for him.

Betty had a brother who worked for her, Carl, who almost always got Dad's coffee. That was about all he could do as he had an accident at some point in his life and had huge scar circling from his forehead to one of his temples. He couldn't see very well, so he held the cup and pot dangerously close to his face and eyes as he poured. When we gave him the money, he carefully laid the coins in the palm of his hand and held them inches from his nose to see what they were.

Betty eventually relocated down to the Hensley's building where she had more room for tables.

Ziph Photography

Ed Ziph, who lived in the Kirschner Addition, had a photography studio in the Valley. He did weddings and special events, and maybe some school photos. But a lot of couples and families went to his studio for formal photos. Mom and Dad and all seven of us children went one time and had a family portrait done. Mom dressed us all up, and she was very proud of that photo. It was the one Bill had redone by Korean artists. Ed was a peculiar person. He was very tall and thin, and was not real outgoing or funny, which seems strange for someone who needed to keep people smiling for photos. But he was a well-known photographer in the South End.

Photo opposite page: 1-Farrell McGinnis; 2-Melanie Hensley Wright; 3-Uncle Sparky; 4-Uncle Bob Pitts; 5-Susan McGinnis; 6-Steven Lamb; 7-John McGinnis; 8-Linda Jurkiewicz; 9-Phil Pitts; 10-Andrew Pitts; 11-Patrick Pitts; 12-Richard Zuptich; 13-Phillip Pitts; 14-James Pitts; 15-Annie McGinnis; 16-Diana Pitts Koelliker; 17-Mike Jurkiewicz and wife, Mary; 18-Rich Lamb; 19-Ted Wolfe; 20-Phyliss Ann Schrorer with Mom to left; 21-Patti Pitts; 22-Joe Zuptich; 23-Jesse Pitts; 24-Amy Row; 25-Jeremiah Wolfe; 26-Matthew Shelor; 27-Jeff Zuptich; 28-Jim Wolfe; 29-Judy Pitts Meyer; 30-Rosanne Zuptich Wolfe; 31-Bob Row; 32-Richard Lamb; 33-Steve Meyer; 34-Gail Zuptich Row; 35-Uncle Charlie Zuptich; 36-Sue Zuptich; 37-Joe Zuptich; 38-April Jurkiewicz; 39-Rachel Jurkiewicz; 40-Robin Hensley Pecora; 41-Jennifer Schroer; 42-Ty Black; 43-Nick Pecora; 44-Debbie Schroer; 45-Valerie Sparks Stehle; 46-Bethanee Boeh; 47-Andrea Sparks Boeh holding daughter Rosalee; 48-William Jurkiewicz holding son Jared; 49-Aunt Rosie Sparks; 50-Lauren Stehle; 51-Kathy Lamb; 52-Aunt Dorothy Hensley; 53-John Boeh; 54-Mikey Stehle; 55-Lynda Jurkiewicz with Aunt Mildred behind her; 56-Susan Hensley holding Nathan; 57-Caleb Jurkiewicz; 58-David Jurkiewicz; 59-Daniel Hensley holding Kevin Pecora; 60-Chuck Hensley; 61-Uncle Charlie Hensley; 62- Jessica Jurkiewicz; 63-Audrey Jurkiewicz.

ME, MY FAMILY, OUR LIVES — 133

1985 Zuptich Reunion.

Kathy and Richard at the 2016 family reunion in Texas near where they lived on Cedar Creek Reservoir.

At the Texas reunion. Back row: Mary and Mike, Richard; 2nd row: Susan, Mary, Bill; 3rd row: Linda, Brendon, Bailey, Kathy; Front row: me, Maggie, Stormy, Steven, Gina.

| 13 |

Christian Brothers High School

I did not like high school. I disliked it intensely.

There are several reasons for that.

First, Christian Brothers High School, where my parents sent me, was all the way across town. We lived in the southwest part of town, and CB, along with LeBlond High School, the girls' Catholic secondary school, was in the northeast, seven miles away. I did not have a car throughout high school, so I rode the bus, as did Mike and Susan.

VARSITY—Row 1: John Cathcart, S. Gilpin, C. Guardado, L. Sanger, B. Nash, T. Thompson, S. Eggleston, B. Guardado, B. Jiminez, M. Neylon, student manager. Row 2: N. Sayles, H. McCullough, P. Pitts, B. Graham, D. Jurkiewicz, B. Jackson, J. Hague, G. Kastner, D. Garrick, G. Davis, M. Schnabel, student manager. Row 3: Coach Meyers, Coach Pawlowski, D. Hensley, B. Swartz, Jim Cathcart, T. Hoffman, G. Kline, B. Brown, M. Przybylski, B. Weddle, D. Echterling. Row 4: Coach Tabor, G. Fry, J. Byrne, S. Marr, D. Chavez, T. Siela, D. Swymeler, F. Rathburn, A. Gatton, M. Sego.

I am in the middle of the second row wearing No. 20. My jersey number at Christian Brothers was 64, and I don't remember why I didn't have that jersey on. I played football all four years. I was a tight end on the freshman team, but played offensive guard part time the other four years. I played sporadically on defense, mostly filling in when someone was hurt.

We watched at 7 a.m. for the bus heading down Fulkerson Street; then we caught it coming back up the street after it made a short loop in the neighborhood. The South End bus didn't go directly to the school. We rode that bus downtown to the main transfer station and waited for another bus that traveled east on Frederick Avenue to the schools. It took 45 to 50 minutes to get to school, and in the afternoon, it took longer to get home, as we had a longer wait at the transfer station. During football season, the time waiting for buses was even longer, and the rides home were made in the dark. I never made good use of the time on the bus, which I see now. I blankly stared out the bus window, wishing I wasn't riding public transportation.

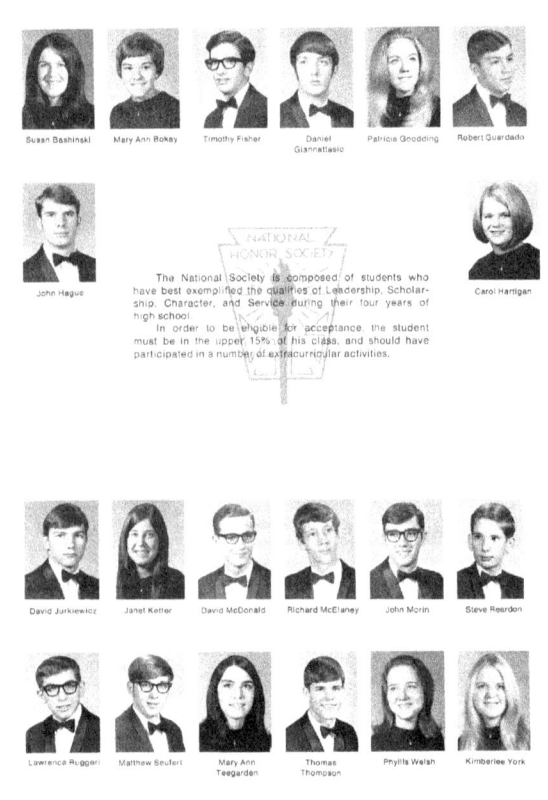

My senior year in high school, I was elected into the National Honor Society. Here I appear on the Honor Society page in the 1970 yearbook that combined the students of LeBlond and Christian Brothers high schools.

Second, there were no girls at CB. Catholic girl students went to LeBlond, which was more than a mile farther east on Frederick Avenue. Most Catholics then believed separating boys and girls at high school age led to a better educational situation as students weren't pestered with thoughts of boy/girl stuff and sex. Actually, that only aggravated our desire and questions about maturation and sexual development. Plus, the separation complicated getting to know girls and dating, especially for me, because I was more shy and quieter than most boys. I didn't date until I was a senior, and then I had only four or five dates, never asking a girl out a second time. I probably never would have gone out with a girl if it wasn't for the National Honor Society. In my junior year, one of the brothers came to me and said that the NHS nominating committee, made up of teachers, considered me for entry, but one of the requirements was involvement in school activities and organizations. Grade wise, I was number nine in a class of about ninety, but I did nothing for three years except play football. So that year, I went out for track and I got involved in drama, which was a joint class and activity that took place at LeBlond my senior year. Those two activities were enough to get me into Honor Society, and I also had a class and interaction with girls. I didn't ask out any of the girls in the drama class, but being in the class increased my confidence.

The high schools did sponsor dances, but I didn't go to many. Susan used to encourage me to go, but I never felt comfortable at them. I didn't know how to dance, and the music was always so loud that a person couldn't hear what the person next to them was saying. A girl by the name of Charlotte Brown is the only girl I can remember dancing with me.

ME, MY FAMILY, OUR LIVES - 137

This is a QUIET family gathering!

Well, it was the only date I could find!

I wish he'd climb down off his soapbox.

But you were a blond last week!

ANYTHING to get into the picture.

My senior year, I took part in a drama class that involved students from the girls Catholic high school. I had a supporting part in a play titled "Unfinished Business," playing an elderly, kind man. In the top photo, I am the one on the left in the bad lighting. In the bottom photo, I started horsing around, and then was labeled a "ham."

She was a nice girl, and nice looking, and I think she liked me, but of course, dancing with her brought teasing from my buddies, and I didn't handle teasing very well then, especially guys who had trouble asking girls to dance too.

Because I did get more involved, my senior year was my most memorable year in high school, and most pleasant. However, the others, I can truly say, were miserable. I wished I was someplace else, and I made the situation worse by reading a lot of adventure novels and travel books. I don't know how I earned decent grades as I spent most days daydreaming about taking off on my own and traveling. I never really thought about what I wanted to become, nor did I work toward a specific goal. When I took a career placement test my junior year, the results came back saying my best fit for the future was with the merchant marine. When Brother Benedict shared the result of the test with me, he made a joke of it and laughed. I must have been the only one recommended to go to sea.

"We love to sing, oh yes we do."

Susan was busy at LeBlond High School, taking part in several activities. Here she is a member of the choral group, on the left end of the middle row in the LeBlond gymnasium. This photo was in the 1969 yearbook, the year she graduated.

It wasn't until near the spring of 1970 when the Christian Brothers basketball team made the state playoffs that I decided to go to the University of Missouri. The playoffs were held in Columbia at the MU arena, and Mike and I rode with Ronnie Peden, who had a car, to watch the games. We stayed with Bill's friend Wally Wells, and I was so impressed with the campus and the thought of college, that I enrolled the minute I returned home.

The third reason I didn't like high school was the angst from being around only guys and the brothers of Christian Brothers. Every day it seemed school was a male combat area. Guys were always challenging guys, one bunch asserting themselves over others by humiliating them. Several times a year, fights would break out in the halls or challengers would make a date for a fight at the park down the street after school. While the brothers naturally frowned on fights and punished students for fighting and bullying, they sometimes engaged in heavy-handed behavior too. They just were not as overt as students.

Coach Suholaski, the football coach, was a bully and mean. He slapped students and got away with it. He and the basketball coach were terrible teachers. Don Tabor, who took over as football coach my junior year, was a big improvement as a coach, but he too was not an inspiring teacher. Brother William, the principal, ruled with tyranny, trying to stay on top of any disciplinary issues. Brother Dennis was creepy. Other boys said he was gay and a pedophile because he managed the locker room, and he did hang around there more than he needed to. Almost all of the non-vocation teachers who were there were terrible. Our math teacher, Mr. Burke was nice, but he was an alcoholic. He came to class drunk several times. Eventually, Brother William told him not to come back. I was done with math by then. Our first Spanish teacher was a meek, docile ex-Peace Corps volunteer who had no control over his classes, and some students made life miserable for him. I forget who, but one student mouthed off to him one day, and the Peace Corps guy finally had had enough. He started punching the smart guy and they rolled and wrestled in the aisle for a while before the Spanish teacher walked away and never came back.

Business staff headed by Gerard Hershewe and Susie Jurkiewicz.

Susan also served on the Business staff in 1969 for the Aerie, the combined CB and LeBlond yearbook.

John Chavez, who taught Spanish and PE and coached track, was a really nice guy. He had a brother my age who went to CB and who was not in any of my classes, Daniel. John was nice to me because I didn't cause trouble and I did pretty well in Spanish. He lettered me in track probably when I didn't deserve it. I didn't place in meets but a few times, and a few other runners said something to me that my letter wasn't earned fairly, but it wasn't my fault. I did my best.

That's not to say there weren't some nice brothers who were good teachers. Brother Justin taught biology. He was old-fashioned and dull, but he knew his subject and the few labs we had could be interesting. Brother Edwin gave me a love for chemistry and physics even though I never was adept at the math. He could be testy and cranky, but he had the best labs, better even than the labs I would take later at the University of Missouri. I especially liked the brother we had for English, Brother Joel. I can't remember how many years he was there, a couple I think, but he had LPs of Shakespeare plays and we listened to them all as we followed along in a play book. He even set up special viewings of new movies that came out as we were studying Shakespeare, *The Taming of the Shrew* with Elizabeth Taylor and Richard Burton, and *Romeo and Juliet* with Olivia Hussey and Michael York at the Missouri Theater. There was a scene in *Romeo and Juliet* in which one of Olivia Hussey's breasts was exposed. A lot of the boys started hooting and making catcalls, and Brother William had the film stopped. He threatened to stop the showing and take us all back to classes if that happened again. That is a perfect example of the crass behavior of a group of boys that I didn't like, even though I admit I was titillated by the scene too.

We had religion classes at CB, but I don't even remember them. We all took religion. And we all had typing too, taught by Brother Aloysius, who was odd, but never got a lot of grief from the students. That's because he was so big, and he was the superintendent.

The fourth reason for not liking high school was that students entering CB were enrolled in a science curriculum or a business curriculum, or for just a few special students, a blend of the two. Each student's status was based solely on their grade school scores. There were only few exceptions to the rule, and for those in either the science or business curriculum, no mixing of the two. Once you were in one, your schedule was fixed, and never did the school try to adopt any new or innovative classes, like the drama

Mike started at Christian Brothers in 1968, and here is his sophomore yearbook photo. CB closed in the spring of 1970, so he finished at LeBlond.

class I took. It was only in my senior year that CB teamed up with LeBlond to try something new, and that was the last year for CB. The next year, CB closed, and the boys attended LeBlond. However, the two schools did have a choral group, and I always wished I had been in it. My problem though was transportation. I couldn't get to the practices which were at LeBlond, and then home.

I went to my first class reunion, the five-year reunion. I had just met Audrey, and we went together. It wasn't very memorable. We all ate at some restaurant and it was very crowded. The two guys I was closest with in high school, Jerry Stock and David Hurst, didn't attend. Only lately, I went to the 50th reunion, which was held a year late because of Covid19.

| 14 |

Minnesota Trips

Dad and Uncle Phil were born the same year, and Mom and Dad played cards with Uncle Phil and Aunt Mildred frequently when we were young. I remember going to a small wood-frame house on a street just north of Mason Road, where Uncle Phil and his family lived before they moved into a newer brick home several blocks away. I don't know that other than cards, Mom and Dad and Uncle Phil and Aunt Mildred did anything together. But one year, our families took a fishing trip to Minnesota together.

We have a photo with a date on it, so I know it was in August 1961, and I would have been 8 years old.

We stopped on the way at Lake Okoboji in northern Iowa to see the lake. It was a big lake, well-known, and had an amusement park. But we didn't go to the park. We just stopped, and Mom was disappointed that there wasn't something interesting to see or do, just another lake. She liked traveling, but this wasn't her idea of an interesting vacation, a fishing trip.

We went to Minnesota because Dad had an old buddy, someone he met in the service or worked with once, who had gone to Minnesota and bought a resort on a lake. Mom said we had gone to the resort once before, when I was nine months old. It was not a fancy resort. It had no frill cabins like the ones we stayed at many summers at Bean Lake or the lake house Dad bought

When I was about 9 months old, I took my first fishing trip to Emily Lake, Minnesota.

at Sugar Lake. Basically, it was an open dorm with four or five beds and a bathroom at the back end with a cotton material curtain for a door.

The resort didn't have much in the way of entertainment either, only a long building by the water with a few items for sale, candy and chips. It didn't even have a pinball machine like the central building at Bean Lake. And you couldn't even swim much at the Minnesota lake because it was mostly fishing. We got in the water a few times in a small area set apart for mostly getting wet nearM one end of the lake building.

The lake was located outside St. Peter, and the name of the lake was Emily. There is an Emily Lake outside St. Peter now. I saw it on Google maps, but the satellite image doesn't show a resort there anymore. It's a public fishing lake.

Mom, me, Mary and Linda in Minnesota at Lake Emily, where a friend of Dad rented cabins, boats and fishing equipment.

The most disappointing thing about the trip was that Dad didn't take Mike and I fishing with him except one time. He and Uncle Phil and Bill went out all the other times and they came back with game fish: bass, northern pike, crappie and walleye. They came back with big ones they cleaned in a small house by the lake strictly for cleaning fish. It had a big table along a wall with a spigot in order to wash fish skins, scales and entrails into the lake after fish were gutted and scaled.

I don't know what the girls did on the trip, but Mike and I did get to go fishing twice. Once, Uncle Phil took us and his son, Jimmy, out, and we fished by some stumps and we caught several big crappie and blue gill, and I caught a big sunfish with a bright orange belly.

The other time we went out, we went with Dad and Bill to one end of the lake, a shallower part, and we caught a big bunch of catfish, hauling in one after another. We weren't out there long though because a big wind came up, and the wind was blowing from the direction of our return. The lake wasn't huge, but the wind whipped up the water and it made rowing back difficult. I don't know why we were in a row boat because I'm sure we went out in a motorized boat with Uncle Phil. But Bill had a hard

Mary holds a stringer of fish that Dad and Uncle Phil caught at Lake Emily. Dad didn't normally fish for game fish, but he enjoyed it the few times he did it in Minnesota.

time rowing and Dad was nervous that we weren't going to make it. I don't remember being too nervous. I guess I had confidence in my big brother and his rowing ability.

Dad didn't need children in the boat while he was fishing, so we children mostly swam and played in the water.

Since we didn't get to fish out on a boat much, I just remember running around the grounds with Mike and Jimmy. We fished sometimes from a wooden dock with wooden posts driven in the mud of the lake. One day we were fishing from the dock, and Mike started horsing around near the water end of the dock. He wasn't paying attention and fell in the lake in his clothes. He started slapping his hands and yelling help, help. Jimmy and I just told him, "You know you can stand up in the lake," which was true. It was not a deep lake, anyway for most of it. And sure enough, Mike found he could stand where he was about 12 feet from the shore.

In August 1970, before I went off to college, Mom, Dad, Linda and I went back to the resort. It was pretty run down, and the lake had degenerated from runoff and silt buildup. Dad and I went out on the lake several times but we didn't catch anything those trips. I caught two little rock bass near the shore on separate mornings. That was it. That's probably why there's no resort there now. I also saw a Minnesota water quality report on the lake which reported on an attempt to revive the lake, and it is now a public lake where people catch mostly perch.

I don't believe the girls went out in a boat at all, so they sat in one along the shore.

In 1970, Dad and I decided one day to try fishing along the Minnesota River near St. Peter since the fishing at Emily Lake was so poor. Dad caught a big snapping turtle that we couldn't get the hook out of. We ended up cutting the line and he crawled back in the water with the hook still in his mouth. I caught a huge carp, about 20 pounds, and we took it back to the resort to show the owner, Dad's friend. He said, "Why did you bring that here?" Minnesotans prefer game fish, and obviously disdain bottom feeders.

The highlight of the trip was Linda breaking her foot running down the slope to the central building in the dark one night. Mom and Dad took her to the hospital where doctors put her foot in a cast. That was a few days before we were set to go home and the doctors there did a bad job setting the break. It had to be recast in St. Joe, but the three nights or so at the lake before we left, Linda moaned and cried the whole time. Mom, Dad and I couldn't sleep because of all the noise she made, and we were pretty upset with her. But it turned out she was in pain for good reason and we felt bad about being upset with her. We had thought she should have been tougher, but she was in a tough way.

| 15 |

New York/Washington D.C. Trip

In 1968, Mary was attending college at the University of New York-Brockport. She was in a special Peace Corps program preparing her for advising and assisting teachers in a foreign country. She would eventually go to La Ceiba, Honduras, where she stayed for one year. Political problems in Honduras led to her coming home before her two-year commitment was up.

But while she was in New York, Mom bugged Dad about taking a trip to see her. Dad mostly said it was too far, but in the end he relented.

However, he was sorry afterward because the first thing Mom said was can we go to Washington D.C., too. Dad told her the two places were not remotely close, but Mom said as long as we were going east, we might as well go to Washington.

Susan, Mike, Linda, and Mom at Lincoln's mausoleum when we stopped in Springfield, Illinois, on our way to visit Mary in Brockport, NY.

In the end, Dad agreed as Mom never let up, but he refused to go to New York City, which Mom also wanted to see.

At that time, Bill was away, and Kathy was married with her own family and kids, so it was Dad, Mom, Susan, me, Mike and Linda traveling in the blue Ford Galaxy. It was crowded in the back seat with us four kids as we were pretty big. Linda or Mike sat up front sometimes with Mom and Dad, but most of the time, we four were back there. Susan would have been 17, me 15, Mike 13, and Linda 9.

Dad bought a used movie camera, a Super 8, from somebody who brought it into the shop. He was excited about his purchase and bought several rolls of film to take on the trip. Mom said something about taking a photo camera because she didn't trust the movie camera or Dad, but Dad didn't think we needed a photo camera. He had the Super 8. He tried it out, panning the merchandise in the store. He moved way too fast though, and the film made us dizzy, and we had a good laugh over his practice movie.

I had a Brownie when I was younger, and developed the negatives and made contact prints from them. The negatives were like 2 x 4 inches, just big enough for viewing well without enlarging. I'm not sure what kind of a camera I had when we went to New York, but it was one that allowed me to hold the shutter open for as long as I wanted so I could take pictures in low light or at night.

We left on the two-week trip in August, driving across northern Missouri on US 36. We stopped first in Hannibal, where we saw Mark Twain's boyhood home, his famous white picket fence, and Cardiff Hill with its lighthouse. We walked up Cardiff Hill, which wasn't much of a climb, but it offered a view of the Mississippi River winding south past several islands. I had read several of Mark Twain's books and short stories in high school, so I was excited to see some of the places in Clemens' life that he incorporated into his stories.

But I was even more excited about our second stop, which was Springfield, Illinois, as I was an even bigger fan of Abraham Lincoln. I had read several books on Lincoln, including one volume of Sandburg's biography of Lincoln. However, there was no library or museum at that time in Springfield, only his home. I don't think we went through the home, though, only saw it from the street. Then we went to see his mausoleum before we continued on.

At the US Niagara Falls, we walked a staircase to the bottom of the falls that required we wear rain gear.

I'm not sure where we stayed that first night, but the second day, we ended up in Cleveland on a busy street at rush hour. When the light changed for us to go, our Ford Galaxy stopped running. Dad tried several times to start it again, but it wouldn't run, and he told us to get out and push. So Susan, Mike and I got out and pushed the Galaxy. It was a heavy car, and we weren't moving very fast. A man got out of his car and helped us, and he said something about it being a rotten time for a car to quit. He said it nicely, as if he felt sorry for us.

The street had a lot of businesses along it, so we weren't far from a motel or a car repair shop. We stayed the night there, and the car was fixed quickly. It was some sort of electrical problem. The car had plenty of gas. It just stopped firing.

It was only a five- or six-hour drive from Cleveland to Brockport. We were able to stay in a school dorm as it was summer and many of the dorms were not being used.

There at Brockport was the first time I ever played soccer. Mary's friends, fellow students, played soccer; I guess because they were all going to Latin America, and they invited us to play. We were there for three or four days, and on one of the days we drove over to Niagara Falls. We stayed one night there, going to the falls in the daytime, and at night as well to see the colored lights display that was shone on the water in the dark. I took photos at night with my camera, and of course,

Dad had been filming us whenever and wherever we stopped. He said we were going to have quite the movie when we got back home.

We had a little dispute over where to go at Niagara as there were several things to see and do on the American and Canadian side of the falls. We all couldn't agree on one thing. Mike and I wanted to go to the Ripley's Believe It or Not house, but in the end, we went to the wax museum. I think it was because that's what Mary wanted to do, and we had come to see and visit her.

The neatest thing we did was take the mist walk on the American side of the falls. We were all given raincoats and rain hats and we walked a wooden stairway that wound along the rocks and spray. We did get pretty wet from the mist that exploded from the water as it hit the rocks at the bottom of the falls and shot up the cataract on gusts of wind created by the watery turmoil.

We left Mary back at Brockport and drove for two days to get to Washington, DC. On the way, we stopped in Corning, NY, to see the glass factory. I remember it having a viewing area with seats so that we could watch workers blowing glass in big kilns. Mike and I wanted to go to Cooperstown to see the Baseball Hall of Fame, but that didn't happen. I remember seeing the Appalachian Mountains in Pennsylvania for the first time, and I wasn't very impressed. They were just big hills there, not high, jagged peaks.

At night at Niagara Falls, colored lights were shone on the cataract. I took this photo with a camera I bought that allowed timed exposures.

In Washington, we had an interesting time, though we were there for only a couple of days. Susan, Mike, Linda, and I walked up the stairs inside the Washington Monument, and we went to the Lincoln and Jefferson memorials. We went inside the U.S. Capitol, but we didn't do the whole tour. I remember standing under the dome, and then a guide or security guard told us to stand on one side of the rotunda. We could hear people whispering on the other side as if we were standing right by them. The dome acted as a natural amplifier or a conduit for the sound to travel.

The neatest thing we saw in Washington, however, was the Smithsonian Museum, which actually is not one museum, but many. There was so much to see and our time was so short that Mom and Dad agreed to do something they normally wouldn't. They let us all go our own way to see what we wanted and we met up back in the lobby of the Natural History building where the big elephant and five-story-tall Foucault pendulum were. I remember walking through the buildings to see as much as I could see. Even though I liked the science and natural history displays, what I remember walking past were the big glassed cases of the fancy dresses worn by the first ladies at their husbands' inaugurations.

From Washington, we headed across Virginia and West Virginia. There the Appalachian Mountains were higher and the roads more twisted and turning and more up and down. Dad complained about the roadway, but that was the shortest way to get back to I-70 in Ohio. We were ready to get home, and tired from the long trip. I remember us sleeping a lot in the back seat leaning on one another. But the roads were so windy and steep that it was hard to sleep. Susan and Linda got so tired that they slept piled together on the back seat floor with the big lump for the driveshaft in the middle.

But Susan was awake and driving when we entered Parkersburg, West Virginia, a town on the border of Ohio by the Ohio River. We wound down a long hill into the middle of town, when one of the back wheels came off the car, axle and all. An old pickup stopped alongside us, and the driver, an older, kind-looking man in a straw hat, rolled down his passenger window and said that he had tried to get our attention about the wheel when we were up the hill, but we didn't hear him honk or at least, didn't know what he was up to. Dad got out and talked to the man, and then Dad told us to load our luggage in the back of the pickup and go with the man. He took us to the downtown hotel, a neat old-style, red-brick hotel with narrow corridors, and Dad arranged for a tow truck and a repair shop to get the Galaxy fixed. I think maybe the man helped with that too, after taking us to the hotel. Dad blamed the steep roads and all the braking required for driving the roads for the breakdown. But it was probably just one of those things that happens.

The rest of the trip was uneventful; however, there was strangely funny and sardonic ending to the New York/Washington, DC, trip.

When we got home, Dad took all of the Super 8 film he took on the trip, and it was several rolls of film, to be developed. I had my photos developed which didn't take long, but mostly, I took photos of buildings, statues and places, not many of us. One of the few of us was a group shot of everyone dressed in their raincoats and rain hats at Niagara Falls. Dad had taken some film of it too, and during the trip, he pointed his movie camera at us wherever we went, telling us to look at the camera and smile and wave. We joked he was going to have a lot of film of us waving when we got home.

My photo of the elephant in the main lobby of the museum of natural sciences at the Smithsonian.

But when he went to pick up the film so we could put it on a projector and view it, the developing place said they had some bad news. They said all the film came out overexposed, not just overexposed, completely exposed. There was something wrong with the camera that it developed a crack or the door didn't close tight, allowing light in through the camera body.

Dad had absolutely nothing to show for all his time and effort. Mom, of course, made that a I-told-you-so moment.

From my sister Linda

It's funny that cameras are a theme for this trip. The one thing that I purchased was a tiny camera when we were in Washington, D.C. It was about 2 inches wide, 1.5 inches tall and about 1 inch deep. I thought it was fascinating, and I did use the one roll of film that came with it. Can't imagine I ever had it processed or that I was ever able to find another roll of film, but it sure was cute.

Before we went to Washington, DC, I had read an article about a professional photographer who had taken photos of the Lincoln Memorial. I mimicked one of the angles of a photo he took.

My most vivid memories of that trip are that mist walk at Niagara Falls. I remember that we had to wear some sort of chamois suit and shoes under the raincoats and pants. The shoes kept us from slipping on the damp steps. It was so exciting to be in all of that mist and see and hear that water thundering next to us. And of course, the yellow rain outfits really stood out in all of that grayness. Kestrel went there two summers ago and he said the raincoats are no longer yellow, probably some cheap version of disposable clear plastic.

I also loved the night lights on the falls, no doubt that was the most amazing thing I had ever seen in my life up to that point.

I also loved that old hotel in Parkersburg; it seemed so fancy and so different.

My memory about the car breaking down, which I believe is correct, is that I guess the man who helped us mentioned that he was divorced (Now why would that come up?) and I remember Mom saying, "Even if he is divorced, he is still a nice man!" The persistence of religion!

I don't remember sleeping on the floor of the car. I do think it was that trip that when we left home there was a very bad rainstorm happening and Mom was anxious about being on the road, so we said the rosary. It felt like we said it over and over, but we probably really didn't!

The Smithsonian, also an eye-opener for me. I remember that pendulum, it was so large and fascinating. I do remember walking up the steps to the top of the Washington Monument. Good thing I did it then. I wouldn't be able to now!

A view I took of Niagara Falls from a tower on the Canada side during our visit there.

From my brother Bill

A lot of the events David recounts I was not a part of because I was grown and had abandoned the homestead. So they are very interesting to me but also familiar. Your observation, Linda, about the divorced man who helped all of you when the wheels fell off the car is right on. Mom's steadfast belief in her religion colored a great deal of what she thought, said and did. Her opinion of Uncle Charlie Zuptich's wife, Aunt Margaret, was less than positive because she had been married and divorced before she married Charlie. Mom was always nice to her, but there were moments when she would make a remark similar to what she said about the divorced Good Samaritan.

From my sister Susan

Reading your account of New York trip, I remember that axle breaking and Dad yelling, "What did you do?"

And I remember Mom so wanting to see the White House, and Dad headed that direction, drove by and pointed. He said, "There it is." And if I recall correctly, he pulled up in front of the Washington Monument, and we jumped out, ran up the steps while he waited in car, right out front.

From my sister Mary

Dad points something out to Mary and Linda at a site along the Niagara River.

I was so happy that Mom and Dad decided to make the trip up to New York and bring Susan, David, Michael and Linda. I was so homesick.

Even though we had classes on the weekends, Harvey let me go up to Niagara Falls with you. I just remember how powerful the Niagara River was! As we stood on the banks and watched it rush by, it almost felt like we were being sucked into the river. Really scary. And so powerful!

| 16 |

Other Trips

Texas to see Bill

We were living on the farm when Bill enlisted in the Army, and we went to Texas, where he was stationed, to see him. My impression was that he was stationed in San Antonio at Fort Sam Houston, and we went there and then to Corpus Christi so we could see the ocean. I don't remember a whole lot about that trip because I was so young, six, but a few things come to mind.

We drove in that Ford station wagon with the turquoise top. It seems like it was fairly new. Linda was not quite a year old, and I don't remember if Kathy was with us. I don't know why she would have stayed home if she did. I remember it was a long, long drive, with all of us piled in the car, even though it was a station wagon. We stayed in motels along the way.

In San Antonio, Bill introduced us to a new food, pizza. That's the first time I remember hearing about it or eating it. He took us to a restaurant, and we had it there. It seems like we should have gone to a Mexican restaurant, but I don't remember eating Mexican.

We went to the Alamo. I was excited because I was a Davy Crockett fan then. At that time, I didn't know what a racist and political extremist he had been. But I remember being disappointed at the Alamo because it was so small. It didn't seem something that important in history could have happened at such a small place.

In Corpus Christi, all I remember is playing in the ocean for an afternoon. I couldn't tell you if it was hot or cold, but I do remember waves. I was disappointed because they were small waves, Texas coastal waves, not big ones like in Hawaii. But all the same, I told my schoolmates at St. James when I returned that I swam in the ocean and how neat it was.

Me, Bill and Mary in the Gulf of Mexico outside Corpus Christi.

I remember swimming, too, in a few motel pools along the way. That was great fun because living on the farm, we didn't drive in to Hyde Park much, so going to a pool was a big thing.

Mom told a story often about that trip, about us getting a motel somewhere along the way. Dad went into the office and paid for a night; then we all got out and started carrying our cardboard boxes of clothes into our room. Mom said the manager saw us and ran out and told us there had been a mistake, we couldn't stay. She always said the manager saw our cardboard boxes and thought we were poor white trash and didn't want us at the motel.

Sedalia and the State Fair

It may have been on the way to or from Texas to see Bill that we stopped in Sedalia, Missouri, to go to the state fair. I was pretty small, and we were driving that turquoise-topped station wagon and heading somewhere, so maybe it was the Texas trip.

I don't know when, but we made a trip to the Ozarks in southern Missouri once, and we walked up the stairway of a forest fire lookout tower. Growing up in the rolling hills of northwest Missouri, we didn't realize that the lower half of Missouri was a mountainous area.

We parked in a sea of vehicles in a huge parking lot, but we were on the edge of the lot, and we all said, we'll be able to find our car on the way out; it's at the end of the cars. From there, we walked a long way to get to the entrance of the fair. There were rides galore, but what caught our eyes as we walked in was big flat disk with cages around the edge. People were in the cages holding onto bars, and the disk spun faster and faster and then it turned on edge, still spinning with the riders held in the cages by centripetal force. We didn't do the rides right away. Mom wanted to see the displays, and we all had to stay together. We walked through the maze of commercial ventures displaying their wares and services, and every one of them was giving away stuff. We were handed bags at the first one, and each of us ended up with pencils and erasers, and rulers and yardsticks, and a lot of literature that we were just going to throw away. I don't remember what all we got, but we took whatever anyone handed out and put it in our bags. I don't remember seeing farm animals or canned goods for judging, or listening to music shows; I just remember the stuff that people were handing out.

Then at the end, all of us kids went on the spinning disk. It seemed like it was as tall as a skyscraper, but it really wasn't all that scary, and it didn't seem to go as fast as it looked like from the ground. To me, the Ferris wheel was scarier than that ride was.

When we left the fair to return to our car, we looked to the back of the lot, but the back of the lot stretched a lot farther than when we came in. Our car was nowhere to be seen. We walked around a while, and then Mom told somebody to get on the back of a truck and look for the turquoise top. One of the girls spotted our car right away.

Bean Lake

When other kids our age were taking family vacations to Colorado, Florida or Disneyland, our parents took us to Bean Lake. We were not poor, but we also were not rich. There were seven of us children, and Dad didn't make enough money for us to go out to eat very often or to take a week's vacation six hundred miles away. He also had his own business, the shoe shop, and he couldn't afford to be closed for a week and lose his customers.

So Dad rented a cabin at Bean Lake, an oxbow lake in the Missouri River valley about 25 miles south of St. Joseph. There are several oxbows along the river in that stretch, including Lake Contrary, Horseshoe Lake, Mud Lake, Sugar Lake and Bean Lake. Bean got its name because of its shape, like a kidney bean, but all oxbows actually have that same shape. They also are very shallow, and muddy, as they silt in easily in the fertile river valley, and to remain lakes, they have to be dredged frequently.

Bean Lake was not a particularly fun lake to swim in. We spent a week there two or three summers, and one summer, Mary, Susan, Mike and I swam across the narrow part of the lake, which was only about two hundred or three hundred feet wide. Every so often across the lake, I reached down with my feet and I could feel the muddy bottom. I could not stand up

Dad, Linda and Mom taking a dip in Bean Lake with a cabin onshore behind them. I don't remember the rental cabins looking that nice. I remember the rentals as having a screened porch on front and weathering to a shabby shade of green.

though, because as with all oxbows, the bottom was so squishy and soft, that I would sink in the mud up to my knees and my head would go under water. The thing we found with swimming in Bean Lake too, was that the mud would turn our toenails yellowish brown within minutes of being in it. The mud was like a dye, and it was gross. Of course, Mike and I and other boys there would scoop it up, throw it at one another, and put it on our arms and chests and heads. We thought that was great fun. The other thing about Bean Lake was that the water, being so shallow, was about the same temperature on the bottom that it was on top, and the mud was warm too. So while other children went to motel pools, clear mountain lakes, and Florida's clear Gulf waters, we went to murky Bean Lake.

Three generations at Royal Gorge, Colorado. Mom and Dad went in the 1940s after marrying. Audrey and I went in 1976 during the US Bicentennial. I returned with Jessica and Noah in 1999, on a trip to Aurora to visit Mike and his family.

But we really didn't know better, and we had a decent time, although Bean Lake did get a little boring at times.

We had a nice cabin, which had lots of spiders and other interesting insects. And sometimes toads came into the cabin. There were always lots of fireflies, and flies, and mosquitos. And we spent all week in swimming trunks and bathing suits. We ran in and out of the cabin, slamming the screen door, letting in more flies, and driving Mom nuts. There was no television, and all we had to entertain us was one pinball machine in the main building where we could also buy popsicles and pop. But we didn't drink much pop in those days, and Mom would make tea.

One summer another family was there, and they had a couple of boys about the same age as Mike and I. I remember their last name, Shipley, and they were from some southern state, like Alabama or Louisiana. We ran and played all that week, but what I remember most about them is that they drank their ice tea sweetened. I know that I had never heard of that before, and they couldn't believe that anyone would drink ice tea unsweetened. However, we kids really never drank ice tea a whole lot anyway. We mostly drank Kool-Aid. But the Shipleys didn't like Kool-Aid, and wouldn't touch it even though it had sugar in it. It was very ironic, us not liking sweetened tea, but liking Kool-Aid, and them liking sugar in their tea, but not Kool-Aid. We would argue about it, the Shipleys telling us we were weird, and us telling the Shipleys they were weird.

Dad would leave each morning to work at the shoe shop, then come back in the evening. One summer, he rented a rowboat that he, Mike and I took out several times to fish. We never caught very much; however, one afternoon on a weekend, we tied up to duck blind at one end of the oxbow. The water was about six feet deep there, and we dropped our lines down just about to the mud. Using worms for bait, we caught one bluegill after another. A lot of them were small, but we caught a lot of pan-sized ones that we put on a stringer. We filled it and we filled another. We were there an hour or so, and we caught more than fifty fish. I don't remember how many we kept, but that's the first time I remember helping to clean fish. Dad didn't want to do it all himself, and he liked to say, "If you catch a fish, then you have to clean it."

One time at Bean Lake, Kathy brought the blind man who she worked for who was an exotic animal buyer and seller. She led him down to the swimming area where we were swimming, and she and the man sat down with Mom who was watching us. We were swimming with a lot of other people who were there that day, and among them were some older girls, teens. I was entering puberty about then, and I remember stealing glances at several of the girls, when all of a sudden, they started screaming and shouting, "Snake, snake," and rushed out of the water onto the shore. They were clustered at the water's edge pointing to the snake about six feet from them. I walked over and looked, and it was just a small brown snake, barely a foot and a half long, wriggling on top of the water searching for a place to escape. I wanted to impress the girls, so I reached down and picked up the snake and held it up. The little rascal turned its head around and bit me right on the knuckle of my middle finger on my right hand. Of course, I dropped it, and the girls gasped, but I grabbed it again and took it to shore away from everybody and let it go. When I was going back to the water, Mom asked me if I was OK. She wanted to look at my hand. I had a mark on my finger, and it was bleeding a little, and she asked Kathy's employer if I could have been bitten by a poisonous snake. The man asked me what the snake looked like, and I told him, and he said it was probably just a bull snake, a nonpoisonous snake which has little sharp teeth to hold its prey. He said that a person could get a bad infection from a bite and I should put some alcohol on it. I sat down and talked to the blind man, and he started telling stories about all the times he had been bitten by poisonous snakes and boa constrictors. He told me the next time that I went to pick up a snake, I needed to grab it very close to its head so that it couldn't turn its head to bite.

Several years ago, probably ten or so, when I was in St. Joseph, I drove down to Bean Lake. It was still there, but not much of the lake was left as it was silting in, and the cabins that we used to stay in were gone. Missouri's wildlife agency turned one end of the "lake" into a conservation area, Little Bean Marsh. There was an RV park across the lake, what was left of it, and a winery had established itself nearby.

Lake of the Ozarks

When I was twelve, maybe a young teenager, a man who shopped at Dad's shoe store told Dad that he had a cabin at Lake of the Ozarks. Dad was not afraid to ask favors of people, and he asked the man if he could take his family there for a few days. The man was quite willing to let us use it, so we loaded up and drove to Central Missouri. We had heard a lot about the Ozarks but never had been there. Friends of ours had been to the lake and Osage Beach, and we were really excited about going, especially since we were going to have our own cabin to stay in. We had just bought the Galaxy 500, and Dad drove 65 and 70 miles an hour on I-70, and I remember Mom telling him to slow down, but Dad said that's what a highway was made for.

We slowed down considerably, however, once we got into the Ozark hills. We wound around forever on narrow roads and were nowhere near Osage Beach when we got to this man's cabin. The Lake of the Ozarks is a dammed up river in a maze of hills, and the lake is the endless stretching of the Osage River and its tributaries. This man's cabin was in a forest of trees with not a sign of civilization around other than the rock road that led to it. It was not a pretty cabin. It was as plain as a barn and barren inside, except for all the spiders that were living there. Dad said it wasn't too bad, but Mom and the girls screamed they were not going to stay there. Dad didn't stand a chance. We never unloaded a suitcase or a box. We went to a motel somewhere close to Osage Beach.

We were only there a day or two, and it was a big disappointment. I think Mom and the girls enjoyed themselves as they went shopping at some of the stores, but I was not impressed. If amusement rides or arcades were there, we didn't go to them. Dad and I and Mike fished a little, but we caught nothing, and we drove home without seeing very much. The deplorable state of the cabin that we put all our hopes in on the first day seemed to have taken all the glamour out of the trip.

Rocky Mountain National Park, 1971

Nature shows increased in number on television in the late 1960s, and in 1970, environmentalists held the first Earth Day observance. Nature always captured my imagination as I was growing up, and then John Denver became popular, and his songs and activism spurred my desire to see mountains, Colorado, and everything natural there.

I did this drawing of John Denver recently, but I was a fan of John Denver soon after he came on the music scene with his first album in 1969. His song about the mountains inspired me to want to go there.

I longed to go to Colorado, and Bill and I drove there over holiday break in early 1971 to see a couple of his friends. But I wanted to go back and get out in the wild. I didn't have a car though, nor much money, and not much time after the spring semester ended at Columbia as I had a job in the wildlife department running tests on lake water. Before I reported to work, though, and I was back home for a few days, I complained to Mom that I wouldn't get a chance to go to Colorado that summer. She liked to travel but never really did much traveling, so she proposed a deal. She said we could go to Colorado and she would pay for food and lodging if I would pay for gas and any repairs that needed to be made to the car while we were gone.

I can't believe I did it, but I was so excited about the chance to go, I agreed to go with my mother. Not only that Mary and Linda wanted to come along, and I had to agree to that. However, I told my mother that I wanted to camp, and unbelievably, she agreed.

So off we went.

As I have stated in the memories of my mother, the transmission fluid leaked out of the car halfway across Kansas, which I would have to pay for. It was relatively easy to fix, although expensive, and we got back on the road in just a few hours.

I'm not sure where we stayed the first night, but we got a campsite at a private campground in Estes Park the second night. I set up a big tent I had bought and we piled in our blankets and sleeping bags for our first camping experience together. It was a beautiful night, maybe a little cool, but Mom's first ever attempt at sleeping out did not go well. She complained she was on a rock, and why didn't I check for rocks before I put up the tent. She couldn't get comfortable, and she moaned and groaned about how hard and uneven the ground was, and what if an animal came and got us all. The girls complained a little too, but Mom made noises all through the night, and in the morning, she proclaimed that we weren't camping anymore. She was going to pay for motels the rest of the trip.

She tried hiking too, when we went into Rocky Mountain National Park, but of course, that was something that no one on the trip wanted to do very long. For me, the trip was somewhat a disaster, but I couldn't complain because I wouldn't have been able to go at all any other way. I learned a lesson that if there is something you really want to do and not be compromised, you have to go it alone.

California, Table Rock Lake, and Silver Dollar City, 1972

The summer after the Colorado trip, I drove out briefly to California. Bill let me take his station wagon, and I drove to Denver, the Grand Canyon, Los Angeles, then up the California coast on Highway 1 to Yosemite. I hiked Half Dome, had my backpack ripped open by a bear one night and my food eaten, and I visited the grove with the giant sequoia trees. I also saw my first brown bears. They sauntered through my campsite at Tuolumne Meadows and sent me rushing into Bill's station wagon where I slept the night. From there I went to San Francisco and stayed with a friend of Bill. I was only there a couple of days, and on one of them, Bill's friend and a couple of his friends took me to a coffee shop where they served Irish coffee, coffee with a helping of strong Irish whiskey and whipped crème on top. We ate at a fancy Italian restaurant; then Bill's friend and I went to a

In 1972, I hiked up Mt. Whitney in California.

restaurant/bar in Oakland. The place featured a belly dancer, a dark-haired lady who came around to the tables to shake and shimmy for dollar bills. Patrons, males of course, stuffed dollar bills in her miserly top and bottom outfit. I only had one dollar, but before she left our table, Bill's friend gave me two other dollar bills. After I left his house the next day, I drove to Mendocino. I camped there on the beach for a couple days before heading back home to work at the state park. I drove through a dust storm in Arizona to get back home, which damaged the paint on Bill's vehicle. It ended up losing its paint over time.

The job at the state park was interesting. I roomed in a cabin with four other guys from mid-June through mid-August. We took turns working the pay booth for the campground, and when we weren't doing that, we picked up trash, painted buildings brown, cleaned bathrooms and pumped out latrines. The great thing about the job had nothing to do with the job, but the campers. Many of them were very kind to us, inviting us to cookouts, giving us a cold soft drinks or tea when we were thirsty, even taking us for rides after work in their boats. Just before my time at the park ended, a pretty, tall blond high school girl from Kansas City took a liking to me, and for several days after work, I ended up at her parents' trailer playing canasta and eating with them. I went out in their boat too. The other guys were all jealous of me, and it was the first time that happened in my life.

On my trip to California in 1972, I stopped at Joshua Tree National Monument. That trip was the first time that I had seen a desert, as I went through western Colorado, Utah and Arizona on the way.

When I had a few days to go, Mom and Dad and Linda came to get me. Dad left his car with Jim Testerman, and Jim let Mom and Dad borrow his pickup and camper. After we left Table Rock, we went to Silver Dollar City. I had worked at Table Rock for a couple months but never had time to get to the park. Mom loved Silver Dollar City, the whole atmosphere of the place. She wanted to go to Shepherd of the Hills, too, but we ran out of time, and there was plenty to see at Silver Dollar City without going anywhere else. Besides Mom and Dad paid a lot of money for Silver Dollar City and didn't want to fork over more money for another attraction. We didn't go to any shows in Branson either, but at that time, there were only two shows to see: The Presleys and The Baldknobbers. Dad probably would have liked the show, but Mom wouldn't have been impressed. Before we headed to St. Joe, we went to Roaring River State Park. Dad wasn't much of a trout fisherman, so he didn't try, and though Mom thought the river was pretty, the water was way too cold for her.

Southern Missouri, 1974

One of the most interesting short trips I have ever been on was a tour of the springs in Southern Missouri. I had come back from West Texas, then driven to Houston in a red pickup Bill and I bought to move Mary and Robert back to Missouri. I said I was taking the pickup to the Ozarks for a little vacation and Mary and Robert asked if they could go along, and so did Linda. So we all took turns sitting in the back of the pickup with Robert and I taking turns driving. We stopped at several places on the Current River, including Round Spring and Big Spring, then traveled to the Jack Fork to visit Alley Spring. We slept out every night on the ground, and I remember one night a big lazy fog developed and the trees were dripping on us all night. Linda and I floated down the Current on our backs, and we weren't watching where we got out. We ended up in a mass of brush and weeds, including poison ivy. I was scratching for weeks after that.

Mary kept saying that she didn't feel well as we were driving on those curvy Ozark highways and roads. It got where she didn't want to ride in the back when it was her turn, but she wasn't doing well in the front either. I don't remember if she knew at the time that she was pregnant with Matthew, but that's what caused the car sickness. That was such a nice trip because the weather was nice, and the rivers and springs in southern Missouri are beautiful to see, plus we learned a lot of history at many of the places we stopped. Friends of mine had been before and talked about the canoeing there, but I had never gone. I had grown up around muddy lakes and rivers, and I didn't think clear streams existed in Missouri.

Omaha and the Horse Races, 1975

Horse racing was a popular sport when I was growing up, and it was the only gambling allowed in those days in some states, except for dog racing in a few others and the casinos in Las Vegas, of course. Then, as now, the Kentucky Derby and other Triple Crown races were big news events in the spring even though we heard practically nothing about horse racing the rest of the year. For some reason, Mom started talking about wanting to see a horse race. Perhaps, she heard people talking about it or the derby had just been held, and she got it in her mind that she wanted to go.

Missouri did not have horse racing, and the closest places we could go were Nebraska, Arkansas, or Oklahoma. Nebraska was the closest, so we went, and it turned into a family affair. Mom and Dad, Mary and Robert, and Mike, Linda and I went, and I think Susan and Farrell may have gone, and what was weird was that we stopped somewhere in Iowa and slept out in a state park. The park was in the hills along the Missouri River, and Linda and I woke up early and took a walk. Everyone was upset with us because we took a long walk and they had wanted to get going, but couldn't find us.

The Omaha racing stands were pretty and well-kept, and the track was made of reddish dirt. The day was all blue skies, but it had rained there the day before so the track was wet. There were ten or so races, and we all went down to the viewing area at one point to see the horses and jockeys displayed before one race. We bought our $2 tickets, and mostly tossed them aside after the races and after we realized we'd lost. I believe I was the only one who won, and I won on the last race, the trifecta. Without knowing anything about horses, I picked a light gray horse who was a medium shot to win, and I correctly chose the second- and third-place horses. I won more than $90 on my $3 ticket. It was nice to go down and collect money at the gate rather than just give it over.

On the way back home, Mom said since I was the winner, I had to buy dinner for everyone. I don't remember where we stopped to eat, but I remember I left half my winnings there.

From my sister Mary

The first thing I remember about San Antonio was the Alamo. It was just in the center of the city, this old decrepit fort that had walls that were crumbling and really, really small! Hard to believe that a war went on there.

Also, right near the Alamo, within walking distance was the River Walk along the San Antonio River. It was so neat, because they had cleaned it up and built restaurants and shops along the river and a nice sidewalk you could walk along. You could sit outside on the patio and eat and see the river and all the lights. I can't remember if there were boats going along in it. I don't think we ate there, too expensive.

But, yes, we did eat pizza. I don't remember if we liked it very much. But Bill talked to Dad and Uncle Phil and asked them to back him on a pizza shop in St. Joe after he returned. They said no, of course. Bill would have been rolling in the dough.

Mike, me and Susan on the beach outside Corpus Christi, Texas.

We particularly liked Corpus Christi and the Gulf of Mexico, although we called it the ocean. We had to crawl down 12 or 13 big steps to the beach during the day and when we returned at night, the tide had come it and the water was lapping over the street curb. They must have a really high tide. I know that years later when they built a new causeway, it was so high. But of course, that port had big ships that came in there, so they had to have enough height to let ships come through.

I thought we went to Sedalia several times over the years. Going to the state fair was an annual thing, but maybe not for us.

Yes, I remember that ride though. I don't remember seeing how it operated before we got on it. If I had, I would NEVER have gotten on it. And we did walk around and look at the animals. Remember there would be kids grooming their pigs and sheep? They had to clean up their messes. Smelled bad too. Mostly, I remember eating a corn dog. When I go to the grocery store, I always consider buying some, but never do. Probably don't taste good except at the fair.

I remember going to the Lake of the Ozarks, but not the cabin of Dad's friend. I probably did complain if it was yucky. All I remember that there was really only one windy road, and cars drove slowly because people were walking along that highway and crossing the road all the time. It's a wonder that people didn't get killed more often there. I thought you and Michael got to drive those little race cars while we girls shopped. Of course, we didn't buy anything, but I never saw so many pairs of earrings and statues and whatnots!

I didn't know you made a deal with Mom about the trip to Colorado. I had just come home from Honduras and was starting a teaching job in the fall at Horace Mann. I don't remember the car breaking down, but of course I wasn't paying for it. Sorry, you got stuck with the bill. Thanks for taking me along. Colorado and Estes Park is really beautiful. I agree it was clear and fresh, and Mom did say you put her bed roll on a rock. Of course, we ALL had rocks. That's what there is in the Rocky Mountains. I just remember all the little chipmunks. They kept popping up all over from every little hole in the ground. That was a nice trip.

I think South Missouri was one of my favorites. I just found out I was pregnant, and I was so sick. I had morning, afternoon and night sickness. But after that trip, sleeping out, it went away, so thank you. I don't think you even set up the tent, did you? The campsite generally had showers so that was nice, and you cooked over the campfire in a coffee can! You were so clever. And the Current River was so clear and cold. I thought I would freeze when we crossed the narrow streams. And the springs were gorgeous too. Some of them deep blues, or turquoise, wow!

Yes, we did go to Aksarben, the name of the race track in Omaha. I asked my friend from Omaha, and you know, they closed it down. Bulldozed down all the buildings. Sad.

I know every time I placed a bet, I lost. I think we all had maybe $5 or $10, but that was losing big for us! Happy to hear you won.

We went to Bean Lake a lot on Sundays with a picnic lunch, but there were always so many people. But it was nice. One summer, we rented a cabin for a week. I think it cost $100, and we had four or five beds and a kitchen, so Mom could cook. There was no running water in the house. We had to pump the water outside and use the outhouse. But the beach house had a shower so we could clean up.

The lake wasn't that clean, but during the week there were few boats and people, so we got to rent inner tubes for the week and we floated out all across the lake. It was wonderful! I think Dad drove down to the lake each night after work and then we went to the little cantina where we could get a Coke or candy bar and they had a bowling machine. I'm sure I didn't appreciate it that much since I was a teenager then, but looking back on it, it was probably one of our better vacations.

Looking back, we really didn't have many vacations, did we? But we played ball during the summer and went to the pool. And we went to the drive-in theater on Lake Contrary Road. And I remember one summer, every week for three or four weeks we got a flat tire at the drive-in movie. Dad kept driving over nails. He was so mad!

From my brother Bill

The trip to San Antonio was probably made in the summer of 1959. I joined the Army in September 1958, and I had about two months of boot camp at Fort Hood, Texas, and then went to Augusta, Georgia (Camp Gordon), for another two months for my training as a military policeman. So I was out of there about Christmastime. Maybe I came home for a short visit then, and proceeded to San Antonio where I was stationed for all of 1959 before being transferred to the 55th Military Police Company near Seoul, Korea. Ouibanju was the town's name, I believe.

So all of you showed up in San Antonio in a white and green Ford station wagon to visit me. That had to be a hectic trip for Mom and Dad. I think Linda was born by then, so you had a whiny little baby serenading you for a couple thousand miles. Somehow, I was able to fit my body into the car with eight other passengers and luggage, and we all travelled to Corpus Christi for a couple days. I don't think anybody was wearing seat belts. And the gulf was a big attraction for us. It was the first time any of us went for a dip in the ocean, except for Dad.

The San Antonio River did run through the middle of downtown San Antonio, but I don't believe the River Walk was much of an attraction at that time. It became a major development later and a tourist hangout. Maybe at that time there was the beginning of the Walk.

I think we went to Bean Lake for a week's vacation for several summers. The cabins we stayed in were dingy, and Mom complained it was more work for her feeding us and worrying about us swimming in that muddy water than just staying home. How none of us drowned is a miracle, but I think we had lots of inner tubes to float on. But that was all they could afford with that many children and somehow it was important to get away from home for a week and have some sort of vacation. Dad loved to fish, of course, and that made lakes attractive to him.

From my sister Susan

Me, Mary, Mike and Susan outside a motel on our Texas trip to see Bill in June 1959.

The thing I remember about the Texas trip was the boxes used as luggage and picking up shells on the beach. We brought them back to the hotel not knowing they still had snails in them and they all started moving. It freaked Mom out and we had to get rid of our treasures!

And our trips to Bean Lake were wonderful to me because we lived in our swim suits, possibly slept in them. And then I don't recall the couple's name who ran the office, but there was a pinball machine in there. I believe it was a nickel to play, and we used to rack up so many free games we had to work hard to use all of our free games before we left.

Also, didn't Mom and Dad acquire the station wagon from inheritance from Grandpa Zuptich?

Susan, Linda, Kathy and Mary in 1998 while in Texas.

Someone obviously did a tie-dye project in 1989, and we gathered for a photo at Susan and Farrell's house: Back: John, Susan, Audrey, Farrell, Matthew. front. Caleb, Annie, Noah, Jessica, and Mary.

| 17 |

Colorado Trip with Bill

When I was on Christmas/New Year's break from the University of Missouri, 1971-1972, Bill asked me if I wanted to go to Colorado with him to visit a couple of his friends. So after our family got together for the holidays, we drove to Denver. It was a quick trip, only a few days, four or five in Colorado, and two days driving. Bill had a station wagon then.

We left from Kansas City and read to one another as we took turns driving. Bill had a novel and I had brought along a book that answered various questions about science and nature. The drive during the day went fine, and it was clear and sunny, but after we crossed the Colorado line towards sunset, we could see a big bank of clouds along the horizon.

Bill said that I ought to look in the book and see if it had anything about weather, and sure enough, there was a section on cloud types and what they portended. The pictures and description in the book of an approaching snowstorm fit the clouds we were seeing and we laughed about it. But after it grew dark, Bill drove the rest of the way through a snowstorm, and there were four or five inches of snow in Denver when we got to the home of Bill Wellisch.

Bill Wellisch, a tall, thin, dark-haired guy with lots of curly hair, was really nice (Susan and I would stay with him for a night when we drove through that coming late May). He and our brother Bill bantered back and forth with friendly insults, as Bill did with other friends. But Bill Wellisch seemed more normal than most of Bill's friends, except that I seem to remember he had just divorced his wife and was living alone in an upstairs apartment in a complex. I believe he was teaching in Denver somewhere and was very knowledgeable about a lot of things.

Bill Wellisch took us to the Denver Museum of Natural History the next day. That was the first time I had seen those beautiful dioramas there. We spent the day downtown, and Bill Wellisch kept talking about the fish that he was preparing in his refrigerator. He was fixing raw fish, not raw really, but fish soaked in onions and lemon juice. The acid in the lemon juice supposedly "cooked" the fish.

Our brother Bill had eaten lemon-cooked fish on Yap Island and he was excited about it too. The two Bills ate the fish that night, but I didn't even try it. It didn't smell right and it didn't look right. I should have tried it, I know, but we weren't brought up to be adventurous eaters. We ate the same things over and over.

A view of Eagle Nest, the lake and the town, in eastern New Mexico, along with the state's highest peak, Wheeler, in background. Bill and I traveled through there in 1971 at night. I always wanted to go back to see it in the daytime, but didn't return until 2011, and took this photo.

We stayed maybe another night with Bill Wellisch in Denver; then we headed to Colorado Springs to see another of Bill's friends.

I don't remember the guy or his wife's name, and I believe they had two children, a boy and a girl. I usually connect with children easily, but I don't remember even talking to these kids.

And I don't know if Bill even called the family ahead of time, because I seem to remember it was a surprise when we got there, and they said they were driving down to Taos, New Mexico, that night and spending the next day there. They said we could go along. I was a little uneasy about it because I just met them and it was going to be crowded for the next night and day in their Volkswagen van, without privacy and thinking about having to go bathroom and all those sorts of things.

But we all piled into the van and headed to New Mexico. We stopped somewhere along the Raton Pass to eat dinner. Bill's friend, the husband, brought along a camp stove and he and his wife fixed spaghetti and meat balls. It took a long time for the spaghetti to get done and they blamed the high altitude for the lengthy cooking time. So it was late and dark by time we went through Raton and Cimarron and turned into Cimarron Pass. We circled around Eagle's Nest, the first time I saw it, and I wouldn't see it in the daytime until 2011, when I went there on a birdwatching trip.

It was really late by time we got to Taos, and we pulled over somewhere along the road or in a park to spend the night. The family slept on a foam bed in the back, and Bill and I slept in hammocks that were set up over the driver and passenger seats. Bill's hammock was a little lower and closer to the windshield than mine. It was cold outside and Bill's friend gave us a couple of sleeping bags saying they were winter sleeping bags and we would be fine. In fact, he said we would stay warmer if we took off our outer clothes and just slept in our underwear. So we did.

I don't think we were asleep very long when we both woke up freezing to death. Those sleeping bags weren't much good, and there was nothing but cold air under us where our bodies flattened out the down in the bags rendering it ineffective. It was snowing outside and there was a heavy frost on the inside of the van from our breath. I heard Bill cussing and rustling around. He was trying to find his clothes. I told him to hand me my clothes too. We made all kind of noise but the sleeping beauties in the van didn't hear a thing. They were snug and warm.

It seemed daybreak took forever to come, and all I did was shiver. Bill didn't sleep either. He cussed and we talked about how cold it was, and if we were going to live to see the sun again.

I think I remember hearing the next day it got down to 20 below that night. I searched some records on Weather Underground. Taos averages about 5 below in January for a minimum, but in January 1972 there was a very cold period in New Mexico and Colorado early in the year. There weren't records for Taos, but in Alamosa, CO, it got down to a minus 31 one night in early January 1972 and for a week or more around that time, every night was below zero.

I remember how happy I felt when the sun finally came up and started shining through the windshield. Bill's friend woke up and started telling us that he had a wonderful sleep even though he had been a little hot with all the bodies on the van bed. He said something about how warm we must have been too in those down bags. When we told him how cold we were, it was like he didn't believe us.

The day stayed sunny, and it warmed up above freezing, which helped to forget the night somewhat. We spent the day visiting the Taos Pueblo and eating at a Mexican restaurant in Taos. We drove back to Colorado Springs that afternoon and evening, and we headed for Missouri from there. Bill wanted to drive through the night, and he told me to get some sleep so that when I woke up, I would drive while he slept.

But I didn't wake up until sunrise the next day and we were on the outskirts of Kansas City. Bill was upset with me. He said he called and called to me several times during the night to wake up and drive, and I would sit up and talk to him a few minutes, then lay down again in the back seat and fall asleep. I don't remember waking up any time in the night, and I don't know how he stayed awake and drove after only getting a couple hours sleep the night before.

What a feat. If Bill had been a pilot and born 50 years earlier, he could have crossed the Atlantic Ocean alone.

Both of these photos are from the 2009 reunion at Hyde Park in St. Joseph. Standing at back: Farrell, Susan, Matthew with William, Andrea, Isaac, Mike, Mary, Maggie, Steven, Gina, Kathy, Blake, Paula, Richard, Audrey, Rachel, me, John Linda. In front: Noah, Kestrel, Rachel, Ahafia, Stormy, Kathy and Bailey, and Rich.

A the top of the platform: Rich, Mike, Blake, Isaac, Bailey, John Miles, Bill, Noah, Kathy, Linda, and Cole. On the steps, top to bottom: Ahafia, Kelsey, Audrey, Mary, Kestrel, Susan, Maggie, and Mary. Bottom, left to right: Rachel, Farrell, Paula, Stormy, William, Matthew, Andrea, me, Kathy, Gina, Steven, and Richard.

| 18 |

The University of Missouri-Columbia

In late August 1970, Mom and Dad took me to Columbia to start school at the University of Missouri. Linda went with us, and Dad drove. We had the Buick then, and I had a couple of suitcases in the trunk, not really a lot of stuff.

My dormitory was one in a complex of several dorms and a cafeteria past the intersection of Hitt and Rollins streets. Those ugly old dormitories are gone now, I imagine. They were in bad shape from years of abuse by college students even then.

There was an easy way to get to the dorms on a thruway that circled south of town, but we went directly through downtown. What we didn't realize in going south on Hitt Street was that the student union with a lot of administrative offices was along that street, and the place was packed. Dad hated traffic anyway, and he became antsy as we had to slow way down and wait for lines of students and parents traipsing across Hitt Street to get to the union. Then we missed a little jog onto Rollins which would have taken us to my dorm, and we ended up circling around by the student union again.

Mom hated the crowd too. She couldn't believe that the school was so big with so many students. I believe when I attended there, 30,000 students were enrolled on the Columbia campus, the main campus for the university. But her main concern was that I would stop going to Sunday mass. She asked me several times to promise that I would go to church. I said yes hoping that she would stop asking.

We eventually found the dorm, and I don't remember its name, but it was the name of a past alumnus, a man. My room was on the third floor, and my roommate was already there. I don't remember his name. He was a short, small, nerdy guy from St. Louis. His parents were there in the room, and he had already taken the bed opposite the door. He had a small television set, radio and lots of gadgets on his desk. All I had was an alarm clock.

His and my parents met and talked a little, but his parents weren't talkative people, and even Mom and Dad felt a little uncomfortable. A lot of people were milling around in the hall and there were guys yelling at one another who knew each other from the year before. We basically left my stuff there, went to get something to eat for a late lunch, during which Mom bugged me about going to church every Sunday; then they took me back to the dorm and left for home. Mom and Dad didn't want to stay with the crowd and noise.

When I got back to my room, I put my stuff away while my roommate watched television. We didn't even talk. I walked out into the hall, and a guy from a room next to mine came out and said, "Lucky you. Your roommate has a TV."

His name was David Doering. He was from a suburb of St. Louis. Most of the guys on my floor were from a suburb of St. Louis. He turned out to be a really nice guy. He was about my height and weight, but he was blond-headed with a hairline that appeared to be receding. I learned later that a gas can had exploded and he permanently lost some hair in the accident. He had a black roommate, a music student, from St. Louis, and his roommate had a nice keyboard all set up. My floor had several black students from St. Louis, the inner city, but most of them roomed together. A few of them were basketball players, and our floor also had a white guy from Iowa, Al Eberhard, who was on the freshman team. He was only six foot five, but he played center, and he was as tough as they come. He saw a lot of playing time during his four years at Missouri, and he ended up playing four years with the Detroit Pistons. The sports guys were always busy at practices, so it was hard to get to know them.

I made friends fairly quickly. Rich Hamra and I got along well, but he was a well-liked guy. He was in his sophomore year, and he was a low-key guy, never caused trouble and was one of our dorm floor advocates. But a couple years later, he had a nervous breakdown and left school to go back home. I ended up moving into an apartment with his two roommates after he left.

Mike Frazee and Rick Hines roomed together two or three rooms down from mine. Rick was from the St. Louis area, and we would share a room in an apartment the next year. A journalism student, Rick did the news on the college television station, but his real interest was sports. He was a Cardinal's fan, of course, and he and Rich and I went to St. Louis for a ball game one time. We went to watch the Cardinals, but we also went to see Willie Mays in his last year. Mays was playing for the New York Mets, and we saw him hit a home run against the Cardinals. Frazee, we all called him Frazee, was the most calm and even-tempered person ever. He was from Alexandria, a small farming community along the Mississippi River in northeast Missouri. Rick tormented Frazee to no end, playing tricks on him, shorting his sheet, putting salt in his bed, and teasing him, but Frazee took it all in stride. Frazee was the only guy Rick pulled pranks on. He never did that with me when we shared a room. We got pretty close, and when he married a few years later, I was one of his groomsmen. Years later, when I was living in Muskogee, he located me, asking me to invest in a sports magazine he wanted to start. I didn't have money, but it was also the start of the internet revolution, and print magazines weren't doing well.

Fosse was another guy known by his last name. His medium length hair was always standing on end, almost an Afro, but he wasn't black. He was a music student, and like Doering's roommate, he had a keyboard. He said he played with rock bands sometimes, filling in for sick musicians. He said he followed the bands around – Captain Beefheart was his favorite group – and I guess they had his number and called him when they needed him. A lot of us went down to his room on evenings and sang while he played.

There was another guy from the St. Louis area who was pretty hard to take because he was so arrogant and proud. But he was a good magician and did lots of card tricks. We'd sit around and he would do one trick after another and brag about himself. He was Jewish and very proud of it. He always talked about being Jewish. When the football homecoming came around, he went around asking guys on the floor if they would go out with his sister, a high-schooler, who was coming up for the big day. He wasn't an exceptionally good-looking guy, he was short and stocky, so most guys were leery about what his sister would look like and especially, her personality since he was so vain. Getting no takers, he came to me and begged me to go with her. His family had some money, so he had rented a car and his sister and I would go with him to a dance that had free food and drinks. I said I'd do it, and the guys on the floor teased me that I was in for a monster. But his sister turned out to be a nice-looking young lady. She was short and stocky like him, but she was pleasant although she was a little loud like her brother. She was also very affectionate, hanging on me, sitting close to me, and she wanted to kiss all the time. She kissed hard too. My mouth was never so worn out as after that date with her.

I liked the dorm OK, but that many guys in a small space was noisy. I didn't join in, but a bunch of the guys on the floor got together for floor hockey games in the hall. I could hear them banging up and down the floor, hitting each other and the walls with sticks and barreling into each other. They busted out so many light bulbs in the hallway, the dorm manager came over to see what was going on. The manager told the guys to stop with the floor hockey in the hall, but they didn't.

The day after Mom and Dad brought me to school, I enrolled in classes. Most students had already enrolled. Returning students enrolled before they left the semester before, and MU had early enrollment for freshman during the summer, but I had not gone to it. I thought I could do it just as well when I got there. What no one in my family told me was that in doing it late, a lot of classes would be closed, and they were.

Enrollment was held in the basketball arena then, with tables set up for the different disciplines and the classes they offered. Students would ask for a class and be given a card with the appropriate information for that card, bundle them all together and turn them in at a registration table. But every time I went to a table to sign up for a class, they would tell me the class was closed. I was trying to take some biology classes in my major and required classes like English or humanities, and I ended up with geography, a math class I actually had tested out of, and German. And all my classes were either very early in the morning or late in the afternoon.

Also no one before I went to school told me about the rip off that college textbooks were. A student paid $35 or $50 even then for a textbook, and when he or she sold it back to the bookstore, they would only give you $5 or $7.50 even when it was still in mint condition. Of course, used books were $20 or $30; the store marked them back up, and in those days, there were no student exchange stores that provided a better deal. You had to deal solely with the university bookstore.

I think I spent as much on books as I did on tuition, and I was really upset about it. I was not prepared for that, I didn't have the money, and I couldn't get all the books I needed because the university bookstore was sold out on some of them. I certainly received a quick education on monopolies and unethical, but legal, business practices. I found out later, some students shared books or sold directly to incoming students. A few years later, some alternative stores were allowed to operate that cut costs for students, but not much.

I survived that first semester despite the challenges, and my classes would count for something toward a degree. I also enrolled early since I was a returning student and I got all the classes I wanted. But purchasing books really bothered me all the time I was in school because my parents had taught me to be frugal and I hated what I had to pay for textbooks.

I believe that first year, my tuition was about $300 a semester and my cost for dorm and the cafeteria was about $900. I was given a $300 government loan, and I took part in Work/Study that provided me about another $600, so I didn't have to come up with much money. When I reported for Work/Study, I was sent to the Chemistry building, where I worked in the lab equipment room washing flasks, beakers, burets, pipettes, and a whole lot of other glassware. It turned out to be a good place to work, and a chemistry professor took an interest in me. We got along and we talked sometimes before he went home in the evenings. Before the year ended, he invited me to his house for dinner, and I ate with him, his wife and young son. His wife fixed spaghetti and meatballs and that was the first time I had spaghetti sauce that was real spaghetti sauce, not the gravy my mother made. I was a bit of a finicky eater then, but I did like the sauce which had mushrooms and peppers in it. After we ate, the chemistry teacher and I played chess.

He ended up getting me a job in the Wildlife Department on campus for the summer. The department needed someone to run tests on water from Thomas Hill Reservoir about 50 miles north of Columbia. A doctoral student was studying the effects of heated effluent from a power plant on the lake, and he collected water samples each week from the reservoir. I tested it for nitrites, nitrates, oxygen, pH, and a few other things. I ended up staying the summer in Columbia, which upset Mom because she thought I ought to come home. It sounded neat to stay, but it actually was a little boring because Columbia was a pretty sleepy town then without all its students.

My summer turned out somewhat exciting as I found a room in an apartment where I planned on staying the next fall with Rick and two other journalism students he knew. The catch that summer was I had to double in an apartment with someone I didn't know. He turned out to be a wild guy from south central Missouri. He was a big guy, over six feet tall and a bit overweight, and he was loud and liked to party. I avoided his partying, but he asked me to go to southern Missouri with him a couple of times on the weekend to canoe on the Current River. I never knew anything like that existed in Missouri, and the streams and mountains captured my imagination after those visits. In fact, I applied the next summer to work with the state parks in southern Missouri and was hired on at Table Rock State Park.

My roommate left a lot of weekends to go home on his own, and one Sunday night, he came back to the apartment with a baby bobcat. He said he hit the mother on the highway returning, and caught the one young cat. He kept it in the apartment for about two weeks until it tore his couch to shreds and he let it go.

As I said, I avoided his parties, but one Friday night, he had one at our apartment. The place was packed with people I didn't know, including girls from Stephens College. I got to know one girl, a nice-looking blond who was in drama at Stephens. We ended up going out a few times. I also dated a few times, a black girl from Stephens that I met at the party. That's the first time I ever dated a black girl. We went to a football game together in the fall. She was a nice girl and athletic.

Our apartment got trashed that night of the party, and when we woke up in the morning, he talked me into going to the Current River to float. I forgot that Jerry Stock and Dave Hurst, friends from St. Joseph who I went to high school with, had called and said they were coming down to visit. I saw them years later, and they said they knocked and knocked and finally went to the building manager who let them into our apartment. They said the manager saw the mess, and shook his head. They were mad that I wasn't there, and they said I should have called and invited them to the party.

Near the end of summer, the graduate assistant whose samples I tested took me to Thomas Hill Reservoir to see the collection process. I had a good day with him and two other students working with him, one a tall, thin guy and the other, a blond who wore short shorts and a halter top. She was nice to me, but she said she had a boyfriend.

The next school year, I roomed with Rick and his two friends. The friends turned out to be creeps, and they were noisy and messy. Rick didn't have a lot to do with them outside of his classes, and I think he was put out by them at times.

My cousin Phillip Pitts came to Columbia that fall, and he came to the apartment to visit me. He started coming regularly, but then he went out for the football team and made it. He was busy after that and I didn't see him much. He ended up playing varsity ball, only he tore up one of his knees and was out a while. His two sons ended up playing for Mizzou too.

Bill came down to visit me and his friend Wally Wells a couple times. So I got to know Wally. I started walking over to his house, which was quite a long walk, a few miles, and spending Saturdays with him. Wally was an affable, funny guy, and very intelligent, and persuasive. He liked to talk about alternative lifestyles, mainly eco-friendly lifestyles and engineering, and we would sit and discuss them in his house. I also helped him finish building a house on the property for his dad, and we walked around his country place near the little town of Hartsburg. I ended up going to his house almost every weekend, and in fact, either he or one of his children would pick me up from school on Friday and take me back to my apartment on Sunday. He had four children. An older girl, Kathy, who lived with a hippie guy. She was a hippie too, but she worked and so did her husband. The next girl, Becky, was tall and beautiful. She had a black boyfriend who stayed at the house and slept with her in her bedroom. Wally and his wife L'Nora were very accepting people. Most of the time Becky picked me up at school. She worked, but her boyfriend didn't if I remember correctly. The next daughter, Wendy, was my age, and she was in college. She had a boyfriend too, a nice enough guy, but he was a bit weird and lazy. Wally's last child, Jon, was a teenage son who was spoiled rotten and was worthless. But Wally and L'Nora gave him money and let him stay in the house.

Wally had me so interested in alternative housing and energy that I took some engineering classes, which ended up being a waste of time because they didn't count toward my major, but I enjoyed them.

The next summer, I didn't stay in Columbia. I worked at Table Rock Lake. When I did return to school, I was disillusioned and depressed. I didn't know actually what I wanted to do. I took classes and ended up living with Fosse and this other guy when Rich Hamra had his nervous breakdown and returned home. I had a nice fall though. I met a dark-haired girl who was an art major, Cindy McBeth. We went out every weekend and even met at times during the week. She would come over to the apartment where I stayed that semester and we'd watch TV and talk. I think Cindy had another guy she was seeing too, another guy named David. I don't she was very serious with him, though, until I left for home at the end of the fall semester. I went back home and stayed with my parents and worked at Farmarco the next spring before I went on my adventure to Houston and West Texas.

When I returned to Columbia more than a year later, I ran into Cindy on the street. We talked, but she didn't seem too interested in me. I didn't ask her out, and I didn't bother to try and see her again.

While I was at Columbia, especially the first two years, protests over the Vietnam War were frequent. I went to a few marches and one sit-in at the county courthouse. We sat outside on the steps all night and into the morning. President Nixon began bombing Cambodia and increasing the bombing of North Vietnam, and of course, young Americans were still fighting there and getting killed in the Asian country's civil war. Some veterans returning from the war and to school would stand silently every Wednesday at noon outside the Student Union. I joined them frequently.

I believed then and still believe now, the Vietnam War was an exercise not only in futility but in poor political judgment. I did not, and still don't, agree with communistic beliefs as espoused by the Soviet Union or China, but about two million North Vietnamese died in the conflict along with almost 50,000 Americans. There were better ways to deal with the division in Vietnam even if it was going to end with a takeover of South Vietnam by Ho Chi Minh, which it did despite our military efforts.

I wasn't long at Columbia after returning from West Texas. I wasn't sure what I wanted to do or major in. The most interesting thing I did while I was there was work in the Anthropology Department about ten hours a week, cataloguing pottery into a computer. Research students had collected pottery from Europe somewhere in an archaeological dig, photographed all the pieces, and assigned numbers to all the characteristics of each piece. My job was to enter the numbers into a computer database that would instantly categorize all the works into type and age.

| 19 |

Ten Fathoms Restaurant

After the fall semester of 1972 at the University of Missouri, I moved back home to St. Joseph and went to work at Farmarco, a soybean oil and mash plant just south of the Power and Light Co. generating plant. I was thinking about joining the Peace Corps and wanted to earn some money. Instead, in the spring of 1973, I decided I wanted to be a sailor.

The Roosevelt Hotel in downtown Houston in 1973, where I stayed that summer working at the Ten Fathoms Restaurant.

By coincidence, Mom had met a lady who lived in Cameron, Mo., about 30 miles east of St. Joe, whose husband, then dead, had been an ambassador for the US government. He had several ambassadorships during his career, including one in Greece. Mom arranged a meeting with the lady, and she, Linda and I went over and ate dinner with her one evening. She fixed an authentic Greek meal, including a dish similar to Polish pig in the blanket, but instead of the meat rolled up in cabbage leaves, the meat was rolled up in grape leaves. Her house was a museum of artwork and decorative pieces from Europe and Asia. I don't remember her name, maybe Linda does, but she was very refined, dignified, and educated. I can't believe she let us into her home, but she was also very kind.

She knew three brothers who immigrated to the United States from Greece after World War II and started a restaurant in Houston. They also owned several ships that brought freight into the Houston Shipping Channel. She contacted the brothers for me, and gave me a hand-written letter to deliver to them asking for a position on a ship.

In late May, I drove back to Kansas City with Bill who was visiting us in St. Joe; then I caught a bus to Houston. I got there late in the evening on a Friday, spent the weekend in Galveston, and went to the restaurant, called Ten Fathoms, on Monday morning. It was located at 740 Polk Avenue, across from the Civic Center. As the name implies, it was mainly a seafood restaurant.

The brother who ran everything, George (I don't remember the last name), said he was expecting me, and put me to work right away as a dishwasher in the restaurant. He said the ships had not been coming in regularly. I don't remember what economic crisis was going on right then, but that was the case. He said it might be a while before a ship docked, but I could work there till then. So I went to work, washing dishes with a couple of nice young black men. Most of the workers in kitchen were black too, and several were gay – the first gay people I had ever been around – but the two main chefs were Greek and Hispanic. The Greek chef had a sour disposition and a foul mouth, but once I got to know him, he really had a heart of gold. He cooked pots of chicken and stew for the kitchen workers, and he took pleasure in it as he did the food he served to patrons.

I don't remember the other brother who was an owner. He wasn't there a lot. He left everything to George. But the third brother, Karl, was the oldest, and he wasn't an owner, but a worker, who sort of managed the kitchen and took payments for meals. He had a big scar across the top of his bald head that ran down his forehead to his left eye. He had been an underground fighter in World War II, and had been shot in the head. He wasn't quite right. He would sit and drink and cry in the restaurant. But he was a nice guy, talkative, and asked me a lot of questions about myself and my family.

I could tell a lot of stories about my time in Houston. I was there for three months. I lived in the Franklin Hotel, paying by the week. It was a dump, old and decrepit, but the young lady at the desk was nice to me – she sewed a split in my jeans knee one time, and the hotel was close to the restaurant. I didn't have a car. I went to Houston Astro baseball games, watched a couple of musicals put on at the park, and went to the zoo frequently.

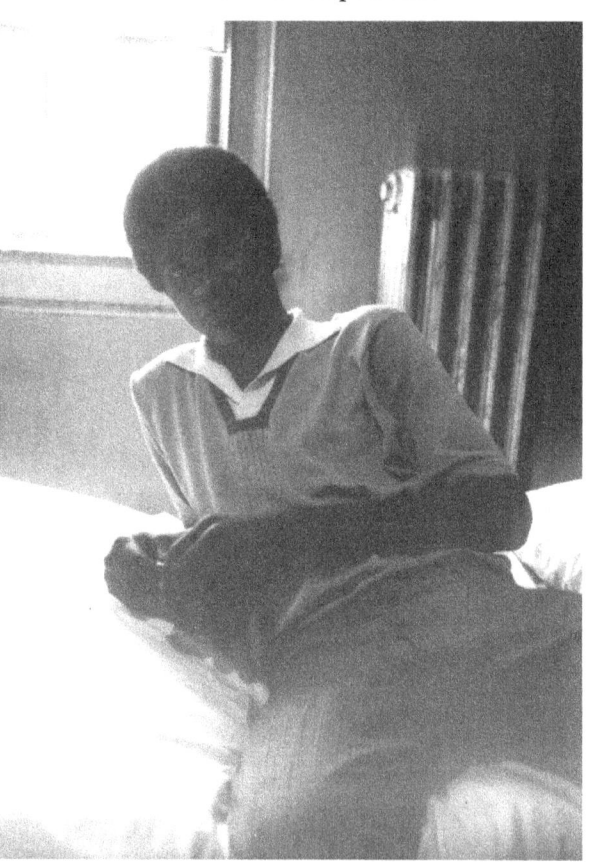

I don't remember his name, but I washed dishes with this young man at Ten Fathoms restaurant. He was a nice guy, and he stopped one day before work at my hotel room.

I didn't wash dishes long. One day a busboy didn't show up for work, and I took his place at the lunch counter and in the evenings, I bussed dinner tables. The place was always busy, and time went fast. There were a lot of nice workers there, and I got along with them all. One elderly black lady who fixed sandwiches at the lunch counter asked me to drive her in her car to San Antonio to visit family once. She took me to her hometown, Waelder, and we ate hot links on the porch of her decaying old childhood home. There were two beautiful ladies in their late twenties who worked as bar maids who were nice to me. They teased me and sat on my lap occasionally, but they wouldn't go out with me even though I asked them several times. The maître de was a super guy who helped me out when I didn't know what I was doing. He even helped clear tables when it got crazy busy.

And there was the Hispanic bartender, Ramon, who I ended up working with for about a month when the bar assistant didn't show up one day. Ramon lived in Chicago at one time, but he said he couldn't take the cold, so he moved back south. And George was a nice guy, though he was an eternal braggart, but I imagine what he said was true. He was a very rich man. He said he had known John F. Kennedy, and visited him several times, and even shared women with him. George said he had sex with lots of women, including Marilyn Monroe. George had an eye for detail, and made sure the restaurant was clean and had plenty of workers. He was good to us, paid well, and he was good to his brother, Karl. However, he often got after Karl when Karl started crying. He would tell Karl to go to the kitchen and cry.

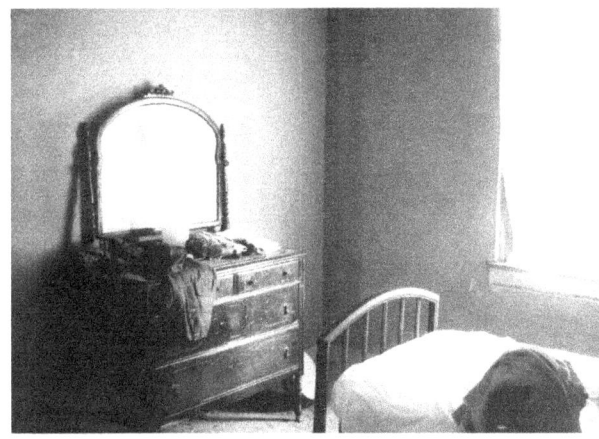

My stark room at the Roosevelt Hotel. It did not have air conditioning, and the heat and humidity in Houston was oppressive. As a result, I left my room window open, and I was constantly barraged with the sounds of the city.

I should mention here that Mary and Robert came to see me in Houston after I'd been there only few weeks. They moved from St. Joseph, where Robert and Mary had been working at the Wesley Center, and they were going to Port Isabel to live. I don't think either one had a job waiting for them, but Robert got a job as a reporter. I believe he worked for the Port Isabel-South Padre Press. Mary and Robert visited with me only a couple days; then they went to Port Isabel. Later in the summer, in August, they came back to Houston, and got an apartment. Robert was managing the apartment complex and I moved in with them.

I ended up leaving Ten Fathoms on Labor Day weekend in September. No ship ever came in, and I was impatient. A few things happened that changed my mind about shipping out as a crew member too. Once at the Ten Fathoms, four guys came in the restaurant late one night half-drunk, poorly dressed, and making a lot of noise. Ramon, speaking Spanish to them, sent them out the door without serving them anything, not even letting them sit down. I asked Ramon what the problem was and he said they were Chilean sailors. He didn't want them in there. If he did, he said trouble would be the result. He said they were sailors, coarse people, uncouth. Then one evening, I was riding the bus home from the park, and a guy sat down next to me. He started talking to me in broken English. He said he was a sailor on a ship. He smelled strongly of alcohol, and was hard to understand, but I asked him questions, trying to be friendly. Only he got too friendly. Before long he was touching me and leaning on me, and wanted to know if I wanted to go someplace with him. I got off the bus and walked from wherever I was to get back to my hotel room. I couldn't help thinking that this would be a problem on board a ship with a bunch of guys. So I decided to hitchhike to California and hike around or maybe look for a more sophisticated shipping adventure there. I told Mary and Robert that I was heading out, and in the morning, Robert drove me outside Houston on Interstate 10. He tried to convince me to stay in Houston with him and Mary, and when Robert let me out, he said, "You sure you want to do this?"

I said yes, and he drove away, and I started hitchhiking west.

A Red Wing shoebox I still have that came from dad's shoe store, and in which I have been storing photos.

A light moment in 2013 while visiting Susan at her house in Overland Park. I'm at front left, and behind me are Annie and Melina, Linda, Audrey, Ahafia, Susan, John, Isaac and Noah.

| 20 |

West Texas Cowboy

After Robert dropped me off along I-10, the first ride I got was with a Catholic priest. He said he was concerned about youth today, and talked to me about the Catholic Church a lot. The second ride was with a pot-smoking young cowboy.

A look across the Chisos Basin in the Chisos Mountains in Big Bend National Park in September 1973.

I had a terrible headache from breathing the smoke from his joints. I didn't smoke with him. I had one or two other rides and made it to San Antonio at noon, making good time. But then on the eastern outskirts of San Antonio, no one wanted to give me a ride. I stood under an underpass as it rained for about an hour before this beat-up, old four-door vehicle pulled over to give me a ride. The driver was a very old-looking Hispanic guy with a much younger woman sitting close by him. They had packages and sacks of stuff in the front and back seat, but he told me to get in. I did, in the back, and we headed down the busy highway with him driving about 35 mph and other cars whizzing by at 70 and 80 and honking at him. Somewhere in the central city, he got off the highway. He said he had to pick up his and his wife's son from school. This old guy, who looked to be in his seventies, was married to the young woman in the car, thirties or forties, and had a child who was in third grade. We picked the boy up. He was a pudgy kid, and he sat in back with me as we drove to the west side of San Antonio. At some point the guy pulled over and didn't say anything. He really didn't talk much the whole way. He just looked at me, and I got out along US 90.

I had a few short rides before an old lady stopped for me. She was well-dressed and had a nice big vehicle. I told her she shouldn't be picking up hitchhikers. She told me I didn't look like someone who would harm people. She said she was a retired teacher and she had spent the last few years translating children's books from English to Spanish. She was driving to Uvalde, and when we got there, she bought me two double hamburgers with large fries and a large Coke from Burger King. Then she left me off at the town square to sit and eat.

Swimming in the Rio Grande River at the entrance to Boquillas Canyon in Big Bend.

I walked through Uvalde and a long way outside town before I got another ride. It was late and I was looking for a place to camp alongside the highway. But a guy in a semi and cattle trailer stopped for me. The driver, a heavy-set guy in his forties said he was going to pick up some cattle outside Sanderson. He was supposed to be there in the morning. It was about 10 o'clock when we got to Del Rio, and he pulled over near the river and we walked across the bridge into Ciudad Acuna, Mexico. He wanted to go to a bar and drink. So we spent three or four hours or more in this bar drinking and listening to Mexican music and dancing with girls. It was about three in the morning when we walked back to his semi, and he drove to Sanderson. It was just getting light when we got there, and he said he could use some help loading the cattle. So I went with him to a ranch that was down the worst rock road in the world almost 50 miles south into desert country towards the Mexican border and the Rio Grande.

We were so sleepy that we were seeing things, and he was dropping off and driving off the worst road into sand and huge rocks. It was a wonder we weren't killed, but we ended up in this beautiful canyon with water and trees, and a little ranch house where an old man and woman lived who raised cattle for an East Texas cattle and land magnate. The rich East Texan wanted some of the cattle back on the ranch near Houston. So we caught a few hours' sleep on the porch, then loaded the cattle and headed out. He wanted me to go back to Houston with him. He said he could get me a job on the East Texas ranch, but I didn't want to go to East

Joe Bishop's ranch south of Marfa, a ranch that Joe's grandfather homesteaded.

Texas. I got out at Sanderson. It took me all afternoon to get a ride almost to Marathon, 50 miles away. Near evening, a young guy in a sports car picked me up and he took me the rest of the way to Marathon. He said he was going to Big Bend National Park. He said I should see it and I thought OK, what's my hurry to get to California, and I rode to the park with him.

There were no campsites left open in the Chisos Mountain Basin when I got there. But a guy, Bill Timberlake, in an old bread truck outfitted for camping, told me I could put up my tent at his site as he saw I was on foot. Bill and I spent several days hiking around Big Bend. He was tall, lanky guy from western North Carolina. He said he mostly hiked in the east, but wanted to get out west. He was also a bit of a druggie, had read Carlos Castenada, and wanted to try peyote. So I went with him as he looked around for peyote buttons, which are hallucinogenic. A lot of people there were after the same thing, but we never found any, and no one we talked to said they found any in the park.

The Delaware Mountains north of Van Horn, where I spent most of my time while working for Joe Bishop.

Bill and I made a mistake one day. We didn't want to pay for Mexicans to row us into Mexico for an afternoon, so we swam the river. We did it in an obvious place. We weren't trying to sneak across, but the Border Patrol was waiting for us on our return swim. The county sheriff was there too, and he was a real nice guy. He laughed about our predicament, but the Border Patrol took it seriously, looking for drugs they thought we may have hidden along the bank. They made us empty Bill's camper out next to the highway. Bill had some drugs in there, and he stuffed the bag in his underwear when they weren't watching. They searched all our things, then told us to load everything back in the van. Bill took his drug bag out of his underwear and hid it in his stuff, again, when they weren't looking. The next day, Border Patrol agents followed us around, and Bill said he couldn't take that, he was going home. He left me in Marathon, and I got a ride right away with an insurance salesman collecting from delinquent payers. He stopped in Alpine and Marfa, and it was late afternoon when we got to Van Horn. He was headed back east, and I told him I was going to head up US 54 because I didn't want to be on I-10. He said very few people took 54 and I would have a hard time getting a ride. He said I should take I-10. I didn't listen and he was right about highway 54.

I walked about four miles with dusk approaching, and I hadn't seen one car. Then this pickup, a white Ford, came barreling from Van Horn. It went past me, then skidded as it came to a stop in a cloud of dust off to the side of the road. I was afraid to get in, but this big guy in a brown cowboy hat yelled to me from an open window to get in.

The guy driving the pickup was Joe Bishop, a cattle rancher from south of Marfa, who had two lease properties north of Van Horn. He was half drunk, and as it turns out he was looking for someone to look after one of those properties.

The block house where I stayed on a 64,000-acre lease north of Van Horn, and 54, my dog.

The first lease he had was in a small group of mountains just ahead.

We stopped there and he put together some groceries for me; then we drove about 30 miles north and he left me at the edge of the Delaware Mountains in a little block cabin several miles east of 54 highway. He showed me, using a sawhorse for a horse, how to saddle a horse, and he said the horses would come down in the morning to the pond – he called it a tank – to drink, and told me put a rope around a horse's neck in order to get me a horse to ride. There was a windmill a couple of miles away, and I was supposed to check to see if it was running. It was powered by a small gasoline engine, and when the tank reservoir was full, I was supposed to switch the pump over to windmill power. He said he'd pay me $300 a month, and he'd be back in a week to bring more food. I didn't see him for another three weeks.

I never did develop a liking to horses while in West Texas, but I rode them a lot.

Joe Bishop was like that. He was not a dependable person. He was subject to fits of anger and alcoholism. He cheated on his wife two or three times in the nine months I was there. I caught him with another woman once, and he bragged about a couple other escapades. He was always scheming too. The whole time I worked for him, he talked of renting irrigated land along the Rio Grande to grow pickle cucumbers. He talked about it because he needed quick money.

He was in debt, and after I left, he would lose the ranch in Marfa that his grandfather had homesteaded. In fact, only a month or so after I started working for him, he couldn't keep up the lease on the property nearest Van Horn and we had to round up all the cattle there. We took some to the leased land farther north, some to Marfa, and some to the market in El Paso. Joe had a partner, a nice, elderly man I met early on. I suspect that he broke ties with Joe after I met him because I never saw him again.

Joe was married. His wife, Virginia Gay, whose maiden name was McMurrey, was a big lady, not heavy, just tall and big boned. She was nice, but she could be sullen, probably as a result of living with Joe. She mentioned once that Joe had been abusive when they were younger. They were in their forties when I knew them.

Virginia, Joe's wife, and their younger son, Tommy.

Jackie, Tommy, and Bailey, the Bishops' three children.

They had three children. Bailey, a boy, was a senior in high school when I was there. Then there was Jackie, a fifth- or sixth-grade student, who favored her mother, and she had been born with a cleft palate. She had a bad scar on her lip from it. She was a very sweet girl. I probably talked to her more than anyone when I was with the family. Tommy, was the youngest, and curiously because it is not genetic, just something that happens by chance, he had been born with a cleft palate too. He was also a sweet kid, fun, funny, curious and active. I learned on a trip to West Texas years later that Tommy died in PE class shortly after I left. It turns out he had a hole in his heart no one knew about until he fell over in the gym.

From September to Christmas, I stayed mainly at the lease north of Van Horn. I didn't see Joe or the family much during that time. I went home for Christmas and returned to Marfa two weeks later. That's when Joe had me spend three days north of Van Horn feeding cattle and looking over the property, then two or three days in Marfa doing the same. I slept in a room separate from the main house with Bailey when I was in Marfa.

The lease land north of Van Horn was 10 miles by 10 miles, 64,000 acres. The east side was bordered by the Delaware Mountains, and the west by US 54. Most of the lease lay in downward slope from the mountains toward salt flats on the other side of the highway. When I first arrived there, the flats were partially covered with water that drained from rainfall to the north and even farther into New Mexico. Joe's business partner told me when I met him that the salt flats were connected by underground caverns all the way to the coast and that's where the salt water came from. Of course, that would be quite a feat for the ocean to push salt water more than six hundred miles through a cavern that came out four thousand feet higher than where the water went in. I don't think he was just pulling my leg. I think he believed it.

I look rugged in this photo from my time in West Texas, but living alone in the mountains, not seeing anyone for days or weeks at a time, was tough.

The Guadalupe Mountains rose up out of the salt flats to the north, and the ancient raised reef is a famous geological formation. Since the whole area was a raised ocean bed, geologists came there for training. In fact, when Noah and I visited the Guadalupe Mountains and Joe's old lease in 1998, a group of oil interests had built a training center for oil engineers, and Mike Capron, who worked there when I was there in the 1970s, ran the operation. He invited Noah and I to eat dinner with a group of trainees at the time, and Noah and I walked up to the ancient Native American site in one of the canyons. It had round depressions in a section of rock where Native women had ground grain and a huge boulder with pictographs etched on it next to caves where Native peoples had slept.

When I was there working for Joe, I could just begin to see the lights of El Paso one hundred miles to the west at night. I could count on one hand the number of visible ranch lights, and on the other hand I could count the number of passenger vehicles traveling US 54 and US 62 coming from El Paso. In daylight, the salt basin shimmered, and a few volcanic sites were visible along the western horizon. The Sierra Diablo was to the south, and reached more than 6,000 feet high, while Guadalupe Peak to the north is the highest point in the state at 8,751 feet.

I was never sure how many acres Joe's ranch south of Marfa had. As I said it was homesteaded by Joe's grandfather, who passed it on to his son, who passed it on to Joe, who borrowed against it trying to expand his business interests, which eventually backfired on him, and he lost it. It was only a few thousand acres, not tens of thousands. The ranch was traversed by Alamito Creek, and the ranch house with its metal roof was on the east side of the narrow stream. Big cottonwoods grew along the creek, and the ones that had died littered the ground forever in the dry desert. There were badgers along the creek, temperamental animals that growled and spit at you. And at night, coyotes howled with wild West Texas abandon. Joe kept goats for milking and butchering, and his wife had an irrigated garden on the north side of the house surrounded by a high fence to keep the goats out. Joe also had guinea fowl that kept up a constant chatter as they pecked around the yard and cow lot. If a snake found its way out of the creek, the guinea fowl cries would alert us that an intruder was present, and at night they climbed in pecking order into one of the high cottonwoods for safety. The house had a heavy wooden fence around it to keep out cattle which roamed the drive and creek bed. There was a big red bull, part Brahman, that Tommy had bottle fed when it was young, and Tommy had ridden it when it was small. But one day, the bull didn't want to be ridden, and he almost gored Tommy's leg, leaving it bruised and sore. Joe didn't have a television. There was no reception in Alamito Creek, and instead of watching television, the family listened to the radio or read the newspaper or books.

Mike Capron and his wife lived on the lease land just north of where I worked for Joe Bishop. In 1998, Noah and I traveled to West Texas, and Mike was still living on the lease that then had become an oil geologists' training area. Here he demonstrates roping to Noah, me and visiting geologists.

While I worked for Joe, the Oakland A's beat the Mets in the World Series. I listened to it on the radio. I heard about Vice President Spiro Agnew resigning, and I followed the news on Watergate by radio and newspaper. Joe's money woes were complicated by Nixon's price controls on meat that depressed cattle prices, and though Joe was a conservative, he didn't like Nixon's handling of the economic crisis. Joe took great pleasure in reading the Watergate developments that would eventually lead to Nixon's resignation.

Bill and Lynda came to see me in December 1973 for a few days. Joe never knew they were there because he never came while they visited. Mom and Dad and Linda came in March 1974 for a few days. Joe was away in Houston at some event, but Mom and Dad visited with Joe's wife.

I was in on five "roundups." Joe was never impressed with my horseback riding, and to tell the truth, I only tolerated it. Riding a horse is hard work, exhausting. Horses sweat, they smell, and they are not comfortable to sit on especially when they are trotting. It's a constant collision of butt coming down and horse coming up to meet butt. I rode a horse named Jose. He was a quarter horse, on the smaller side and slow. He dragged his hooves a lot and sometimes fell asleep while walking. When it was hot, I could fall asleep riding too, and I almost fell off Jose a few times when he stumbled. I also rode a mule named Mr. Brown. He was a big, tall mule, that was easy to ride, but he smelled terrible when sweaty, and he was afraid of his own shadow.

El Capitan with the higher Guadalupe Peak behind it, both in the Guadalupe Mountains National Park.

Joe was not good at explaining anything. He simply expected me and others who occasionally worked there to know what he was thinking or wanted. I don't know why I stayed so long for such a cantankerous person. I think maybe for the adventure that it was. Thinking back, I should have gone to another ranch and worked for someone who was pleasant and ran an efficient operation.

Before I left, Joe said he was going to give me six head of cattle to take with me, and then when I took him up on it, he kept back two months of my pay for the cattle. I didn't want to argue with him. Kathy and Richard came for me in a pickup pulling a trailer. We took the cattle to Kathy and Richard's farm on Turner Road in Missouri, where one died. Kathy and Richard said then that they didn't want them anymore, and I sold the five for half what I paid for them.

I enjoyed my time in West Texas despite Joe Bishop. I enjoyed Joe's kids. I played games with Tommy and Jackie a lot. I took a lot of hikes in the mountains and deserts. I saw a lot of beautiful burning sunsets; a lot of wild animals, bobcats, and different kinds of snakes, birds, and insects.

The red Brahma bull that Tommy rode when the bull was small. The bull always seemed complacent, but once Tommy got on it when I was there, and the bull swung its head around, hitting Tommy in his shoulder with a horn, giving Tommy a good bruise.

I was out in a dust storm with winds gusting from 80 to 100 mph. I rode a horse five miles to Mike Capron's home to phone Joe that the well pump went out one evening. Then I rode back to the cabin in the dark, the horse following the trail because I had no idea where we were going. I went into Mexico a few times for different things, once to take a Mexican worker to a doctor after he injured an eye working for Joe. Joe took me into El Paso a couple of times for a day off, and we went bar hopping one night. He ended up really drunk, and got in a fight in one bar. I got thrown out with him. He drank even more after that, and I had a hard time getting him back to the motel where we were staying.

Joe's final story is sad. Besides hearing about the death of Tommy, I read in a Texas online magazine much later that Joe committed suicide. In 2014, Virginia Bishop died in San Angelo. She is buried in the Cedar Hill Cemetery in Ozona, Texas. I was there in 2020. The Ozona cemetery is a very well kept cemetery with lots of tall cedar and live oak trees.

On our visit to West Texas in 1998, Noah opens a gate as drive into the Delaware Mountains to look for the huge stone with native petroglyphs on it. The Guadalupe Mountains are in the background.

Thanksgiving dinner at Kathy and Richard's house on Cedar Creek Reservoir in Texas in 1998. Left circling to right: Kathy, a church friend of Kathy's, Paula, Rich, Audrey, Noah, another friend, Richard, Steven, Kathy, Jessica, Christian, Jeff, Kymrie, and Blake.

| 21 |

Meeting Audrey McKinnon

I was pretty aimless after coming back from West Texas.

I stayed in St. Joseph with Mom and Dad for about a month or so; then I decided to go back to school in Columbia. I took a couple of summer courses, Anthropology and something else. I ended up working Work/Study in the Anthropology Lab, and I lived with Bill and Lynda in Ashland, in a home they rented. Mom and Dad loaned me money for a white Volkswagen beetle.

Audrey worked for Dan Garvin's insurance agency a few blocks from my dad's shoe shop.

That summer, Bill and Lynda adopted Rachel, and I was there to help take care of her a little. Bill and Lynda also bought some property farther south toward the Missouri River near Hartsburg, and they were able to finance the construction of a new home. So I helped with building that house some. A construction company did the foundation and put up the frame, and Bill and his friend, Wally Wells, and I put on the roof. I helped run the electric and finish out the inside. Bill and Lynda moved into it before it was done, and I stayed with them a while, before moving out.

I didn't take classes in the fall because I didn't know what I wanted to do. I ended up with a job at Cheesebrough-Ponds, a manufacturing company which made a lot of makeup and personal products in Jefferson City. I worked in the shipping department, third shift, loading pallets of products into trailers. I moved into Wally Wells' old farmhouse in Hartsburg, not far from Bill and Lynda. Wally didn't charge me anything. I kept the place mowed, and Wally talked about turning the big old wooden barn there into motel and center for alternative living conferences. Wally was a visionary, but not a serious doer. He never followed up on any of his ideas, or brought them to fruition. I started building little apartments or motel rooms in the loft, framing out a couple and insulating one, but that was as far as I got because Wally expected me to scrounge around for materials; he didn't come up with money to finance it.

I liked Wally, who was a sociologist at the female college, Stephens, in Columbia. He was funny, irreverent quite a bit, and had all kinds of ideas on how to change the world. He had a subscription to Mother Earth News and could talk about green energy and communal living, but he wasn't committed to it. He actually had a soft life with a professorship teaching pretty, young, rich girls at a prestigious school; a nice, comfortable home outside Columbia; and his wife earned a good living, too, as a managerial nurse at the local hospital.

Next to the best truck I've ever owned.

They had four children, two of whom were pretty spoiled and irresponsible, and I realized that what Wally wanted was for someone to spend his or her life doing what he was not willing to commit to. I still liked Wally, but I left at Christmastime and went back to St. Joseph.

Dad wanted to spend less time at the shop and asked me to work with him. It was a nice arrangement, but it really wasn't enough money for me. All that winter, I kept thinking I am 22 years old, I am living with my parents, and I'm never going to get anywhere. By spring, I was antsy and I decided I wanted to go live in Wyoming, live in the West and the mountains.

Audrey and I at the Bucket Shop, a restaurant in South St. Joe.

Mary said she had a friend in Gillette who had a business drywalling. The coal boom was on there, and Wyoming was building homes to accommodate all the workers in the coal and oil and gas industries. Mary and Robert had moved back to Missouri, to Columbia. I went to Houston in a truck Bill and I had bought to move them.

So I told Dad what I had in mind, and he was pretty disappointed. But like always, he didn't say anything.

Then on May 10, Mom, Dad and I went to Roman Cupryk's wedding reception. They received the invitation and asked me to go along with them. I really wasn't keen on it because I hadn't been around much for nearly five years. But I went and while we were in the reception line going in, Dad started talking to Dan Garvin, an insurance salesman, who was behind us. Dan and his wife had a pretty girl my age with him who turned out to be his secretary and I started talking to her, and her name was Audrey Jo McKinnon.

In the back of the shoe shop that I helped Mom and Dad convert to an apartment.

What I didn't know was that Dan had talked to Audrey about me. I had been going to the pool at Missouri Western State College to swim and Dan was taking a swimming class. I ran into him there several times, and according to Audrey, he told her who I was.

After wishing the newlyweds and their families well, Mom, Dad and I filled plates with food from the buffet line, and as we moved to a table, Dan Garvin called out, "Bill, Bill, come sit with us."

Dad went to sit with him and Mom and I followed, setting our food and drinks down across from Dan, his wife, and Audrey. When I put my drink down, I inadvertently set it down on the neck of a spoon, and the cup overturned, spilling pop all over the table which quickly made the paper tablecloth a soggy mess. Of course, I was embarrassed and it made for a memorable first meeting. After the meal, Audrey and I danced and talked. We went for a walk outside, and Audrey took me for a drive in her Plymouth Satellite Sebring, a car she just purchased and was proud of.

I was still planning on going to Wyoming, so after meeting Audrey, I did not call her or go to Dan Garvin's insurance agency to see her. However, she came to the shop because there was some sort of paper for Dad to sign on insurance. I wasn't there, and Dad told me she stopped by. She came a few days later then to have a moccasin sewed, which I did while she waited. Dad gave me a funny look that time, but then Audrey came again with another shoe complaining that it was squeaking and could we fix it.

Dad told her there wasn't anything to do about it, and after we talked a little bit, she left. Dad told me that Audrey was chasing me and I should ask her out. I didn't, but I did want to. I just was confused because I was still planning on going to Wyoming.

A few days later, I was in the shop by myself, and this kid about nine or ten years old came in and was looking all around. It was a quiet day. I asked him if he wanted anything and he said no. He finally parked himself by the main counter where we took in shoes. The counter was a glass case in which Dad had a bunch of old antique stuff, a handgun or two and knives. Audrey happened in then, and she came to the counter and stood and we started talking. That kid, and to this day I have no idea who he was, stopped looking at the stuff in the case and started watching us, as if he could tell there was something between us and wanted to know more about it. It was like an Opie moment from *The Andy Griffith Show*, where Opie is waiting for Andy to ask a lady out and Opie's smiling and turning his head like an inquisitive dog with great interest.

That kid made me nervous. As Audrey and I talked, I wanted to ask her out, but I wanted to wait until that kid left. But obviously, he wasn't going to. He was going to stay to see if I did, and maybe even tell me, "You dummy, ask her out."

So I did, and the kid smiled and left.

I picked up Audrey in my Volkswagen. She lived with her mother on Diagonal Street in Kirschner Addition just a block south of her grandparents' house. They rented the house, and it was a small, narrow, white house with a second-floor so it looked top heavy. And to go with the look, it leaned slightly toward the back. Audrey's mother, Audrey June, answered the door, and told me that Audrey wasn't ready yet. I think I waited fifteen minutes or more before she came down the steps. I sat down on a couch they had in the front room, and the couch had a plastic cover on it. It was so slick that I felt as if I would slip off onto the floor.

Barbosa's Castillo on Sylvanie Street in St. Joseph, where Audrey and I ate on our first date. The medieval-looking home was built in 1891, and sold to the Knights of Columbus in 1944. In 1974, the Barbosas bought it and remodeled it into a restaurant. The Barbosas have since closed this location.

We went to eat at Barbosa's Restaurant, the old red stone "castle," on Ninth Street. After we ate, we sat and talked for a long time, longer than other customers, and we had a good time talking. I could sense right away that Audrey was in many ways the same kind of person I was, a little unsure of the future, a little lonely, both of us living with parents, looking for a close, lasting relationship with a person from the other sex, not just a husband or wife. When she asked me what I wanted from life, I said something stupid, just the opposite of what I was looking for. I said, "I want to date lots of beautiful women."

Afterwards, I wondered whether she took that as a compliment or an insult, but I think she did know I was trying to be funny.

We went out a few times more soon after that, and I also took Audrey to my five-year high school reunion, the only one beside the 50th that I've been to since graduating from Christian Brothers. We got along well, but I kept thinking that I'm supposed to be heading to Wyoming. May turned into June, and June was close to turning into July, and I finally took off for the west, telling Audrey I was going just a few days before I left. Mom and Dad had sold their house and moved to the cabin at Sugar Lake, and I was staying with them. I left from Sugar Lake and headed across the bridge to Atchison, Kansas, and Wyoming.

I had sold my white Beetle, and bought an old Chevy pickup, a 1957, I think. It was a mess, and I paid too much for it. It had a lot of slack in the steering linkage, so I was constantly moving the wheel to the left and right to keep it on the road. It also had a busted spring on right side, so it leaned, and the blue green paint was peeling and the body was rusty in many places. But the pickup made it out to Wyoming. I made it in three days to Laramie, and I spent a couple of days hiking in the Medicine Bow National Forest. I left there and went through Casper, which was hosting the Wyoming State Fair.

Audrey and I on our wedding day, January 10, 1976.

I decided to stop at the fair, and I was glad I did. I spent the whole afternoon and evening there. There were plenty of exhibits and musicians, and of course, farm animals to look at. I was going to leave when it came evening, but the rodeo and music shows were free. So I sat in the stands and watched, and after the rodeo, Waylon Jennings performed. But before Jennings came on, there was the best dog act I have ever seen. The handler sat in the press box while the dog worked the show in the middle of the arena. The owner would tell the dog over the PA system to do something, and the dog would do the complete opposite of what he was told to do. If he was supposed to sit up, he would lay down. If he was supposed to play dead, he would bark and jump up and down. He did some other comical things to some of the rodeo people still inside the arena. The crowd loved him and the dog got a bigger ovation than Waylon did later. I ended up staying at the fair until past midnight, and I slept in my truck on the fairgrounds. Nobody said anything.

The next day, I drove to Gillette. Though it was midsummer, the weather turned windy, cold and wet. I looked for the drywall business, found it, but they were closed because of the holiday weekend. It was Friday, July 1. I got a motel because of the weather and I had slept out for a week. The next day, Saturday, I checked at the business again even though I knew they would be closed, which they were, and I headed for Devil's Tower. I had always wanted to see it, and I stayed there for a week, walking around the tower every day and thinking about Audrey and what I wanted to do.

I finally decided that I wanted to see Yellowstone park before I made up my mind, return to St. Joe or go to Gillette about a job. So that's what I did. I drove across northern Wyoming, the Bighorn National Forest and mountains to Cody and on to Yellowstone. I had a great four days there, but at the end of them, I called Audrey late in the evening from a phone booth inside the park. The sun was setting and four or five deer were grazing near the phone booth. I asked Audrey if she would come join me out in Wyoming and go with me to see about a job and find a place and stay with me there. She said she wouldn't do that, leave home, so I told her that I was coming home. I got in the truck and I drove all night and most of the next day, stopping to sleep overnight in a state park somewhere in western Nebraska. The truck battery went dead, so I had to park on a hill so I could kickstart it the next morning. The next day, I drove all day and into the night to get back to Sugar Lake. When I got there, Mom said that I had just missed Audrey. She had driven down to the lake to visit with Mom and Dad and wait on me, but I took too long to get there.

Audrey holds onto her hair in high winds at Petrified Forest National Park. Audrey and I took a trip out West the summer after we were married.

I got a job teaching fifth grade at St. James for the next year, and in October, I asked Audrey to marry me. I bought an engagement ring for $75 from a pawn shop – it was a nice ring, it really was and it didn't have another name etched into it – and Audrey told me she would have to think about my proposal. I was decidedly depressed for a day or two while she made up her mind. Here I had come home from Wyoming and gotten a steady job, and she wasn't sure that she wanted to marry me.

It was a little more complicated than that, as she had accepted a marriage proposal not long before meeting me, and then called off the wedding a few days before it was supposed to happen. Audrey told me she wanted to be sure this time. She made her decision, and I told her that I wanted to get married on Halloween so we could dress up. She said she wanted to wait a year. I told her I couldn't wait that long, so we settled on January 10, the next year. It turned out to be a terrible choice. It snowed before the wedding and it was freezing cold on our honeymoon in Kansas City. Most years afterward, our anniversary has been on some of the coldest days of the year. Several times there were snowstorms or ice that prevented us from celebrating on our anniversary day.

This photo would be the spring sometime after our 25th anniversary.

| 22 |

William Joseph Jurkiewicz

I looked up to my brother Bill as I was growing up. He was my hero.

Since he was almost 13 years older than I was, my first strong memories of him are Mom and Dad getting after him for running around late at night. He was eighteen and out of high school, and I wasn't even six years old. Then the next thing I knew, Mom was crying because he had joined the Army and was leaving for basic training.

I don't remember Mom doing much for us younger children at Halloween, but apparently, when Bill and Kathy were young, she went all out one year.

I didn't know the reason that Bill had joined the Army at the time: He hated the farm where we lived, and he had lost the free tuition for junior college because our family had moved outside the city limits. I just knew he was off on a big adventure, and he was a member of the US Army's Military Police.

We went to visit him in San Antonio, where he was stationed, and we even went to the Gulf to swim in the ocean with him. We had never traveled so far, and we owed our good fortune to his enlistment. Then months later, after we returned home, he was off to South Korea and the Far East. We started receiving letters with stamps we didn't recognize and gifts at Christmas that came in big boxes marked from Japan.

After his time in the service, he wasn't home long before he was off on another adventure, this time to Venezuela for a two-year stint with the Peace Corps. When he came home, he could speak Spanish and he had stories that were as mesmerizing as the tales of Rudyard Kipling. He was home a while this time, and he reconnected with his St. Joe friends, Dean Shepherd and Arthur

Treu, and they were over at our house playing poker and pitch, drinking, telling jokes, laughing and having fun. They let Mike and I sit with them as they played cards, and they joked with us and teased us as if we were equals even though they didn't let us play.

Bill was friendly, funny, adventurous. What was there about him for a younger brother not to look up to?

Then he was off to the South Pacific, to Yap Island to improve the lives of the people living there in poverty. I was in high school, and when I thought about the future, I knew I wanted to imitate my older brother.

When Bill came home from the Pacific, he stayed around this time, landing a job in Kansas City, and we developed a pretty good relationship. I graduated from high school, and was off to Columbia, Missouri, for college, but I saw him often as he came to visit me and his friend Wally Wells. We talked and played cribbage. Eventually, he moved to the Columbia area, and I lived with him and Lynda for a while. I was there when they adopted Rachel, and I helped Bill build his first home. I didn't do those things because I felt obliged, but because he was a good brother and he had qualities that I admired.

It's a fact of life that as you progress from childhood to adulthood, you discover your heroes are only human. And after I married, Bill and I went separate ways, but I have always appreciated my older brother's humor, geniality and opinions. Heroes are hard to come by, but so are good humans. Bill was in the first category when I was a child, but in my adulthood, I recognized him for the good person he is, not the hero character we create in our mind.

I took this photo of Bill at a get-together in 1989, maybe Mom's 70th birthday. He put two aspirin tablets between his lips for a rabbit look. We all laughed, but Mom took it as silliness, something she didn't like.

My brother Bill was born January 30, 1941, and after leaving St. Louis, he relocated to Roxboro, North Carolina, with his wife Lynda to be near their son, Jared, who lives nearby in Durham. Bill has two daughters, Rachel and April in Missouri, as well as a granddaughter, Kelsey, Rachel's daughter.

Bill wrote the following summary of his life for a Peace Corps reunion in 2002, and has since added to it:

From my brother Bill

When I joined the Peace Corps, I had completed only two years of college. My first priority when I returned to the states from Venezuela in 1966 was to get a degree, so I returned to Kansas City and began working on a BA in English at the University of Missouri-Kansas City. Ken Ritterspach and I roomed together in KC. Ken got a job teaching in a private girl's high school, so we spent a lot of time engaged in cultural and upper-class activities. For example, the parents of the girls at this exclusive school vacationed a lot and they always needed house-sitters to make their million-dollar homes appear inhabited while they were away. Clean-cut, all-American boy Ritterspach became a favorite house-sitter of the KC high rollers. Naturally, his friend, me, would visit him in these palaces from time to time, and wouldn't you know it, other "close" friends would drop in and before long, a party would break out! Of course, we always threw out the beer cans and unconscious partygoers before the family returned.

Bill and his daughter Rachel in 1989. Rachel was born July 10, 1974, and adopted by Bill and Lynda while they lived in Ashland, Missouri.

After I graduated from UMKC, I got a job as a reporter on the Kansas City Star. I had visions of becoming the next Ernest Hemingway, who also once served as a reporter at the Star. Ken had departed Kansas City and enrolled at Stanford, where he would eventually get his PhD. There were several women I was dating, and I had a great bachelor loft with wall-to-wall mattresses and black lights in the bedroom. I was making $5,000 a year as a reporter and was writing up obituaries like a storm as well as covering police activities. These are the jobs, apparently, of all beginning reporters.

I received a call one day from Saipan at the City Desk. It was Fred Perry, a friend who had also been in the Peace Corps in Thailand and who was working now at Office of Economic Opportunity in Washington, D.C. Fred was in Micronesia recruiting people for jobs in the Carolina Islands. He said there was an opening for the director of the Yap Island Poverty Program. The pay was lousy but it was, after all, a tropical island with sandy beaches and a blue lagoon. The women wore only grass skirts. He said he needed a decision pretty quickly.

So here I was in Kansas City in November 1968. Nixon had just got elected. It was cold outside and snow was in the forecast. I had just broken up with my girlfriend. It took me about three minutes to make a decision.

Our family celebrated Bill's 60th birthday with a party in St. Louis. Here, Susan and Annie hold a rope starting a game of limbo. Bill's granddaughter, Kelsey, is to his left and Noah McGinnis is to her left. Our cousin Phil Pitts is seated in the background.

The Yap Community Action Program director job turned out to be a no job. I had 24 employees who never showed up for work. I spent a year and a half alone in a hut on the lagoon completing the reports required by the feds so the money would keep rolling in. Our total budget was $75,000 a year. Some of my most creative writing occurred during this period. I had a small white dog, a motorcycle, a catamaran, a stereo and lots of companionship, male as well as female, including Peace Corps volunteers assigned to Micronesia. It's as close as I ever have come, or probably will come, to Paradise. It got boring.

Also, Lynda showed up in Yap. She was the last girl I had dated in Kansas City before leaving for Yap. She was beautiful. An ex-Playboy bunny, she was also smart, caring and interested in me. She spent her vacation flying 7,000 miles to come see me. Lynda was there for almost a month and then flew back to the Midwest. I wasn't long catching that plane behind her.

We bought an old mansion in St. Joseph, my hometown, and got married in front of a justice of the peace in Chicago. I got a job working for an ad agency, and Lynda was working for Family Services while we refurbished the mansion. It turned out to be a white elephant. Less than a month after getting married, I was fired by the ad agency. I was out of work for quite a while, and Darryl Kramer, recently back from a tour in Vietnam, stopped by for a three-month visit. He was very helpful in the repairs on the old house. When I finally found a job, it was in Kansas City evaluating new housing for the Model Cities Program.

We sold the mansion at a loss, and Lynda went back to UMKC to get a master's in sociology while I evaluated the housing allowance program in KC and Wilmington, Delaware. The housing program later became Section 8 housing. My evaluations were generally favorable, so maybe I can take some small credit for the continuation of the program.

Jobs that I have held

I hate to admit how many jobs I've failed at. Here's the list in chronological order after leaving Venezuela.

Janitor at exclusive girl's school: Lasted five months.

Research Assistant with community studies firm: Had government grant to study War on Poverty. Set record in Guinness Book of World Records for number of boring community meetings attended.

Bill with his son Jared at the 1990 Grand Lake Reunion.

Private Detective: Part-time at car repossessing while going to school. Quit when they wouldn't let me wear a gun.

Newspaper Reporter: Authored big story of pot parties in city park. Firsthand observation.

Poverty Program Director, Yap Island: Even the blue lagoon gets boring when there's no other place to go and only turtle and taro to eat.

Bartender: Lasted a few months. I was no Tom Cruise.

Copywriter: Ad firm for agricultural products. You just try writing creative copy for fertilizer.

Research Assistant: Studied Model Cities Program. First job where program failed before I did.

Director of Morbidity and Vital Statistics: First of two Missouri state jobs I held. Counted stuff like nursing homes, doctors, cases of syphilis, etc. Wrote exciting reports full of numbers.

Assistant Director, Missouri Energy Conservation Program: Didn't even know what BTU stood for. Hired because the Energy director was ex-Peace Corps too, which once again proves it's who you know.

Director of Van Service for People with Disabilities with Care Cab, St. Louis: Prior to this, the longest job I had held was two years. This one lasted 23 years. It grew from 15 vehicles to more than 100 vans and buses. We daily transported about 2,000 people with disabilities in St. Louis to sheltered workshops, life skills programs, therapies, etc. This job gave me an ulcer, but I loved being the boss and I loved the people we were helping. I took an early out in June 2001. I decided to make some money.

Entrepreneur: After leaving Care Cab, I invested my meager savings in a company a friend started five years previous. It was called Rock Technologies. Our only product was drilling large holes in rock. Don't laugh. Lots of people and businesses, such as utility companies, elevator installers, and bridge builders, need holes in the ground to plant things. And they needed help when they hit rock. When the going got tough, they called us. It was a good, old boy network, the drilling industry.

Family

Lynda and I were in Kansas City from 1971 to 1974. It was a rocky time. We got divorced. I took up golf. After a year of being unmarried, Lynda and I started dating again. We remarried. I had a good friend, Wally Wells, who taught at Stephen's College in Columbia, Missouri. Wally had been talking to me and others for eight years about starting an intentional community. When my job with Model Cities fizzled, Lynda and I packed up all our belongings and moved to rural Missouri near Columbia, where we bought some property and began building a house. Wally had a 100-acre farm close to us but he lived with his wife and his children in Columbia where he taught sociology. Wally's farm was a good place to talk about alternative lifestyles, to sing folk songs and barbecue, but a community never materialized.

Jared, Lynda, Kelsey and Rachel. Jared now works for Cisco, and Kelsey graduated from the University of Missouri-Rolla and works for a chemical company.

Lynda and I were now in our early thirties. We tried to have a child but had no luck. We decided to adopt. Family Services said it would take a while to find us a kid, but soon after we went through filling out forms and training, we got a call that a six-week-old girl, with a history of cystic fibrosis in the family, was available. Chances were good she didn't have the disease, but did we want to take a chance? We talked about it for maybe an hour before we told them yes. So, Rachel moved into our household.

We had also agreed to be foster parents. Before long, we had a three-year-old girl who had been abandoned by her mother. April lived with us for over five years before she was able to be adopted. So we adopted her. Then a miracle happened. Lynda got pregnant. Jared was born in 1977, our first and only natural child. I discovered how much I really like little children. We, mainly I, spoiled all of them.

In 1980, we moved to Winfield, Missouri, where we bought 15 acres and built another house. I took the director job of Care Cab in St. Louis and began a commute of 50 miles each way each day that lasted until 2001. Lynda wanted to live in the country with her animals and to keep the kids in a safer environment.

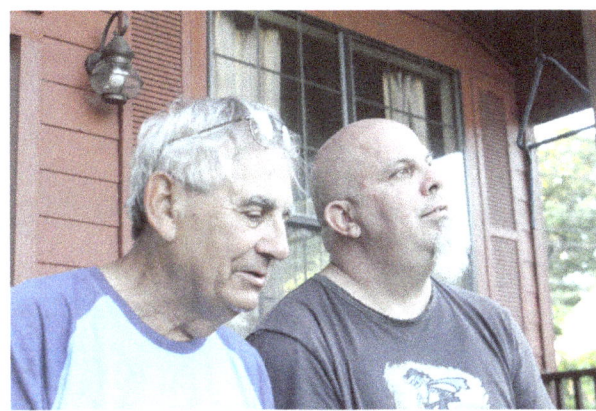

Bill with Rich at a reunion we held in Texas in 2016. Rich died the next year after a battle with cancer.

Lynda worked for 20 years as a state employee with the Division of Family Services, then with Mental Retardation. She took early retirement from that job. At that point, she had three horses and two ponies and rode nearly every day on her Arab gelding, Shalimar. Jared graduated from the University of Missouri-Rolla in 2000, summa cum laude, with a degree in computer engineering. He went right to work for IBM in Raleigh, North Carolina, bought a house, and acquired a girlfriend, two cats and a sports car. Rachel got married to a hardworking journeyman, and they gave us our only grandchild, Kelsey. Rachel went to work as a bank teller and is a wonderful mother and lives in Missouri. April lives in Missouri, too.

Passion and Avocations

I discovered golf when I was 30 years old. So I've been whacking a ball around for 50 years and I still haven't tired of the game. I play at least twice a week when the weather permits and shoot in the mid-eighties. The game, I feel, has a social dimension which makes it unique. Ken Ritterspach and I, over the past twenty years, have gotten together at least once a year to play golf and re-bond. We've played some great courses, and some crappy ones. It's always more fun to play with other people and of course, what if I got a hole in one and there wasn't a witness!

I'm still passionate about politics and stay current on world events. I have stayed a liberal Democrat all these years, but I'm no bleeding heart. But it's still hard for me to stomach Republicans, like John Ashcroft or George W, whose views and ideas are simplistic and sometimes plain wrong. How could some people listen to and agree with Rush Limbaugh, who is nothing but a fat, egotistical windbag? My dad always warned me to be suspicious of people who tell you how smart they are.

My love right now is my granddaughter, Kelsey, who can fill me with joy by simply seeing her or hearing her. Children really are special. I want Kelsey to feel loved and to experience all the good things life offers. Everything is new and special to her and it makes me realize again their value as well, through her. For example, I got one of those revolving balls which lights up with several colors, bought a CD with the divas of disco on it, and Kelsey and I danced around in our living room to "I Love the Night Life" and "I Will Survive" with little technique but lots of energy. Maybe that's the secret to life, just "Keep on Dancing."

The Turn of the Century and Old Age

I visited Bill at his home in Roxboro, North Carolina, in 2017, and we took a drive on the Blue Ridge Parkway just north of Danville, Virginia.

Lynda and I are living in Roxboro, North Carolina, where we relocated after leaving St. Louis in 2009. The drilling business I invested in when I retired from Care Cab didn't work out very well. The guy who owned the business, Dennis Maxey, had been a friend for well over ten years. We were not only golfing partners, I stuck by him when he got in legal trouble and lost his insurance business. But Dennis was a player, knew how to make money, and my goal was to team up with him and earn enough to retire, be able to travel and not worry about money. What I learned, already knew but disregarded, was that self-interest almost always trumps friendship, even family. The money the company made flowed in only one direction, toward Dennis.

After a year of wasted time and money with Dennis, another friend who owned County Cab and Yellow Cab, the largest cab companies in St. Louis, hired me to work for him. Tom Gregerson wasn't a close friend, but we had done business together when I was running Care Cab. He, Dennis and I had played golf together over several years and when Tom saw my financial predicament, he offered me a job. At first I worked as a customer relations person, handling phone calls, inquiries and complaints. Tom had over 200 taxicabs in his fleet, so there were quite a few customers to deal with. That lasted about three years.

Tom really only worked part-time and eventually turned the day-to-day operations of his business over to his daughter and her husband. I eventually was told my position was being discontinued. However, probably at Tom's suggestion, I was offered a job as a cab driver.

Few people understand how cab driving works. Cab drivers are not employees of the cab company; they are independent contractors. The cab company rents the cars to the drivers. The company also provides a dispatching service, insures the cabs and has in-house mechanics to repair them. If a driver works six days a week, usually 10 to 12 hours a day, most of the money in the first two days will cover his pro (rent) and gasoline. The rest of the money the driver earns in that week goes in his pocket. I probably averaged a net amount of $500 a week while I was a cab driver.

Meanwhile, Lynda and I decided to move to North Carolina to be near our son, Jared. Maybe there just wasn't that much left for us in Missouri, except for our daughters, and we both liked the warmer weather in the South. Maybe it was just time for a change after living in Missouri for the past 30 plus years.

Lynda was still obsessed with having horses and living in a rural area, so we ended up buying

Bill's son, Jared, in his Guardian of the Galaxy collection room at his home in Durham in 2017.

a small house on 25 acres with four-board fences around the pasture. I drove the cab in St. Louis for three years before I joined Lynda in North Carolina. And then I got a job at the Roxboro Elks Lodge as a bartender that I kept for almost ten years. We finally sold the house in Missouri, at a loss, but our son did so much to help us during that period. He helped rehab the house in Roxboro, and when we finally evicted the non-paying renters in Missouri, he took time off his job to renovate the home in Winfield. He makes more money than I ever did in my jobs, but he was not obligated to support his parents. He poured thousands of dollars, not to mention his labor, into both homes over a period of several years.

Jared now works for Cisco Systems as a system analyst. He doesn't want to be a manager, but he has such great technical skills, he keeps getting raises and bonuses. I know how smart he is. When I was working at County Cab, he came to St. Louis for a visit and he was on his way to the airport to catch a plane back. We had stopped at County Cab on the way and discovered that their computer system which allows the company to direct cabs to customers had broken down. Jared offered to take a look at the problem which had been plaguing them a full day and in less than an hour, he had the system back up and operating. He is a world-class problem solver when it comes to technical matters and Cisco recognizes that.

Maybe the biggest highlight of my time in North Carolina was when I was playing in a benefit golf tournament and got a hole in one on a par three. The prize for doing that was a new car. No one I knew had ever done that. It was all luck, of course, just like winning the lottery. I never drove the car. We took the money instead to pay off all the bills that had mounted up from the move to North Carolina.

Grandpa Bill with his granddaughter, Kelsey, a few months after her birth in 1997.

First and Last Thoughts

We all like to think our lives have meaning. Our family was raised in a religious, Catholic, environment. Our mother liked going to mass. When I was in elementary school, Mom and I went to mass every morning during the summer. We completed a nine-week novena lauding the Virgin Mary at a Latino Catholic church. According to the priest, doing the novena insured us of last-minute salvation, no matter how bad we might be in our lives. When I began high school, I was certain I was destined to be a foreign missionary and went to the Maryknoll Seminary in St. Louis to become a priest. That only lasted two years until I developed an overriding interest in females.

I didn't realize how devout and insufferable I was until I reached adulthood. Drinking one evening in a bar, I ran into a grade school classmate of mine who was a radio announcer in Kansas City. Mike and I spoke for quite a while getting reacquainted, and he was surprised that I had served in the Army, went to Venezuela, chased girls and used cuss words from time to time. "You know," he said, "you were one of the most pious shitheads I've ever met. I'm surprised you became a real human being."

The 1960's changed me a lot. The assassinations of Jack and Bobby Kennedy, then of Martin Luther King, not to mention the insanity of the Vietnam War, turned me against the establishment, especially Republicans. Southern Democrats switched to the Republican party when the Democrats took a stand for civil rights. We grew up in a middle-class, sheltered community in Missouri so I didn't know that much about the Jim Crow laws until the Civil Rights movement began. What a travesty of justice that was. And racism still exists in our country, almost two centuries after the American Civil War.

About the only thing I've retained from my Catholic upbringing is a strong sense of right and wrong. The Church was not always on the right side of fairness and justice, but I think that Jesus Christ was. Most of the New Testament tends to ring true. Jesus, in my mind, stood up for the poor, the disenfranchised, the underdog. His opinion of the rich, clerics, politicians, bullies, vain and greedy individuals is clearly stated in the second part of what he said is the most important commandment, love thy neighbor as thyself.

When and if you future Jurkiewicz descendants read this, and who knows what the world will be like then, just know we cared about truth and justice, and we tried to bring about needed changes. Like Bob Seger sang, "I'm a lot older now, but I'm still running against the wind."

Bill and I along the Blue Ridge Parkway somewhere.

When I die — To my children

All funeral arrangements made with Rupp funeral home + paid for. All policies + important papers in gray box in bedroom closet + large envelope underneath has funeral policy. Things to be done for funeral left to do.

I'd like a light blue dress, my Ladies of Charity Cross around my neck. ~~I want~~ a silver rosary. Tell Julia to put a smile on my lips. No flowers. If you wish to buy me some I want no more than a spray of pink + white carnations from you all on the casket. Ask Julia if pall bearers, servers + choir expect a gift. You should give the Priest $50.00 for having the mass.

Don't put off funeral for more than 2 days. Put notice in paper + ask relatives please not to buy flowers but to give a donation to the Cancer fund or charity of their choice or to the Food Bank to feed the poor.

Pall bearers — my grandsons — Richie - Jeff - Steven - Jared - John Michael - Matthew and Caleb

At Mass I wish the choir would sing "Be not Afraid"
"Hosea"
"On Eagles Wings"
and at the end of Mass the usual "When Oh When Will I see thee". Have a dinner by the Altar Society in Church basement. Buy the meat + give them a donation of $100.00 for their kindness.

Michael I was not aware till lately that Social Security will pay $255.00 for funeral expenses. So call + let them know of my death + claim this.

Give any organs that will be accepted to the living + eye bank.

I have a right to die will with Dr. Merlin Brown. When they decide I can not get well I do not want artificial means to keep me alive.

The will is in the gray box. Also all insurance policies. Everything is to be divided evenly among you. Even small items of mine if someone asks for a certain thing, be fair and share. Please be careful and pay everyone who says I owe them something.

God Bless you all. See you in Heaven. Be sure an get there   mom

Mom left a hand-written note detailing her burial and funeral wishes. Most interesting is the ending admonition to be sure and join her in heaven.

One of the nicer short trips with Mom and Dad came on a visit to see Bill in Hartsburg. Here, Mom and I are with Rachel at Bill's house, but we also went to Jefferson City to see the state capitol, which they had not seen before.

| 23 |

Kathleen Anne (Jurkiewicz) Lamb

Sometimes we used to say Kathy was the black sheep of the family, but that wasn't true. She was just ornery and daring, fun-loving and adventurous. She did get in more trouble than the rest of us because of that, but at the same time, she was intensely loyal and protective.

Kathy and Linda show off their youthful figures during the 1961 Minnesota fishing trip to Emily Lake.

She was the oldest girl, born January 15, 1943, and therefore, she also was the most "motherly" toward the rest of us younger children. Mary has told me at times that Kathy used to watch over her at school and stand up for her to other kids.

She became a mother, too, when I was finishing grade school, marrying Richard and having Rich and Jeff soon afterward. They lived close to us on King Hill, and we saw them frequently. We went down to their house just to play with the boys, and we were always welcome there. Richard played baseball with Mike and I, hitting towering fly balls to us on Hosea playground.

When Kathy and Richard built a house on Turner Road, we went there and visited too. We all went mushroom hunting in the spring with them. Jeff was the best mushroom hunter. He could see them when all we saw were leaves and brush. One time as Richard was driving down a country road, Jeff and Rich and me were riding in the bed of a truck, and Jeff started yelling stop, stop. He had seen a mushroom along the side and made his dad back up about a quarter mile where Jeff had spotted a huge morel mushroom.

When I was ready to come home from West Texas, Kathy and Richard came to get me. We drove a thousand miles pulling their old trailer with six West Texas Brahman mix cattle and a dog.

Kathy is a fun-loving person, and in 1998, on a visit to see Mary in Tucson, she pretended to be falling down a rocky hill.

Kathy and Richard decided to move to Texas about the time Audrey and I met, so we didn't see each other for several years. But after Audrey and I moved to Oklahoma and established ourselves in Muskogee, we began visiting Kathy and Richard a couple of times a year, and they came up to visit us several times too. They were living on the Cedar Creek Reservoir in the little cabin then, and our children loved to visit them.

We have fond memories of staying several days at a time with them, fishing from their dock, riding their watercraft, and Richard fixing a brisket on hot coals. They had a pop machine outside the cabin that was always stocked, and we drank whatever we wanted. We went to Rich, Jeff, and Steven's weddings; Noah was the ring bearer at Rich and Paula's wedding, and Kathy made him a little suit to wear.

Kathy always has been creative, sewing, gardening, doing ceramics, woodworking, and she and Richard built a beautiful house, eventually, next to the little cabin. While Kathy was doing all that and raising her family, she went back to college, and earned a master's degree. She worked with special needs children in elementary schools and was a diagnostician. Kathy has always been interested in children and their development, and enjoys discussing that topic.

Kathy and Richard and their boys, Jeff, Steven, and Rich. I don't know the year, but the time is 10:15.

| 24 |

Mary Draga (Jurkiewicz) Shelor

Mary, who was born, January 30, 1948, was Dad's favorite. We all knew it. However, our father was not a demonstrative person, nor did he know how to express his emotions. So while Mary was Dad's favorite, he really didn't know how to tell her very well and mostly he displayed it by having high expectations of her.

Mary after her First Communion at St. James. The rest of us children usually said she was Dad's favorite, and though Dad never said, I'm sure she was one of the top two of his favorites.

His favoritism was subtle in other ways. He didn't get after her as much as the rest of us. Now, Mary was a compliant and sympathetic child, so she probably didn't need discipline as much as the rest of us, but that's exactly why Dad treated her differently. Bill and Kathy could be rebellious and ornery at times, and I'm sure that Dad appreciated Mary's gentle nature.

Dad also loved polka music, and Mary played the accordion. In fact, she played very well, and Dad was very proud of Mary. Whenever we had friends or family over for a visit, Dad would have Mary get out her accordion and play. I believe that he also got her involved in the polka band with the Dobosch brothers. Mary stopped playing the accordion, and it probably had to do with developing new interests in life, but it surely also was the result of being made a spectacle for years. Mary never complained though, which says a lot about her good nature and love for her dad.

I also have admired over the years, Mary's adaptability, loyalty, and determination. Her marriage ended, and she raised Matthew pretty much on her own. Matthew is admirable in his own way, intelligent, amiable, and a dedicated family man.

In 2013, Mary and I took a trip to Honduras, where she had been more than forty years before with the Peace Corps. Seated next to her is Mario Thuma, a Peace Corps friend of hers who stayed in Honduras and started a school. Mary speaks to one of the classes in Mario's school.

Mary, like many people, including me, discovered teaching children wasn't for her. So she turned to sales, persevered and succeeded, then turned to managing a budding temp company. Eventually, Mary returned to education, but this time, at about 40 years of age, she went back to school, earning a doctorate while working, and then began teaching in college. I really admire her for all that she accomplished.

In 1989, Audrey, the kids and I went out to Arizona to visit Mary and Matthew, and Michael and his family, too, in Tucson. We had one of the best trips as a family on that trip, and Noah and I went a few times afterward, having a good time visiting with Mary and seeing the sights of southeastern Arizona. I developed even a deeper respect for Mary in 2013, when we took a trip together to Honduras. We had quite an adventure, seeing where she lived and worked in Honduras while she was in the Peace Corps, and visiting one of her old friends who still lived there. In 2017, we took a trip to Vancouver, British Columbia, to meet another of her Peace Corps friends, and again had an adventurous, fun time.

From my sister Mary

Like all of my brothers and sisters I grew up in St Joseph, Missouri, went to St. James School and Church, and spent most of my early years with family and friends. But I was offered an opportunity in 1968 that changed my life. But first, a little background.

I don't remember having any strong ideas of what I wanted to be when I grew up. When I was little, I wanted to be a cowgirl because I was in love with Roy Rogers. Of course, I found out later in life that I was scared to death of horses, and I had several bad experiences on horses, so it was a good thing I didn't become a cowgirl. I really loved driving a car and one idea was to become a truck driver. I could drive, doing something I loved, and see the country. What more could you want? However, I found out that I hated being on the highway with big rigs that scared the poo out of me. So that career never happened.

So I became a teacher. Actually, I fell into being a teacher by accident. I didn't choose it; it chose me. When I was in college at Missouri Western College (now Missouri Western State University), I saw an announcement hanging on one of the bulletin boards in the grotto that said Peace Corps/College Degree Program. I was familiar with Peace Corps. My brother Bill had joined the Peace Corps and was stationed in Venezuela working with peanut farmers. I don't remember hearing too much about his experience, but since I had no idea if and where I wanted to finish college, I tore off one of the five-by-six cards, filled it out and mailed it. I didn't think too much of it, but a few weeks later, I started to receive more forms and letters that needed to be completed. Before long I was receiving information that I was being considered for one of the 50 positions that they had.

Mary says her first dream was of becoming a cowgirl, which is strange in that I can't ever remember her like being dirty or outdoorsy.

I was accepted as one of the candidates. I was going to finish my degree at the State University College of New York in Brockport. I had no idea where Brockport, New York, was so obviously, I took out our encyclopedia and looked it up. It looked like a nice place, right on Lake Ontario and close by Niagara Falls. I was excited about the possibility of living there. However, I failed to read all the fine print. The program was for future math and science teachers. My major was political science. Luckily though, I had had four years of math and science in high school, and I had completed all the courses a degree-seeking student would need at the undergraduate level, with a fairly high GPA. I guess they thought I would be a good candidate.

Graduation was in late May of 1968, and early in June, I caught an airplane to Rochester, New York, that stopped in Chicago. Flying back and forth to school was part of the program that was paid. This was great! Flying was great! I had a summer job at Rosecrans Field right out of high school where I worked for a pilot. He flew 150 and 175 Cessnas, moving cargo and teaching people how to fly. It was a fun job and exciting because periodically I got to take the wheel once we were airborne on some of the deliveries or even help people with their flight plans. So I was not new to flying. But now I would be flying in jets and farther than Missouri and Kansas. This was definitely going to be a new adventure.

Mary with her son, Matthew, who was born in 1975 in Columbia, Missouri.

While flying from Chicago to Rochester, I had a wonderful view of the countryside from my window seat. However, I remembered in my history classes that we read how crowded the East was becoming so people started to wagon train out west to settle into new land. As I looked down from 35,000 feet, I saw lots of empty space. Maybe people just didn't like neighbors to be too close.

Living with and going to school with those 50 young people from all over the country was a once-in-a-lifetime experience. We were all idealistic, thinking that maybe we could make a difference in the world. We all had left friends and family, and we were going to band together and learn what we could to complete college and be changers in another country's educational system. We were so naïve.

The educational experience in our host country that we were all hoping for never materialized. For the entire 15-month program of completing college, we prepared for living in the Dominican Republic, where we thought we would be working. In fact, we visited the DR during spring break. But at the end of our training, we were sent to Honduras and Peru. We had been told at the beginning of our 15-month training program we needed to be flexible. That wasn't the half of it. After only a short time, we were told the education program that we were taken to those countries to work in had been dismantled. We were not needed. If we found something we would like to do, fine. If not, maybe it would be best to go back to the US. I managed to keep myself busy for a while. I went to the local hospital and worked in the children's ward, assisting my nurse Peace Corps volunteers. Then I met a group of sisters who needed help teaching English and music to some young girls, and I did that. I even had a preschool in my house for little kids in the neighborhood. I told stories and helped them with their letters and numbers, and we did a lot of singing, dancing and artwork.

But that wasn't what I had trained for, and hoped for. Over the years, as I met again with some of the young people I had trained with and as we shared our experiences, we all felt like failures. We had been vetted to become "specially" trained volunteers who would excel. It was demoralizing. Not really wanting to leave Honduras, I checked out the American school there in La Ceiba that was operated by the Standard Fruit Company. They offered me a teaching position in the fifth and sixth grades. In addition to $400/month salary, I would be provided a furnished house, plus all expenses each year, plus one free passage to and from the US on a banana boat. I almost took that position.

In 2013,, Mary and I visited La Ceiba, Honduras, where she spent her Peace Corps days. While there, we took a day trip to the Cayos Cochinos off the coast.

But after spending ten months in Honduras, I returned to the United States and moved back home to St. Joseph. Again, teaching beckoned me. Mom knew the superintendent of the St. Joseph School District. He was a Croatian boy who lived down off King Hill, and she went with me to apply for a teaching job. I was offered a job at Horace Mann Middle School, supposedly the worst school in the district, because that's where all the kids went to school as a last resort. Many of these young people had been in and out of jail, and several of the girls were pregnant or had had a baby. Needless to say, I lost the majority of my enthusiasm for teaching that first year. I was barely 21 years old, and the boys were young men looking at me as fair game, and the girls were jealous of me! Getting punched in the nose the first week trying to break up a fight did not help matters. I was so happy when the school year ended.

The next teaching job was for Wesley Community Center running a day care for three-, four- and five-year-old children. That was a nice experience and after that I did teach part time at St. James. I taught seventh- and eighth-grade science and math. I'll never forget the first time, and probably last time, that Monsignor Moriarty came to visit my class and all the desks were moved to one side of the room. All the children were on the floor drawing, coloring and creating a timeline on brown butcher paper that extended from one end of the classroom to the other.

Mary and Matthew in their Tucson home after his high school graduation in 1996.

After that I gave up on teaching for a while and I tried my hand at a number of jobs. I wish that I had kept all the resumes that I had created over the years. Some jobs were so short that it would not look good on a resume. But maybe because I had never decided I wanted to be a teacher, this became a time for me to try out a number of things. Wherever I lived, I always signed up with a number of temporary services so I could try a variety of places to work, and also it was a great way to find a permanent job. In Houston, for instance, I did lots of secretarial work at hospitals, attorney offices and banks. After a temp job at the Houston Chronicle, I was hired as the Secretary to the Vice President of Operations. It was kind of funny how I got hired. After filling in for a few weeks, Mr. McCarty called me into his office with his booming voice one Friday afternoon to ask why I had not left him crying, like all the other temps. I said, "My daddy had a big voice and yelled, so I wasn't afraid of yours!" He offered me the job.

I tried sales too, which our Mom said I would never be able to do. She said, "You're afraid to talk to people first." Well, I proved her wrong. I took a job at KSFT radio station, selling radio advertising, which is a difficult thing to sell since it is so hard to determine if it worked. But I did fairly well.

But when I went to work for a business machine office, I found my place. In 1982, IBM came out with the first memory typewriter. Since I knew what type of work a secretary had to do, all I had to do was show the secretary what my typewriter could do, and they would tell their boss, "I want that typewriter. Buy it!" I was top salesperson for the last quarter of the year, which didn't make the other three salespersons happy because they were men. They even got a company car, but not me. My boss said no company buys new equipment at the end of the year because they have spent their budgets. My boss wanted to know how I did it. I told him I had no choice. I have to make sales to feed my son. He told me he really didn't want to hire me because I was divorced, but from now on he would hire divorced women. They're hungry!

Alice Campbell, who owned a personnel company, was the person who got me the job at the typewriter company. We became friends and she shared her desire to open a temporary business out in Arizona. I asked her if she would want to partner up with me, but since I didn't have any money to put into a business, I would be the working partner. So in 1985, I moved out west to Tucson, Arizona, and set up Alice & Mary Temporary Service. I worked hard and established a fairly profitable business within the first five years, but Alice was greedy. After a few years, her youngest son graduated from Arizona State University and she asked me to train him to run the business. Within a few months she was finding reasons for me to leave. Not having the money to fight her, I left quietly. But I had had time to check out the business and educational opportunities in those five years and I was ready to finally get established in my career. Alice and Mary had a contract with the University of Arizona which helped me meet lots of different people there. And I had already applied to graduate school and talked to a number of deans about which direction I wanted to go.

Mary with her Vancouver, British Columbia, and former Peace Corps, friend Lynn (Wood) Brookes, on a trip there in 2017.

This was actually the fulfillment of a dream I had twenty years prior to that when I was in Peace Corps training in Brockport, New York. During the school year there, I had a work/study job in the College of Education. My boss was a delight, and I saw firsthand the responsibilities of a college professor. She was treated as a responsible professional. She chose the classes she wanted to teach, and she chose the days and hours when she wanted to teach. Right then and there I decided that one day, I wanted that job, and here was my opportunity in Tucson.

Yes, I was a certified 7-12 science teacher. But once I spoke to different departments in the College of Education, I realized if I had knowledge of the instructional strategies that were taught in Reading, I would have been a better science teacher. So I applied to the Department of Language, Reading and Culture. I took classes for a few semesters and then finally landed a job in the College of Education as a project coordinator for a program much like I had participated in in New York with the Peace Corps. I liked the job. It didn't pay well, but I was able to take a class for only $10/class, and Matthew was able to attend classes at the UA for one-third of the cost each semester plus other benefits. It was a win-win situation.

Working with Dr. Fuentevilla in the College of Education also opened up doors for me in all the schools within and surrounding the city of Tucson. Numerous times administrators would ask, "Why didn't you apply for a teaching position at my school?" And I would answer, "No one knew me. I never received an interview." It really does matter who you know.

Matthew with his mother at his wedding.

I also met and worked with professors and administrators from Pima Community College. Several semesters before I was hired on permanently, I taught adjunct classes there at several of the six campuses across the city. Over several years, I met many of the faculty and administrators of that institution and was finally offered a full-time reading position at the Desert Vista Campus, on the southwest side of town where the majority of students were Hispanic and my knowledge of Spanish would again be valuable.

Teaching at Pima Community College proved to be the best job I had ever had. I ended up teaching there for 19 years, and I retired in 2017.

Over the years PCC not only offered a career, but I also met people who were compassionate and committed to educating young people and who became dear and lifelong friends. We just didn't teach at the same institution, we learned together, discussed students' needs, planned new curricula and supported each other when times were tough. We worked on committees together and even traveled together as we went to conferences and other educational events. After I became department chair, I was responsible for hiring adjunct faculty, and the teachers/students I knew from UA and graduate school were always first on my list to hire. Once hired, our department of faculty met monthly at my house for a potluck to share our successes and to strategize how to deal with our problems. We were a true community of learners who cared about our students and tried to offer them the best we could. I never felt alone while teaching and working at Pima. Some of them are still my best friends. What more could one ask for?

Child and grandchildren

I married Robert in April of 1972. I was twenty-four years old, but still immature and not sure of who I was or what I wanted in life. I'm not proud of that, but we had Matthew in March of 1975 and that makes it perfect. Matthew is a wonderful, caring and thoughtful son. He studied hard in school, played baseball, and always chose some of the nicest young boys as his friends. I'm so proud of him. My life would have been a waste if I didn't have him. And in 2004, he married Andrea. The following year William was born, and then Brady in 2009. I am blessed.

Mary with grandsons, William and Brady, in 2018 at Williams' school during an awards ceremony.

Mom and Dad on their wedding day. Newlyweds today usually exhibit close affection in their wedding photos, but this photo portrays an anti-PDA, 1940s decorum.

| 25 |

Susan Joanna (Jurkiewicz) McGinnis

Only one year and four months older than I am, Susan, born July 27, 1951, is closest in age to me. Because of that and because we played together quite a bit as children, we were quite close. Susan liked to role play a lot, as most girls do, so I sat through a lot of tea parties. But we played games together too, war and slapjack, Life and Monopoly.

Susan in her home on East Joseph Street in St. Joseph in 1987. She always has been the best cook and the best at welcoming us all into her home.

We fought, of course. Susan usually got the best of me because whether I picked a fight or she did, she would run to Mom after the first words or blows and say, "Mom, David's going to hit me." I always seemed to get in trouble for any fracas, and probably, I deserved it as I was bigger.

Like Kathy, Susan was protective of me; however, we went to different high schools; I went to the boys school and she to the girls. But in elementary, we walked to and from school together, and Mike became another companion when he started school. I'll always remember us each taking turns to jump and slap the low-hanging paint sign on the side of Valley Lumberyard along King Hill.

Susan always had a lot of friends, and I envied her for that as we grew up. In high school, she was more involved in activities and sang in the choral group. She sang alto. Although she never played an instrument except for beginning piano lessons, she could and still can find the alto line on about any song.

Susan has always been a very generous person. She and I purchased a vehicle together, my first, because I never had the money to do it. I ended up driving the car more than she did. After she married Farrell, we spent a lot of time at her house on Joseph Street swimming in their pool and eating their food. She and Farrell never complained.

We all spent time in Susan and Farrell's pool, and Susan was usually fixing food or cleaning up after us as we were enjoying ourselves in the water.

They had a big garden with every vegetable imaginable and raspberries and gooseberries, and I'm sure Susan did the most of the gardening. Susan is the best cook of all of us, and she's far and away the best host.

Susan and Farrell also employed their nephews who were of age at their electric company during the summers. Caleb worked there one summer, staying with them in their home, and he has good memories of that time.

They had boats too, and we all rode in them. If you went camping with anyone, you wanted to go camping with Susan because she brought the most and best food. One summer, our families met in Arkansas on Beaver Lake, camping at a state park. We fished, and Farrell motored us about the lake until a heavy rain came for a full day and night. When it was still pouring the next day, we all gave up and went home, but we had had several good days together. Susan and Farrell brought their boat to Eufaula Lake one time, as well, and I know they spent several days taking our kids all around the lake.

Of all of us, Susan has had a strongest sense of family, enjoying the planning of outings and get-togethers. She was the closest to our aunts, stopping in to visit them often as she lived in St. Joseph the longest. She also has remained the closest to our cousins who still live in St. Joseph and the area.

Susan is a good mother, and she and Farrell took care of his two children, Shane and Angela, from a previous marriage part of the year and also adopted two children of their own, Annie and John. She and Farrell also raised two other children as their own, Isaac and Noah. Undeniably, the best thing she did was to take care of our mother in her old age when Mom developed Alzheimer's. The ordeal lasted several years. That was a heavy load to carry, one that no one else wanted or tried to take on. Thanks, Susan.

Susan and Farrell came to visit us in Muskogee several times. They and Noah and Isaac came this time during Easter 2000.

| 26 |

Michael John Jurkiewicz

Mike was born two years and one week behind me, November 28, 1954. He was always smaller and skinnier than I was, and he could run faster than I could run. He was a better baseball player too, and he did wheelies on his 20-inch bicycle with the banana seat. I never could do a wheelie. I'm pretty sure that he had more girlfriends than I had too. In fact, when I was home from college one weekend, a girl called for him when he was out. She asked me if I was his brother, and I said yes. She asked me if I wanted to go out with her. We did, and she was nice looking and we had a pleasant time. Mike had good taste in women.

I took this photo of Mike one day outside the back of the shoe shop in the late 1960s. Mike is sitting on the fender of the work truck driven by Jim Testerman, a friend of Dad who used to come into the shop frequently.

Mike and I were close as boys, as we were constantly playing, and wrestling. Mom told people that Mike and I would be sitting across the room quietly doing something; then next thing she knew, we were rolling on the floor, knocking over furniture and lamp stands.

We did do other things together. In the summer, we played catch with a baseball in the yard, and we took turns batting fly balls to each other at Hosea school grounds. We played catch with a football in the fall and winter, and we had one-on-one games in the back yard.

We slept in the same bed for way too long. I mentioned that in an earlier chapter. When we lived on King Hill and slept together in that upstairs sun room, we went on adventurous excursions, crawling between the mattress and the box springs from one side of the bed to the other. The objective was to make it to the opposite side of the bed and back on top of the mattress without falling off the bed and into the crocodile pit. Mike and I, of course, pushed and shoved each other, trying to help the other into the crocodile pit which ended up generating a lot of bed vibrations and floor thumps right above where Mom and Dad slept in their bedroom below. Most nights, Dad was yelling at us to "Cut it out, and go to sleep."

Mike with Maggie and Cole. This photo was taken on a trip Jessica, Noah and I took to see them when they lived in Aurora. Mike was in his Tom Selleck phase.

Mike and I developed a mime skit we liked to perform occasionally for the family. It was called "Carpenter and Son." Mike was the carpenter, I was the simpleton son, and we accidentally hit each other with boards and hammers in Three Stooges slapstick-like humor. I don't believe our programs ever ended with a climax and resolution. They only ended when our audience tired of our masochistic schtick, and we sensed their loss of interest. "Carpenter and Son" died out before we turned teens, but we probably should have developed it into an act. Who knows, we could have been the next Smothers Brothers.

Mike always has had an inquiring mind. He asks good questions, and he has always been genuinely interested in people, which is evident by the number of friends he has and the good relationship he has with his in-laws.

Mike had a clearer view of what he wanted and how the world worked than I had. He finished college and got a good job with the St. Joseph Fire Department. He moved on to the Tucson Fire Department, and in Tucson, found a partner for life, Mary Fulton. Mike has been a devoted husband, and he moved to Denver so Mary, his wife, could be close to her family. Nobody else in our family did that. The rest of us moved farther away from our in-laws.

Mike has been a devoted father too. Cole and Maggie love him, and I notice too that Maggie laughs at all his jokes.

This black-and-white photo was one Mike sent to us from Tucson after meeting Mary Fulton.

| 27 |

Linda Elizabeth Jurkiewicz

I remember well the birth of my youngest sister, Linda, in 1958, and I related a memory of that in a previous chapter. Another strong memory of Linda's arrival that has an application here is Mike's disappointment of the addition of another girl to our family. Mike and I both wanted a brother since we had three older sisters whom we believed mothered, or bossed, us way too much. I have noticed that's a pretty common feeling of boys with older sisters, rightly or wrongly.

Mom, and Dad, with her pride and joy at Hyde Park the summer following Linda's birth.

So when Kathy received news by phone from Dad that "we had another sister," Mike, who was two months short of four years old, began crying. In fact, he was inconsolable for several days. I did not cry, but I must admit that I was a little disappointed too.

However, I have noticed that the youngest child in a large family is usually the most affable, most even tempered, and easiest to get along with of all the siblings. That certainly is true of Linda.

Because no other child came along to spoil her standing as youngest, Mom definitely favored Linda over the rest of us over the years. We complained about it sometimes, but that never affected Linda's character or behavior. She always has been the best of the seven of us. Growing up, Linda was more cheery and more willing to get along with others, and she was more accommodating in play, and in times of crisis, more understanding, patient and thoughtful.

She has also been the most creative and most focused. She took piano lessons as a child and continued musical training into adulthood, becoming an accomplished musician and music teacher. She developed a love for visual art and has turned that passion into a unique style all her own, and she impressed her love of music and art on her children, Ahafia and Kestrel.

For Linda and I, our bonding moment occurred the summer in 1974 when with Mary and Robert, we took a camping trip to the springs and clear rivers of south central Missouri. We discovered on that trip our shared interests in travel, history and nature. It has continued to the present, and over the years, we have taken short trips together to various parks in Missouri and Oklahoma, as well as Cornwall, England, and Chaco Culture National Historical Park in New Mexico.

From my sister Linda

I appreciate the opportunity to express myself and to tell my story for this book that David has taken time and much effort to put together. I appreciate his commitment to this idea and the fruition of it. It doesn't surprise me that David is the one to do this. In our home growing up there was not a big emphasis on creativity. We did the normal things that kids do: took piano lessons; Mary played the accordion; we played a little bit of sports, mostly the boys; but nothing like the plethora of activities children get signed up for now. Mostly we just played with our friends who lived in our neighborhood.

But David's creativity could be seen if you looked hard enough for it.

I emptied the trash every Saturday morning, and I remember as I dumped his trash can into the one outside, I would find his drawings of the comic strips that were published in the St. Joe News-Press. I mostly remember Beetle Bailey drawings. They were accurate and I was impressed. Also, he painted the solar system on the ceiling in the attic – I thought that was neat.

And yet, David's drawings, Bill's storytelling, and a nude painting that Kathy did of herself when I was quite young, cast a spell over me. I didn't really understand creativity; we grew up in a very utilitarian type of household; all actions pretty much headed towards the same goal, survival and keeping things in order – I'm not sure which came first. But it piqued my interest and now that I am in my sixties, creating is where I spend a significant part of my daily life.

Linda with her cake on her first birthday in the dining room on our farm. It looks as if no one is there to celebrate it with her. Unfortunately, or maybe fortunately, her older brothers and sisters were gone from home during her teenage years.

When I arrived at Missouri Western State College to sign up for my freshman year, they asked me what I wanted to major in. I had no idea, so they asked me what I knew how to do. I said, "I play the piano." So they said, you will be a music major! (Interesting approach to college planning.)

I ended up getting a Bachelor's in Music Education with an emphasis in Music Therapy. When I finished my last section, an internship at William S. Hall Psychiatric Institute in Columbia, South Carolina, I visited an art museum. I saw a painting and thought, "That's what I want to do." Of course, I lamented that fact that I had just spent six years completing a music degree.

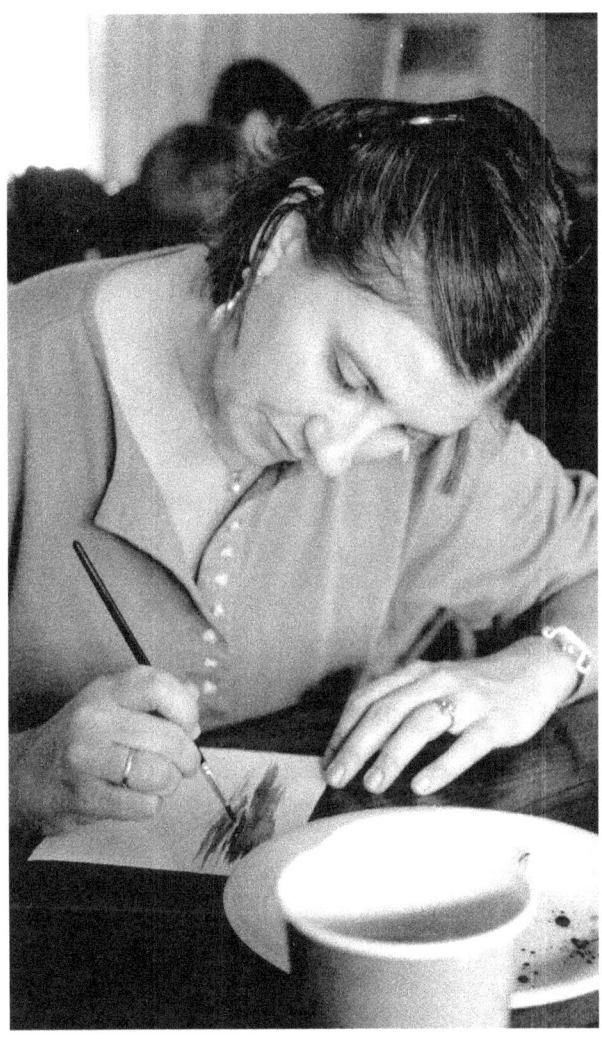

Linda in 1989 doing a practice exercise with watercolors.

So began my feeble attempt to create visual arts. This resulted in taking classes wherever I could afford them for about the next 25 years, practicing different skills.

In those 25 years I also grew up. I met John Miles and lived with him for 30 years and then realized this was not the correct relationship for me. As a couple we did have an amazing year in 1992, when we quit our jobs and traveled for ten months around the southern and western part of the United States.

Together we had two children, Ahafia and Kestrel. I had the pleasure of homeschooling them, which was a turning point for me in terms of how I viewed life. In my goal of teaching them, I became aware of how much I loved to learn, with my goal of instilling in my kids the love of learning.

Both Ahafia and Kestrel seemed to discover their passions in their younger lives. Ahafia studied classical piano since the age of five and is a fabulous musician and has expanded into a variety of musical styles. Kestrel began sewing when he was five and is now in a master's program at the University of Missouri-Kansas City studying costume design.

As Ahafia and Kestrel grew up, I began to have a little more time to explore my artistic interests. I began weaving in 2003, and by 2010, I had discovered that I was more able to express my ideas through fiber art.

In retrospect, working in fiber for me was not really a surprise. Mom was an amazing seamstress and embroiderer. So, I already had a fair amount of skill in working with fabric. Mom would work on her stitching almost every night while Dad was watching TV or watching the cars drive down King Hill Avenue. I always thought that Mom just didn't know how to sit still and do nothing, which may be true, but now I understand the pleasure and the sense of calmness and meditation the act of stitching brings. She never really valued her creations, but I wish that she would have because they were beautiful, and she was incredibly thoughtful about her choices. In fact, one time she had embroidered this lovely pillowcase with flowers, and after it was done, she didn't like her color choices, so she removed the stitches and started again. It would have been easier to have bought a new pillowcase and printed the pattern again, but Mom was never one to waste anything.

Linda on Bodmin Moor with our English friend Richard Thorn in spring 2018. Typical of Linda, she became fast friends with Richard, showing an interest in all things Cornwall. She listened intently and asked questions about everything we saw.

The thing that has been wonderful about my textile journey is that I have been able to use my pieces as an opportunity to express and work through many difficult questions that I have had in my life. And in the end, I have a piece of art!

I am a storyteller in my work, and many of my stories are about Mom and women in general. Being born in 1958, I was on the cusp of the Women's Liberation movement in the 1970s. Also, Mary was very influential in my knowledge of this; she was making choices as a female that were showing her independence and desire to live a life of her choice. But I am saddened for the women of my mom's generation, their lack of choice, the cultural limitations they faced, the expectations of women at that time, and religion's requirements of women in general.

Raising my own children, growing up, and becoming aware of what women have had to do to break out of the cultural barriers has helped me understand my mom more clearly. She was a product of her environment, just as we all are.

I am excited to continue my exploration of fiber and stories in my creative work. The act of creation is a balm for the soul.

Lastly, I would like to share with you one of the most recent pieces I have made, "Anna, Tomorrow Your Knight in Shining Armor will Arrive." This piece is about Anne and Draga killing and dressing 100 chickens the day before Mom and Dad were married.

Linda's textile piece "Anna, Tomorrow Your Knight in Shining Armor will Arrive" was accepted in the art show "Tangled Roots" at the Interurban Art House, Overland Park, Kansas, in 2021.

Linda with her children, Ahafia (a namesake of Grandma Jurkiewicz) and Kestrel (named after a little falcon).

| 28 |

Audrey Jo (McKinnon) Jurkiewicz, in her words

I once told David that someday I would write a story of my life, and he said, "That would really be interesting." Well David, I'm doing it and you actually asked me to do it.

Audrey on Mother's Day in 1999.

Once upon a time there was a little girl named Audrey Jo, and she lived with her mother, her grandmother and grandfather, and her sister.

Her grandparents had raised their seven children, and within a year or two after their last child was married and out of the house, their daughter came back home with two little girls ages five and four. Growing up she was kind of embarrassed that she lived with her grandparents, but really it was the best thing for her in many ways. It was a good arrangement. There was built in childcare for a working mother, and there was a piano with a grandmother who made sure practice happened right after school before any playing.

I lived in a house nicer than I ever could have lived in raised by a single parent. And right here, I will say that I was born in the first year of my mom and dad's marriage. And I was a preemie. So life was serious right away for a newly married couple. And then 14 months later my sister, Jennie was born.

My dad had problems, I guess, with finding a job that he liked. He drove a bus and then moved on to trucks. I think my dad loved trucks, and that was the old days when men would be gone for days and days, and I think it was just too much for him to take care of a family. He would come to see us once a year or maybe a little more often. He would call my mom, but my grandmother would answer and knew it was him, and naturally, she had pretty strong feelings about how he was treating his family.

Audrey's parents, Jack and Audrey June, in 1954.

So my mom would talk to him, and we would go meet him and then go to see my Grandma McKinnon, too. He would hand us a dollar, and we thought he was great not knowing that he never really supported us. But I have to say my mother never did talk badly about him so we didn't have bad feeling towards him.

I grew up in Kirschner Addition in South St. Joseph. I later met the Kirschners when I worked for Neal Arnold at Irwin's Grocery Store. The Kirschners I knew were three brothers who farmed and owned a lot of farm land. I think they probably owned the property where our new elementary school, Lake Contrary, was built.

My grandparents had been in their house since about 1926. Some of their friends still lived in the neighborhood, but there were also younger families so I knew, or knew of, almost all the kids in that approximately five-block square neighborhood. My grandparents were charter members of Kirschner Community Church, so I went to that church from the time I was born. Off and on over the years some of them would come to church. When we would go trick or treating, we would walk the whole neighborhood, and we trusted and knew who all the people were who gave us candy.

Again, I was kind of embarrassed that I didn't have a dad who lived with us, but no one ever really said anything about it. It was just my feeling. What this feeling did for me though was cause me as a teenage girl to pray many times for a husband who would stay with me and would want to stay with his children. More about that later.

One childhood Christmas for Audrey Jo and Jennie.

So just a little more about my family. My mother worked full time, and when she was home she was totally in charge of us. We were her life. We had church activities to keep us busy. And since we lived with our grandparents, whenever they had any company it was our company too. During my childhood only one of my mother's siblings stayed in St. Joe. Three of her siblings lived in Chicago at the same time. Since my grandfather worked for the Burlington Railroad, we could take a trip at half fare. So we went to Chicago several times when I was growing up. And when I was eight years old, my mom's youngest sister lived in California, so we went to visit on the train and we went to Disneyland which would have been about 1961 (Disneyland opened in 1955). Then one at a time my mom's siblings came back to St. Joe over the years (except for one aunt) and we began having Christmas Eve together at our/my house. One Christmas Eve we counted 50 family coming and going through the evening of eating, talking, an impromptu program, reading of the Christmas story and gift exchange. Nice family time.

Audrey Jo's grandparents, Roy and Josephine Blakely, at their house on Diagonal Street in the Kirschner Addition, St. Joseph, in the late 1950s.

I went to Benton High School and so I never knew the Jurkiewiczes. I never did know about Bill's Shoe Shop. In south St. Joe there were two main little shopping areas: The Junction, (Ilinois Avenue area, probably called the Junction because the city bus stopped there) and the Valley (King Hill Avenue area). Whereas the Jurkiewiczes went to Marty's Hardware, we went to Scanlan's Hardware. Our doctor's office was at the Junction and our pharmacy was Wrinkle's. We only went to Fox Department Store in the Valley a few times. They were too expensive I think. I don't even remember any other stores in the Valley, except I think there was a place to take your chickens to be butchered and maybe then you came back to get them. I think I went one time with my grandparents to take some chickens. They didn't want to do it themselves any more. And we had a grocery store in our neighborhood so we had what we needed close.

We would go downtown shopping for clothes at the big stores, Penney's, Paris and Townsend's. And drive to Sears in a different location. Also, it was always fun to go to United Department Store in the basement where they had toys, Woolworth's and Kresge's. Christmas shopping in the evening was always special. Of course, when East Hills opened it was a pretty big deal, the end of Downtown as we knew it. Never quite the same.

Another fond memory was going to the Auditorium for city basketball games. My mom would take us and we usually sat with her and really watched the game. I didn't walk around the whole time like my childhood friend did. She would go with us and then meet up with us at the end of the game. I really did like basketball. The games were exciting, the rivalry was fun, and getting to sit in the upper level you had a good view of the game and cute boys playing or roaming around. The whole place was so noisy when people would stomp on the wooden floors. Sometimes we would stop at The Spot Café on the way home which was always a treat and choose a song on the jukebox.

I remember starting high school with a certain amount of apprehension. Our elementary did not feed into Spring Garden School which was the junior high in south St. Joe. So I went all eight grades with the same 25-30 students. Then at Benton, many of the kids from two or three elementary schools already knew each other because they had been in school at Spring Garden. I was very shy. I remember that my mom was concerned about my shyness and told me she thought I should take Speech when I would be choosing classes for probably my junior year. She thought it would be good for me. I shudder to think of the anxiety that would have caused me. And if I had cried and carried on, maybe she would not have forced me. But something wonderful happened, Divine Intervention? They made Speech a mandatory class for one semester instead of an elective for the whole year. And it was good for me – I lived through it.

Of course, my shyness affected my whole life. I didn't talk to boys and didn't feel like I could or that I had interesting things to say. And I had crushes on boys all the time, but they never noticed me because I never talked. I had one "date" in high school and that was with a guy younger than me. We went with another couple to a musical at another high school. I never did go to a prom.

Audrey at her desk at Dan Garvin's Insurance Agency in early 1975.

My first job was at the Thirsty Drive-In. I started out as a carhop; then I worked the fountain area, dishing ice cream, filling drinks, sending orders out. After the seasonal closing and after graduation, I went to work at the grocery store. Little by little I became more outgoing because of my job. My "love life" was at a standstill though, and even as an 18-year-old, I felt like the clock was ticking. One of my fears was being an old maid. That was kind of a real thing back in the 1970s. A lot of girls still got married straight out of high school. And because I didn't really know any career I was interested in, I didn't pursue college. I knew if I went to college I would have to work at the same time to be able to pay for it.

So work and church activities kept me busy, and having a crush on a guy from church who was very confused himself occupied my next couple of years. Then I met and dated a few guys from the church Jennie was going to, King Hill Baptist, with her boyfriend and then husband. And I sang with a group there and went on two trips to Washington and Oregon with them.

One day a guy from one of the factories came into the store and ended up asking me out. Very quickly, he was serious and it was flattering to have someone want to spend time with me. When he proposed, I thought I was ready to be married. Looking back I realize I had many insecurities and I was naïve. I was too trusting and not intelligent about men. It was kind of an emotional roller coaster time. I thought I was happy, but there were warning signs that bothered me but I didn't pay attention to. As the wedding grew near though, I began to get cold feet. I believe the Holy Spirit was answering my many prayers from the years before, and I decided I couldn't go through with the wedding. I called it off. I never could set another date.

I began 1975 hoping it would be a better year. After the grocery store for almost three years, I worked at Bill Kenney Pharmacy for about 3 months, then Dan Garvin Insurance Agency. Jennie had worked for him, and I knew him for that reason and King Hill Baptist Church.

These are my memories of getting to know David: In the spring, Dan was taking a swimming class at Missouri Western and so was David. Dan told me about David and told David about me. I had to take a paper to Bill's Shoe Shop because David was not carrying insurance on his car but living with his parents. He was in the second-highest category of higher risk drivers. So Mr. Jurkiewicz needed to sign an exclusion which said that if David was driving any of his dad's cars insured with Dan, there would be no coverage. I remember taking the form, and I think David was in the shop and smiled at me.

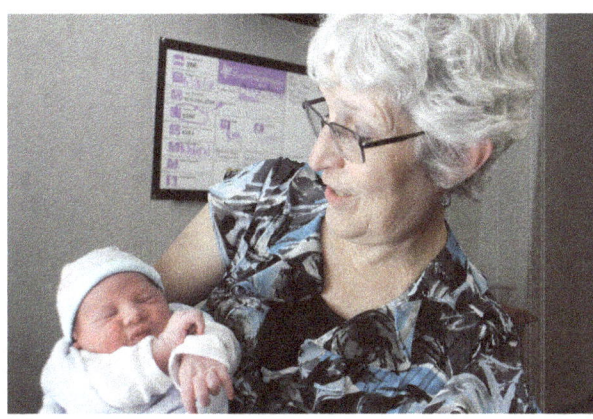

Audrey with her most recent grandchild, Cameron Michael Jurkiewicz.

Then the most fortunate thing happened. There was a wedding for a favorite client of Dan's, Roman Cupryk. He invited Dan and Carma Lee and me to the wedding on May 10, 1975. We went to the wedding and then home, and then back for the reception at the CIO Hall. And David filled in the details on that. I remember David saying at the end of the evening, "We'll have to get together some time." He didn't set any kind of date for that to happen, and he mentioned going somewhere the next weekend so by that next week I felt I had to be proactive, for the first time in my life with guys that is. So I took my moccasin into the shop to see if anything could be done with the stitching. David was there and fixed it for me no charge, and asked me if I liked Chinese food. I said I thought I did, and he asked me out for Saturday. As it turned out though, we changed it to Barbosa's and that was our first date May 24th.

Looking back, I see there was such contrast between my dating life before David and with David. With David there were no inconsistencies, no confusion, no strings attached. He liked me, then loved me from the beginning and I had feelings of happiness, belonging, stability and faithfulness.

I felt welcome in the Jurkiewicz family. Even though I knew Anne would have liked for David to marry a good Catholic girl, she never did say anything to me about it. She was the stronger personality to be sure. Bill was pleasant and likable, and I think he liked for life to be simple. He had raised seven children, and I think he was tired and just wanted to relax. He liked people, and I think he was proud of his children. Those children have strong personalities, but also an interest in the world and in people, and a strong sense of family which I find admirable.

I tell David we were "destined" to be together. He just rolls his eyes but consider: My favorite TV actor growing up was David Janssen. I never missed *The Fugitive*. I even saved the *TV Guide* talking about the last episode.

So, David Janssen, initials DJ (David's initials), and Lieutenant Gerard was always chasing Richard Kimble, (David's middle name is Gerard), and the time I was born was 11:52 a.m. (David was born November 1952 (11/52). I rest my case.

Audrey with Jessica, Caleb and Noah at LaFortune Park in Tulsa, long before we moved there.

Heston, Jackson and Hannah horsing around at Noah and Sarah's house.

| 29 |

Birdwatching

As a child, I was always interested in nature.

I carried that interest into adulthood even though I didn't pursue a career in science or nature.

In 1980 or thereabouts, while Audrey and I were living in Castile, New York, I bought a bird field guide and started to document the birds I saw. That was in winter, and I remember that the first bird I ticked off in the book was the American crow. I did not get far, however, only adding ten or fifteen other birds, as we were busy with starting a family, and the effort died quickly.

Noah chronicles his bird sightings at Palo Duro State Park near Amarillo, Texas, in 2007 on our first extended birdwatching trip together.

After I began working for the Muskogee Phoenix in 1995 and began writing nature stories in addition to historical and cultural stories, I met members of the Indian Nations Audubon Society. The local group had members across northeastern Oklahoma, but the first ones I met were Jim Norman of Muskogee and Jeri McMahon of Fort Gibson. Jim and Jeri both were very knowledgeable and dedicated people. Jim worked for years at a nursery and besides being an ornithology expert, he was a wildflower expert. Jeri had a life list longer than anyone in Oklahoma. Her husband had a successful car business, and she traveled the world on birdwatching trips, so her life list numbered in the thousands. When I first met her, she was leaving on a trip to Antarctica. Jim and Jeri were fastidious and exacting in their hobby, Jeri more than Jim, but they still welcomed newcomers into the group and were helpful and willing to share their knowledge.

I did a few stories about their work in northeast Oklahoma, and I joined them first at Black Mesa in the Oklahoma Panhandle for a wildflower tour, which also included birdwatching. Noah and Jimmy Fields went with me.

Over the next few years, Noah went with me to a few of the Indian Nations' outings; another I remember was in the Wichita Mountains National Wildlife Refuge, which was another mainly wildflower tour. But one of the best for birds was a shorebird watch at the Salt Plains National Wildlife Refuge near Enid.

On our 2007 trip, we traveled from the Texas Panhandle into New Mexico and the Bitter Lakes National Wildlife Refuge outside Roswell.

In 2006, Noah was attending college at Oklahoma State University. He made friends with Professor Tim O'Connell, a very outgoing and popular teacher in the Department of Natural Resource Ecology and Management. O'Connell is a rabid birdwatcher, and a frequent president of the Payne County Audubon Society.

Noah began going with him and other students on birdwatching outings, and Noah became very interested in it, including starting life and year lists of birds that he saw. When he told me that, I decided to do the same thing, and we went together on some local birding outings. He was living in the cabin I built on the three acres we bought in Stillwater, and he recorded red-breasted nuthatches there and watched two yellow-crowned night herons nesting there. I would go over to Stillwater, and we would hike trails at Lake Carl Blackwell and other sites looking for birds.

In March 2007, Noah and I decided to take a lengthy birding trip over Spring Break. We only had five or six days, so we went to New Mexico, the farthest point from Stillwater being about 600 miles. That was one of the nicest trips that I've gone on, and Noah and I saw many interesting birds for the first time and had some interesting experiences. We stopped first at Palo Duro State

Park outside Amarillo, where we saw turkeys and recorded for the first time golden-fronted woodpeckers. We stopped next at Oasis State Park in eastern New Mexico. That is a little diamond in the desert. The oasis is a big spring that had been circled by a concrete wall where residents come to fish for stocked trout. In the night, we woke up to the sounds of a great-horned owl hooting. We crawled out of the tent, and the owl was perched in a low tree right beside our tent. Noah had Sarah's camera, and he steadied it against the concrete picnic table. He took several shots of the owl's silhouette against the near full moon-lightened sky. Unfortunately, the next day, when he looked at the camera, the photos he took to that point had somehow been erased.

Caleb was never interested in birding, but he and I did share a liking for heights and climbing. In 2008, we went rappelling in the Wichita Mountain National Wildlife Refuge in southwestern Oklahoma.

We told a ranger at the park about the owl the night before, and he took us to a shed where mowers and other equipment was stored. In the far corner, the owl sat on top of a roof rafter where he spent his days, according to the ranger. We drove the next day to Roswell and the Bitter Lakes National Wildlife Refuge. On the road to the refuge from Roswell, we saw scaled quail and tree swallows. At the refuge, we met a ranger coming out who we talked to for a few minutes and lo and behold, he had just moved from Oklahoma and from the wildlife refuge closest to Muskogee, the Sequoyah refuge. That first time at Bitter Lakes was phenomenal. There were thousands and thousands of geese, ducks and shorebirds. I have been back four or five times since then, and the western drought has decimated the numbers, but we caught a great year and recorded a dozen or more species we saw for the first time.

After Roswell and a visit to the downtown UFO museum, we drove through Ruidoso to a camp in the White Mountain Wilderness Area. We had read that visitors could pan for gold there, and so we brought along cake pans to do that. We did, and we learned quickly how difficult it is. The water was freezing cold, and it was cloudy and sprinkling, and we didn't really know how to pan for gold, which eluded us. The next morning we awoke and took off for a hike up a high mountain. We started off energetically and walked along a tumbling brook where Noah spotted a dipper, which kept flying ahead of us, but we got several very good looks at it. The brook and glades of aspen and beech ended and we came to the tree line where the snow turned very deep. We tried to walk to the peak, but the snow was up to our thighs in several places and we couldn't trudge any farther. We did reach a saddle between two peaks and there we disturbed a wolf that had been lying in the snow. He was very skinny and ran off over the edge so quickly that we couldn't get a photo. That night back at the campsite, it drizzled and got colder. We were miserable by morning, and we left, driving to Carrizozo down the mountains to the west and the Malpais-Valley of Fires area. On the way down, we saw our first mountain bluebirds, and at the Malpais, we saw cactus wrens. The warm shower I had at the campground was the best shower I ever took because of how cold I had been just hours earlier.

Jessica did not become a birdwatcher, but she loves traveling. Jessica and Heston invited Audrey, Caleb and me to join them on a trip to Iceland, and on one excursion, we stopped to spend a few minutes with Icelandic horses.

We left the next day for Santa Rosa, where we planned to finish our birding. But as we approached the town of Vaughn, we saw a strange patch of white among the constant tannish brown of the winter desert. As we approached Vaughn closer, we discovered that a severe storm had dumped several inches of hail and the storm had not quit. It was still dumping heavy rain and large hailstones that were several inches deep on the ground. I was driving my small, white Nissan pickup and I quickly pulled under the canopy of a defunct gas station. The hailstones pummeled the old tin of the canopy and we stayed there about ten or fifteen minutes waiting out the storm. The hail stopped, but the rain didn't. We moved on, wanting to get to Santa Rosa by nightfall. I was driving through several inches of water rushing down the highway carrying hailstones that crunched as we drove. Other vehicles were trying to get going too, and the traffic in the little town was heavy. In the rush of semis and farm trucks splashing water and hailstones everywhere, I missed the turn to Santa Rosa and instead headed south toward Roswell. We had gone about 20 or 25 miles before we realized we were heading the wrong direction and backtracked to Vaughn, which had some semblance of normality by this time. It was late when we made it to Santa Rosa, and a cold front was moving through following the storm. We left Stillwater with temperatures in the high 80s and now it was down into the 30s with 20s predicted. We had seen many birds – I recorded 31 species of birds for the first time for the year on the trip as well as seeing dozens of other species – and had a good time, so we headed home, Noah driving most of the way into the early hours of the next day.

Some people, including some people in my family, have said they don't understand my fascination with birds.

Well, I say I don't understand people's lack of fascination with birds.

On a trip to Honduras in 2013, I saw my first toucan in the Lancetilla Botanical Garden outside Tela.

Every bird, from the smallest hummingbird to a huge eagle, is a marvel in flight. Many move from one place on the globe to another and back again in a year's time, and repeat that flight for many, many years, transporting themselves thousands of miles without a map or GPS. Most of them change their appearance during the year, dropping worn feathers for bright colors and interesting patterns, then switching back to their basic look. They sing with beauty and abandon, and it would be a poor world without waking up to the multitude of sounds and songs of birds.

And you may go a day or two without seeing a rabbit or a squirrel, and a person may go a lifetime without seeing a fox, a wolf, or a bear, but few people don't go many hours without witnessing a bird. Birds are all around us, moving through our yards and our trees, through the space above us, constantly in view, so it seems very odd that they would not raise an interest in everyone. Even though birdwatching has become very popular in recent years, most people here in America have 200 or 300 species pass by them in a year, and still won't see or can't name more than 10 or 20 species. They can't even distinguish between the 20 or so species of ducks they might see, only calling them all "ducks" even though they are widely different.

It's no wonder that humans are destroying the natural environment. Most know nothing about it, even the things that should be the most familiar.

Since that first trip to New Mexico with Noah, I have been back there probably ten times on birding trips. I have been to California two times; Colorado half a dozen times; Vancouver, BC, once; Maine and Canada once; Honduras four times; Mexico three times; England, Iceland, and Croatia once; Arkansas every spring for the last ten years, and I've traveled about every road in Oklahoma looking for birds. Every time I take a trip, even if birdwatching is not my main reason for going, I look for birds. I am continually amazed by bird's wide diversity and curious habits.

Why wouldn't you be? You don't have to be an expert, and I'm not by any means, but I find reading and learning about birds as interesting as reading and learning about human history, and definitely much more interesting than knowing something about Kim Kardashian or Britney Spears.

www.ingramcontent.com/pod-product-compliance
Lightning Source LLC
Chambersburg PA
CBHW080847020526
44118CB00037B/2282